DEREK KIRK KIM
AND LES McCLAINE

BOOK 2
STILL LIFE

:01

First Second

NEW YORK

PREVIOUSLY,

IN TUNE: VANISHING POINT

ANDY GO DROPS OUT.

Look, the point is, I can draw! I can paint! I don't see why I have to go through another year of watercolor blends and contrapastos just to get a piece of paper that says I can.

In fact, I already sent my portfolio out to a bunch of publishers and magazines. It's only a matter of days before the offers start pouring in.

You can probably guess what happened next. 2 months later, I was sitting on my ass watching infomercials at 2 o' clock on a Wednesday afternoon.

click click

Still living with my parents, of course.

ANDY GO FINDS LO

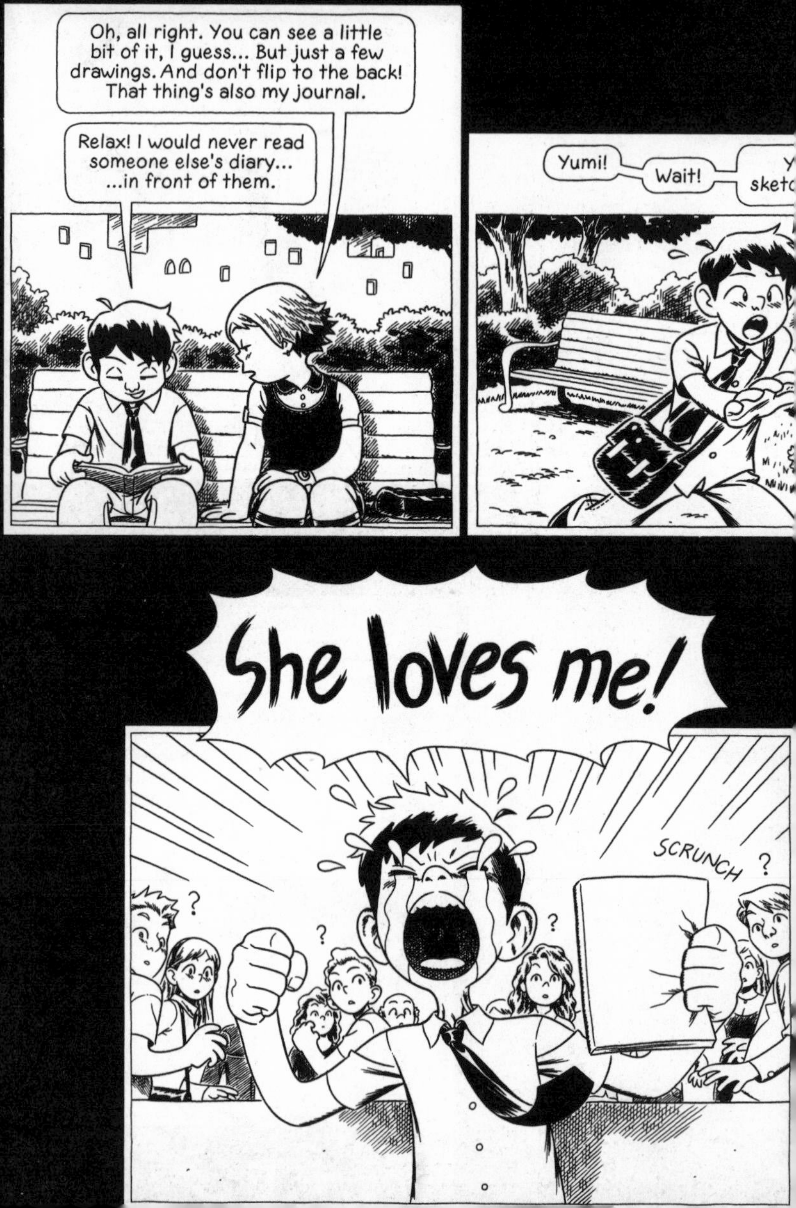

Oh, all right. You can see a little bit of it, I guess... But just a few drawings. And don't flip to the back! That thing's also my journal.
Relax! I would never read someone else's diary... ...in front of them.
Yumi!
Wait!
She loves me!
SCRUNCH

ANDY GO GETS A JOB.

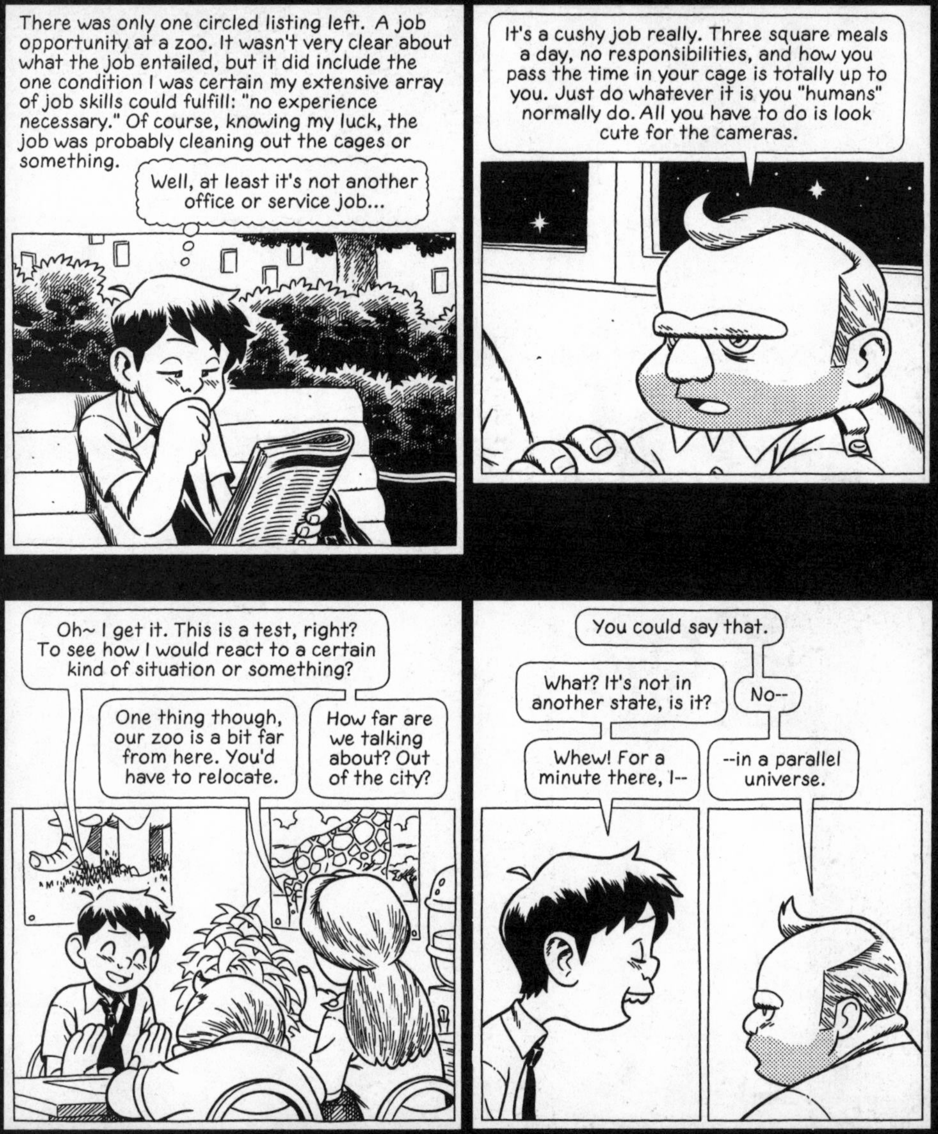
There was only one circled listing left. A job opportunity at a zoo. It wasn't very clear about what the job entailed, but it did include the one condition I was certain my extensive array of job skills could fulfill: "no experience necessary." Of course, knowing my luck, the job was probably cleaning out the cages or something.
Well, at least it's not another office or service job...
It's a cushy job really. Three square meals a day, no responsibilities, and how you pass the time in your cage is totally up to you. Just do whatever it is you "humans" normally do. All you have to do is look cute for the cameras.
Oh~ I get it. This is a test, right? To see how I would react to a certain kind of situation or something?
One thing though, our zoo is a bit far from here. You'd have to relocate.
How far are we talking about? Out of the city?
You could say that.
What? It's not in another state, is it?
No--
Whew! For a minute there, I--
--in a parallel universe.

WHAT'S NEXT FOR ANDY GO?

CHAPTER
11

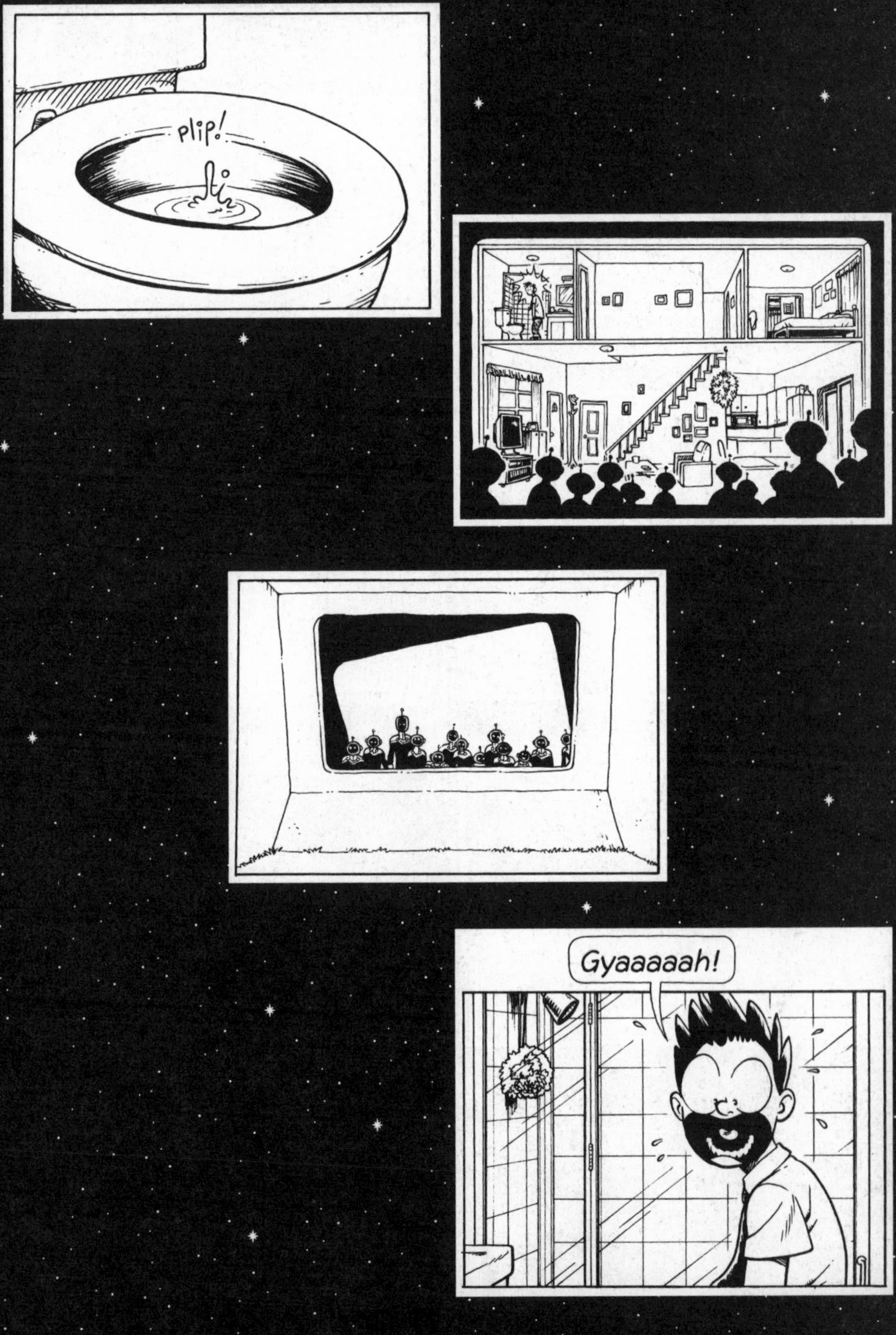
plip!
Gyaaaaah!

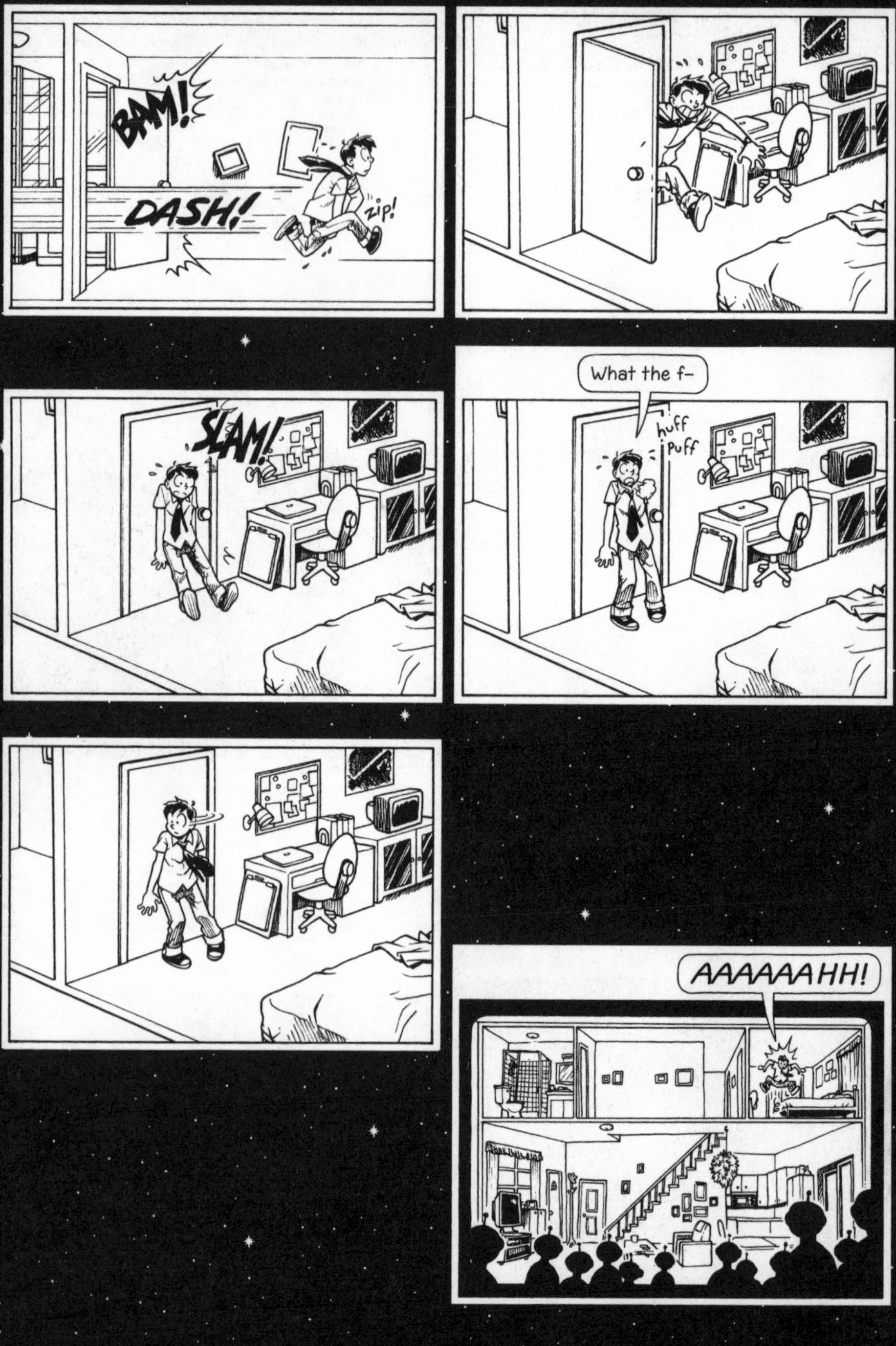
BAM!
DASH!
zip!
SLAM!
What the f–
huff
puff
AAAAAAHH!

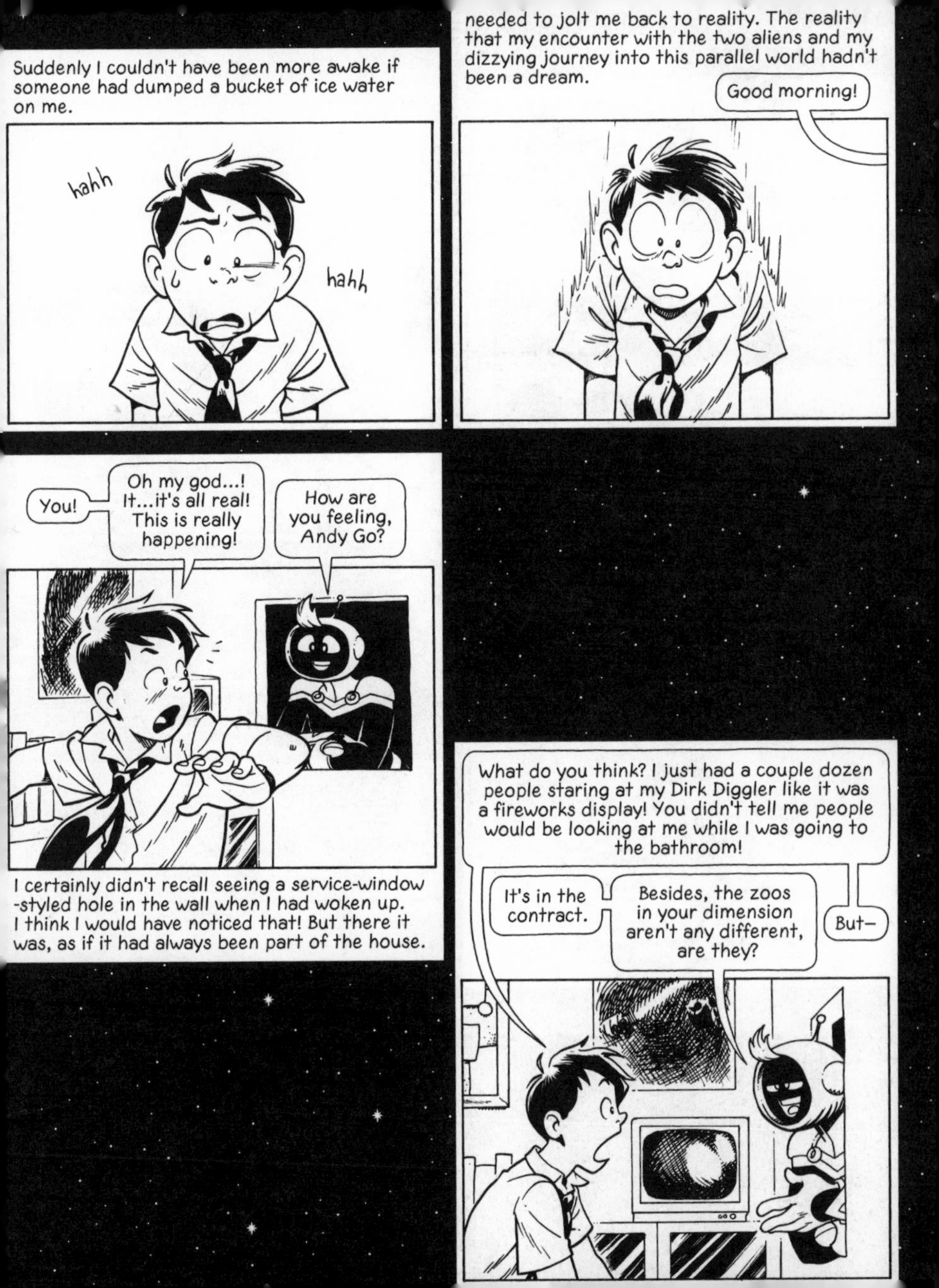
Suddenly I couldn't have been more awake if someone had dumped a bucket of ice water on me.
hahh
hahh
needed to jolt me back to reality. The reality that my encounter with the two aliens and my dizzying journey into this parallel world hadn't been a dream.
Good morning!
You!
Oh my god...! It...it's all real! This is really happening!
How are you feeling, Andy Go?
I certainly didn't recall seeing a service-window -styled hole in the wall when I had woken up. I think I would have noticed that! But there it was, as if it had always been part of the house.
What do you think? I just had a couple dozen people staring at my Dirk Diggler like it was a fireworks display! You didn't tell me people would be looking at me while I was going to the bathroom!
It's in the contract.
Besides, the zoos in your dimension aren't any different, are they?
But–

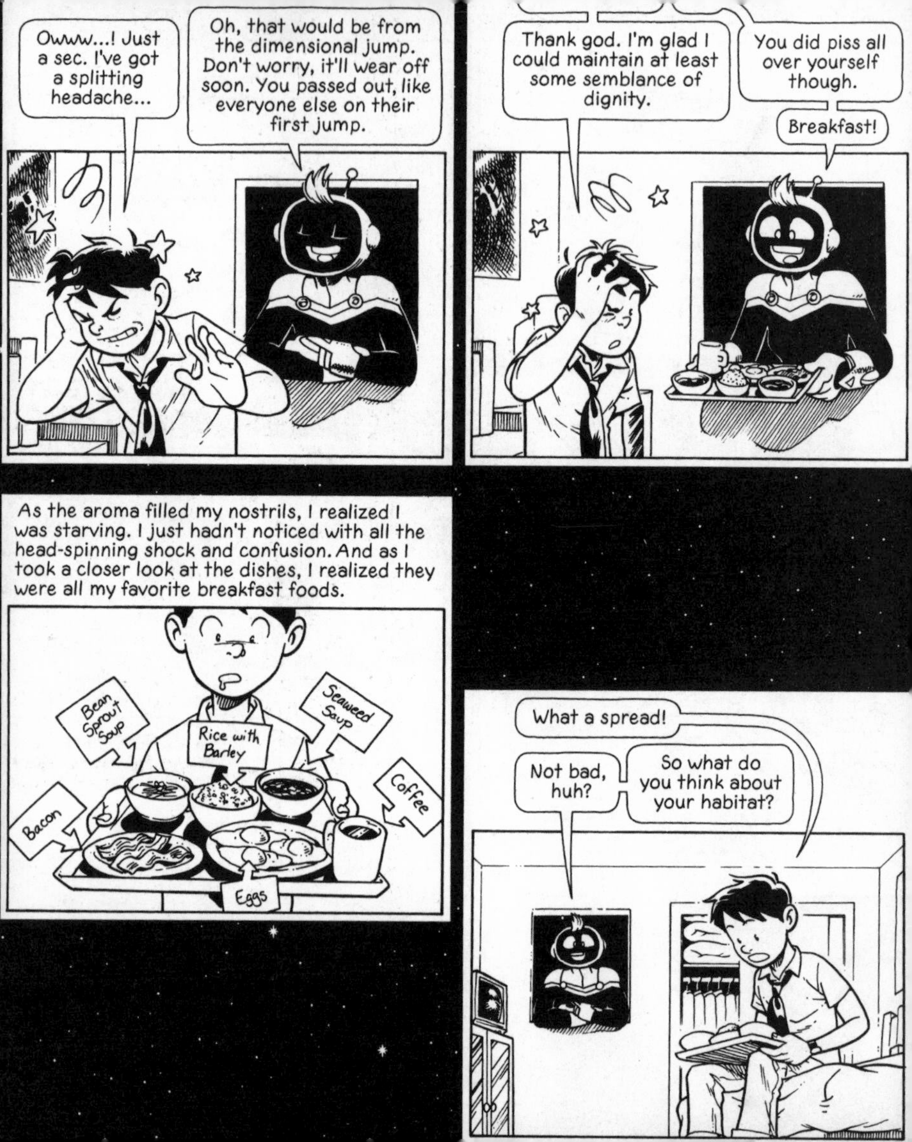

Owww...! Just a sec. I've got a splitting headache...
Oh, that would be from the dimensional jump. Don't worry, it'll wear off soon. You passed out, like everyone else on their first jump.
Thank god. I'm glad I could maintain at least some semblance of dignity.
You did piss all over yourself though.
Breakfast!
As the aroma filled my nostrils, I realized I was starving. I just hadn't noticed with all the head-spinning shock and confusion. And as I took a closer look at the dishes, I realized they were all my favorite breakfast foods.
Bean Sprout Soup
Rice with Barley
Seaweed Soup
Bacon
Coffee
Eggs
What a spread!
Not bad, huh?
So what do you think about your habitat?

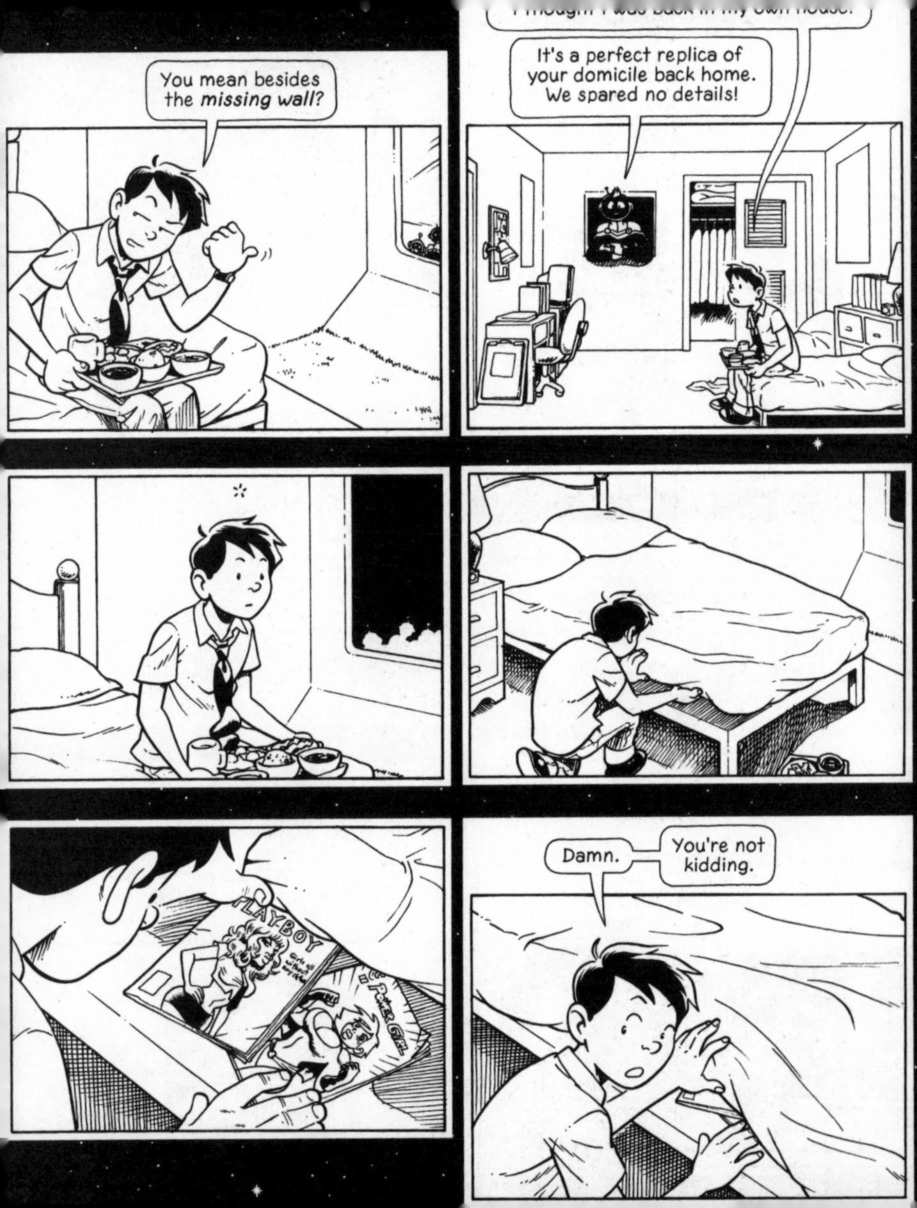
You mean besides the *missing wall*?
It's a perfect replica of your domicile back home. We spared no details!
PLAYBOY
Damn.
You're not kidding.

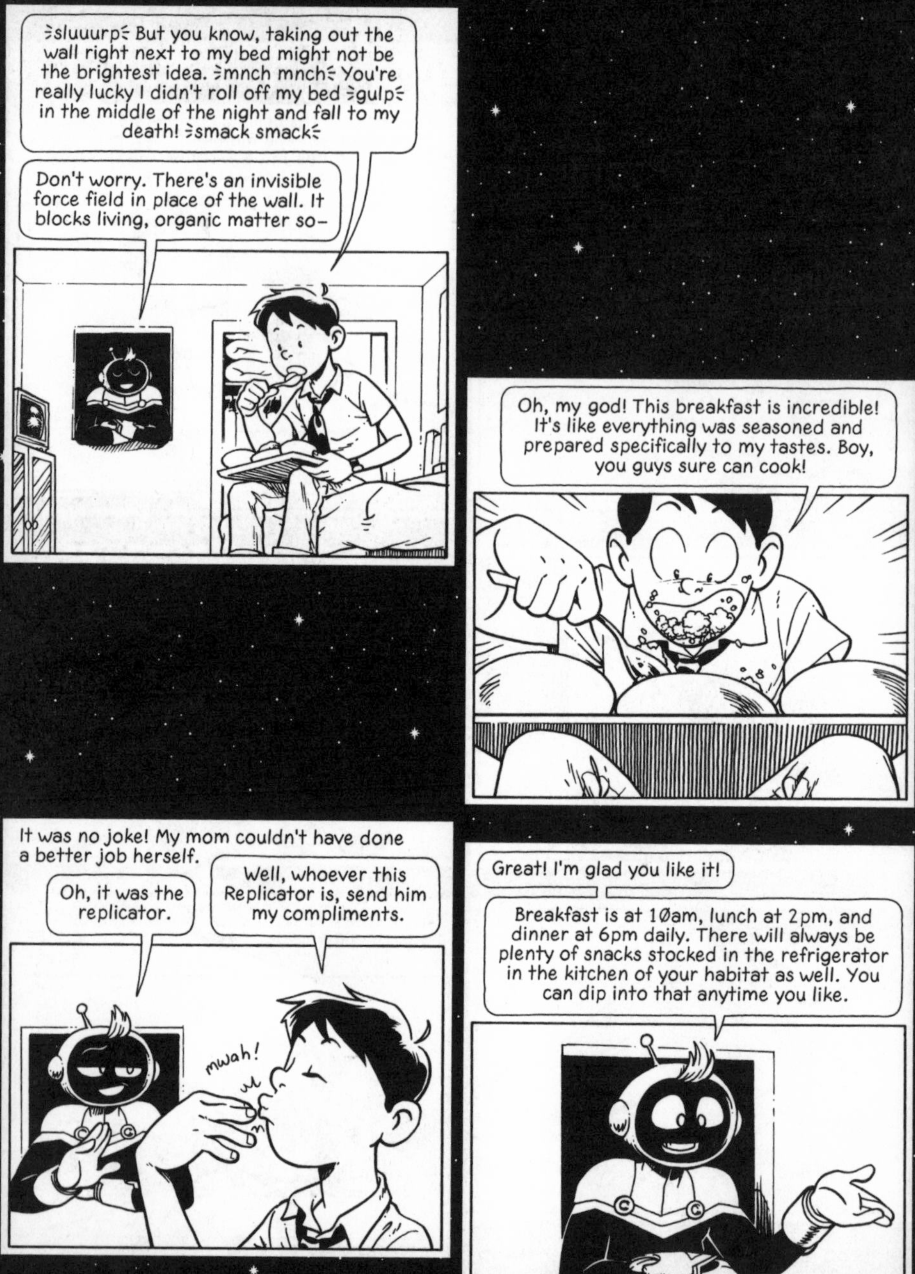
sluuurp But you know, taking out the wall right next to my bed might not be the brightest idea. mnch mnch You're really lucky I didn't roll off my bed gulp in the middle of the night and fall to my death! smack smack
Don't worry. There's an invisible force field in place of the wall. It blocks living, organic matter so–
Oh, my god! This breakfast is incredible! It's like everything was seasoned and prepared specifically to my tastes. Boy, you guys sure can cook!
It was no joke! My mom couldn't have done a better job herself.
Oh, it was the replicator.
Well, whoever this Replicator is, send him my compliments.
mwah!
Great! I'm glad you like it!
Breakfast is at 10am, lunch at 2pm, and dinner at 6pm daily. There will always be plenty of snacks stocked in the refrigerator in the kitchen of your habitat as well. You can dip into that anytime you like.

Fabulous!

Ahh! I feel much better now.

WHUMP

I gazed up at the ceiling, completely relaxed and content for the moment. Even my headache seemed to have subsided.

Pat

Pat

My alien zookeeper just continued standing there, grinning at me. I felt like a gorilla in the mist to her Jane Goodall.

This was going to take some getting used to.

...what now?

What do you mean?

...do. I just sit around in here eating and pissing?

Yup, pretty much. We just want to observe your everyday behavior in your natural environment.

Really? There's nothing else to the job? No goals? No problems to solve? Nothing to keep me motivated? Nothing to challenge me or my skills in any way?

Nope.

Hooray!!

Hey, does this thing have cable?

500 channels worth. Just like the big TV downstairs in the living room.

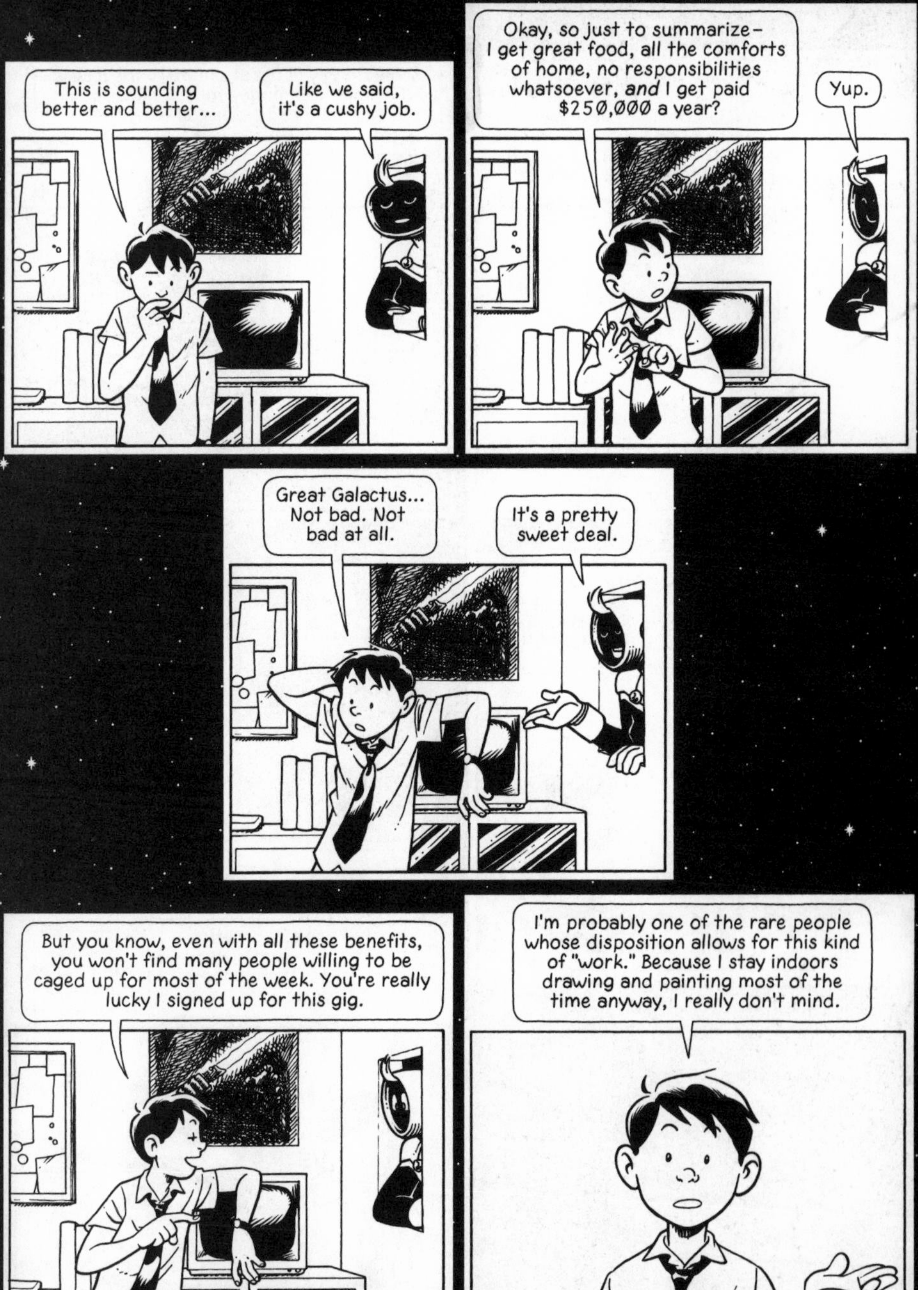

This is sounding better and better...
Like we said, it's a cushy job.
Okay, so just to summarize- I get great food, all the comforts of home, no responsibilities whatsoever, *and* I get paid $250,000 a year?
Yup.
Great Galactus... Not bad. Not bad at all.
It's a pretty sweet deal.
But you know, even with all these benefits, you won't find many people willing to be caged up for most of the week. You're really lucky I signed up for this gig.
I'm probably one of the rare people whose disposition allows for this kind of "work." Because I stay indoors drawing and painting most of the time anyway, I really don't mind.

In fact, I've always thought going to prison would be a huge boost to my work. I think it would liberate me creatively because I wouldn't have to worry about what would sell. I could focus solely on following my muse.

With the free room and board, I wouldn't have to constantly worry about taking on some crappy illustration job just because I needed the money for rent and food. All that applies to this zoo gig as well— minus the anal rape and tossed salads.

Uh-huh...

Perhaps like Martin Luther King Jr., Nelson Mandela, and the Marquis de Sade before me, I'll create my greatest works under imprisonment!

z

I can't wait to tell my parents. I think they'll finally be happy.

That's great! It's certainly important to make your parents happy.

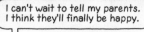

I hope Yumi's okay with this.

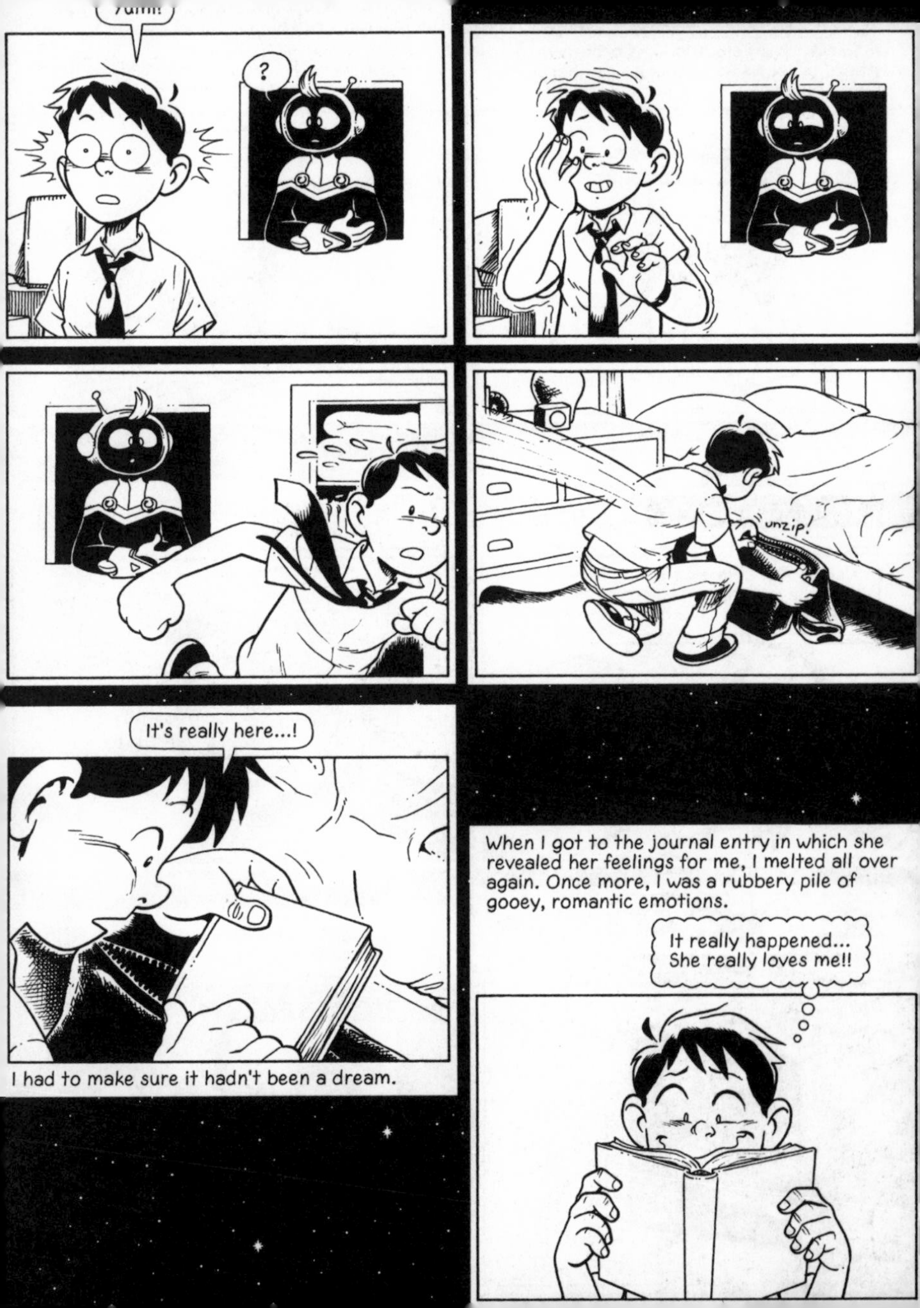
?
unzip!
It's really here...!
I had to make sure it hadn't been a dream.
When I got to the journal entry in which she revealed her feelings for me, I melted all over again. Once more, I was a rubbery pile of gooey, romantic emotions.
It really happened... She really loves me!!

Then like a jolt of electricity, it occurred to me that I never had a chance to call her before I left for this gig!

whipped my cell phone out of my pocket.

I have to call her right now! I have to hear her voice!

God, you are such an idiot. Did you really think AT&T was going to have service in another *dimension*? You're on the basic plan, for Christ's sake!

503(4)-0717.04.23.B101! Get over here!

We were supposed to be off on another recruiting mission 7 minutes and 14 seconds ago!

Coming!

Wait! Wait! I need to make a phone call!

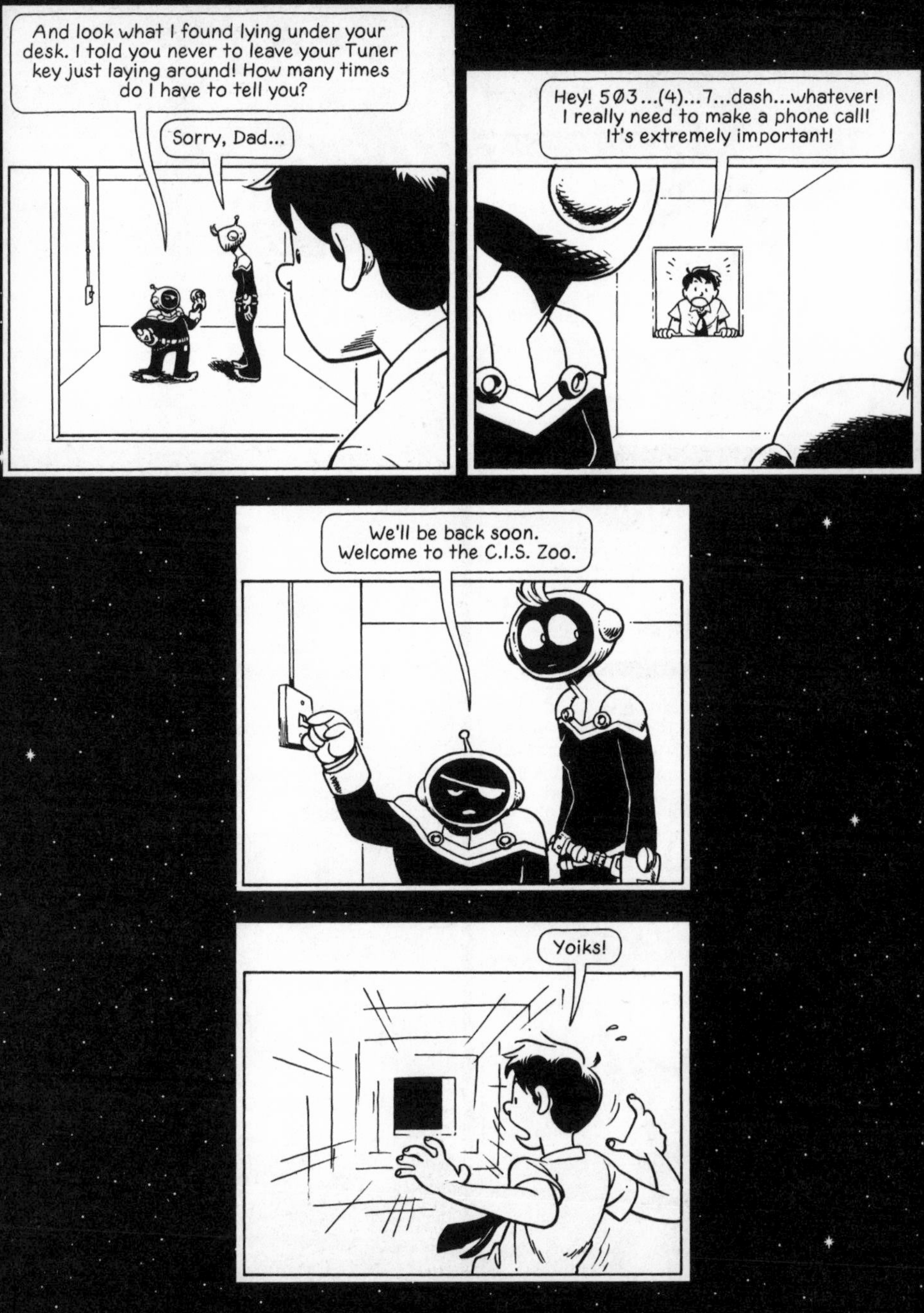
And look what I found lying under your desk. I told you never to leave your Tuner key just laying around! How many times do I have to tell you?
Sorry, Dad...
Hey! 5Ø3...(4)...7...dash...whatever! I really need to make a phone call! It's extremely important!
We'll be back soon. Welcome to the C.I.S. Zoo.
Yoiks!

The window shrank and sealed itself shut without leaving a trace on the wall. Not even a seam or a crack—it was as if the small portal had never been there.

Hey! Come on! Just one phone call! This isn't a prison, you know!

Hell, even in prison you get one phone call!

POUND! POUND!

I continued pleading and banging on the wall a bit longer, but soon it became apparent that they were gone.

Rrr...

Well, I guess there's nothing else to do but chill out and wait for them to return.

Relax. As long as Yumi doesn't hook up with some other dweeb in the next few hours, you have nothing to worry about.

Hm... How do we know if they can even make an interdimensional phone call?

Hey, if they can get the Golf Channel from our dimension, I don't see why they couldn't make a phone call happen.

16

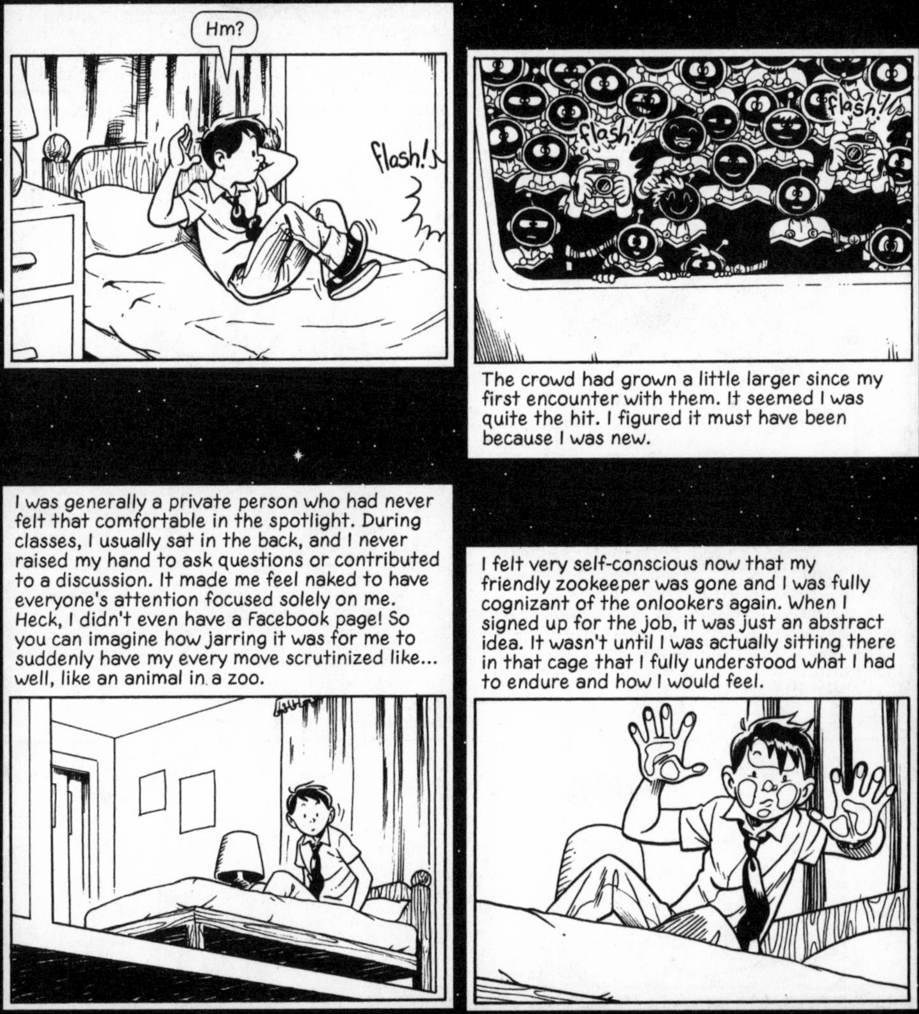
Hm?
flash!
flash!
flash!
The crowd had grown a little larger since my first encounter with them. It seemed I was quite the hit. I figured it must have been because I was new.
I was generally a private person who had never felt that comfortable in the spotlight. During classes, I usually sat in the back, and I never raised my hand to ask questions or contributed to a discussion. It made me feel naked to have everyone's attention focused solely on me. Heck, I didn't even have a Facebook page! So you can imagine how jarring it was for me to suddenly have my every move scrutinized like... well, like an animal in a zoo.
I felt very self-conscious now that my friendly zookeeper was gone and I was fully cognizant of the onlookers again. When I signed up for the job, it was just an abstract idea. It wasn't until I was actually sitting there in that cage that I fully understood what I had to endure and how I would feel.

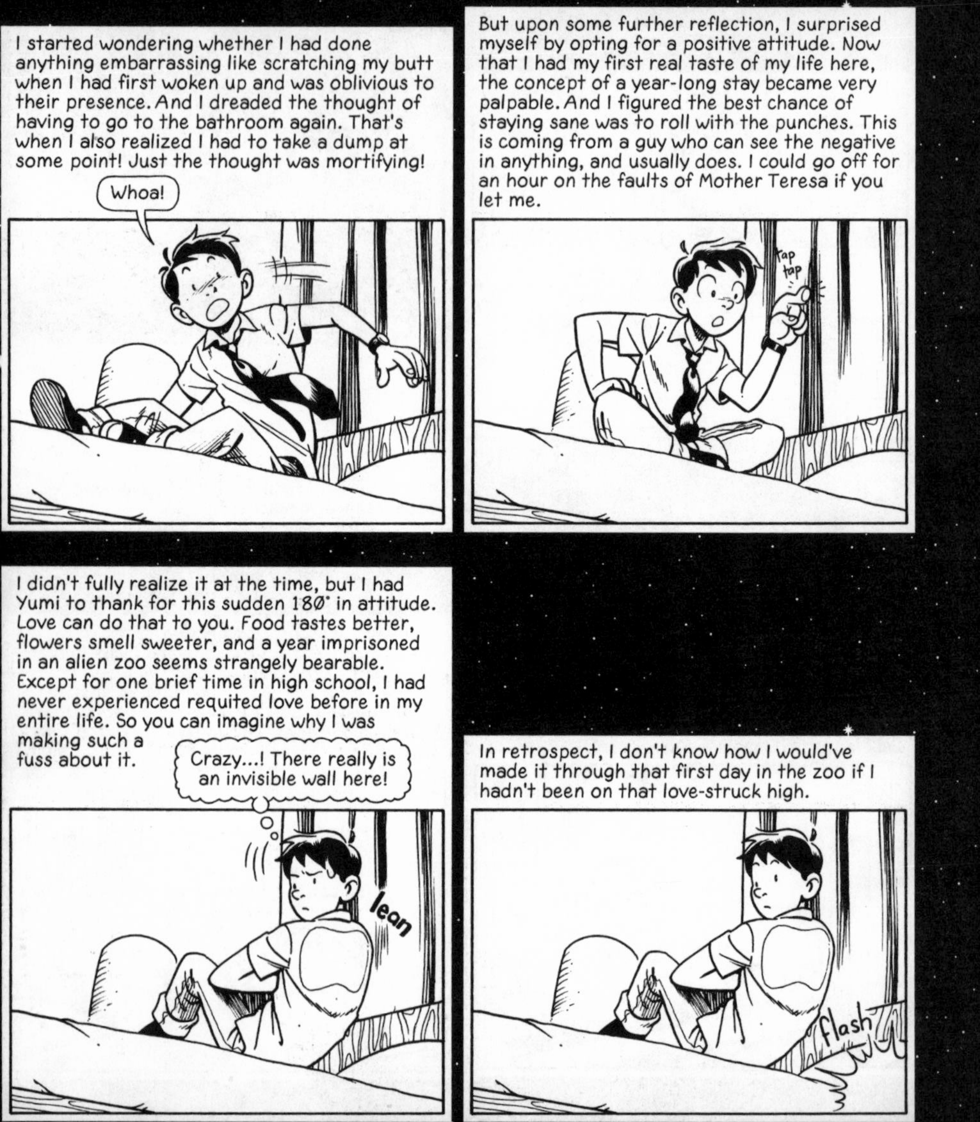
I started wondering whether I had done anything embarrassing like scratching my butt when I had first woken up and was oblivious to their presence. And I dreaded the thought of having to go to the bathroom again. That's when I also realized I had to take a dump at some point! Just the thought was mortifying!
Whoa!
But upon some further reflection, I surprised myself by opting for a positive attitude. Now that I had my first real taste of my life here, the concept of a year-long stay became very palpable. And I figured the best chance of staying sane was to roll with the punches. This is coming from a guy who can see the negative in anything, and usually does. I could go off for an hour on the faults of Mother Teresa if you let me.
tap tap
I didn't fully realize it at the time, but I had Yumi to thank for this sudden 180° in attitude. Love can do that to you. Food tastes better, flowers smell sweeter, and a year imprisoned in an alien zoo seems strangely bearable. Except for one brief time in high school, I had never experienced requited love before in my entire life. So you can imagine why I was making such a fuss about it.
Crazy...! There really is an invisible wall here!
lean
In retrospect, I don't know how I would've made it through that first day in the zoo if I hadn't been on that love-struck high.
flash

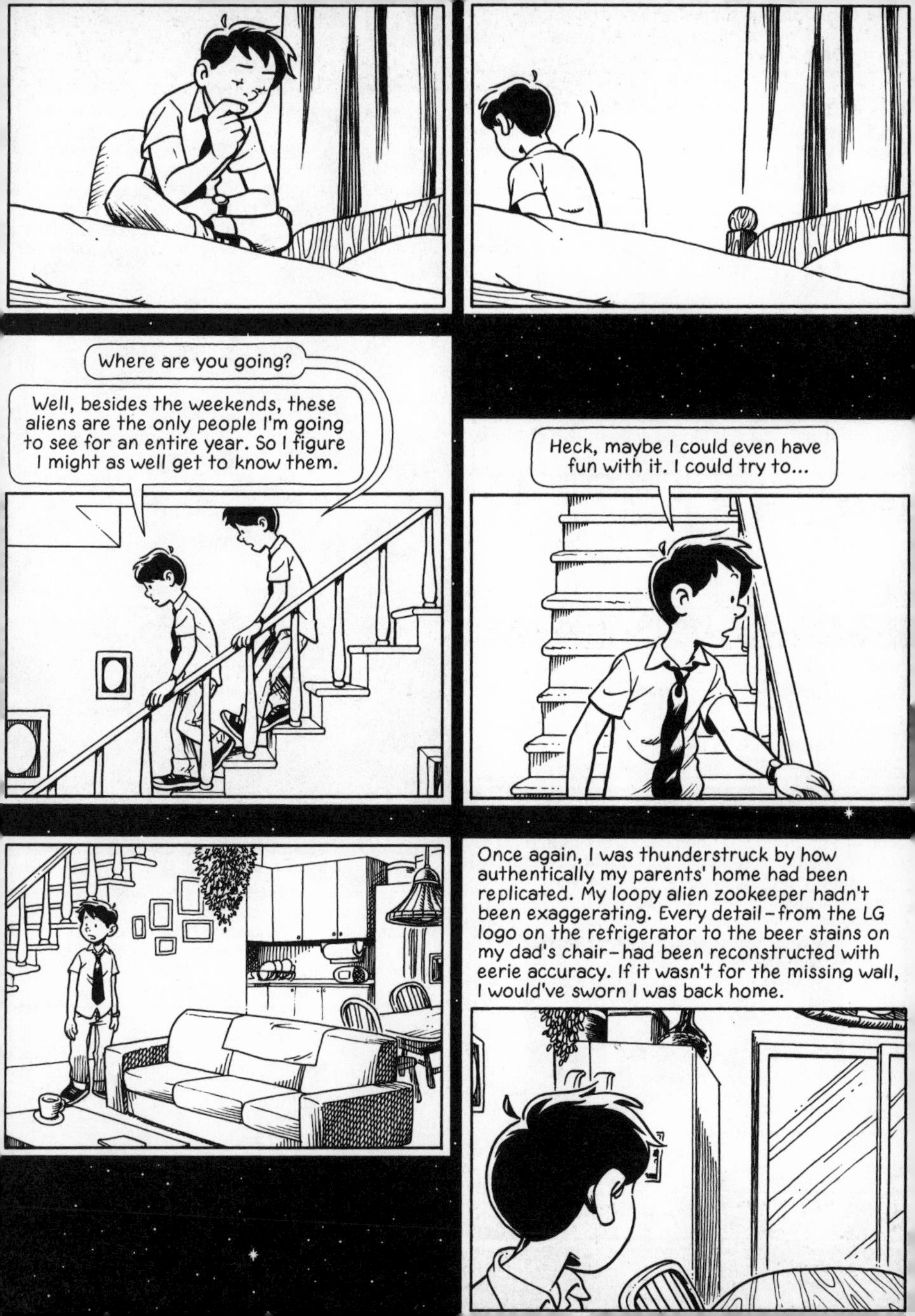
Where are you going?
Well, besides the weekends, these aliens are the only people I'm going to see for an entire year. So I figure I might as well get to know them.
Heck, maybe I could even have fun with it. I could try to...
Once again, I was thunderstruck by how authentically my parents' home had been replicated. My loopy alien zookeeper hadn't been exaggerating. Every detail–from the LG logo on the refrigerator to the beer stains on my dad's chair–had been reconstructed with eerie accuracy. If it wasn't for the missing wall, I would've sworn I was back home.

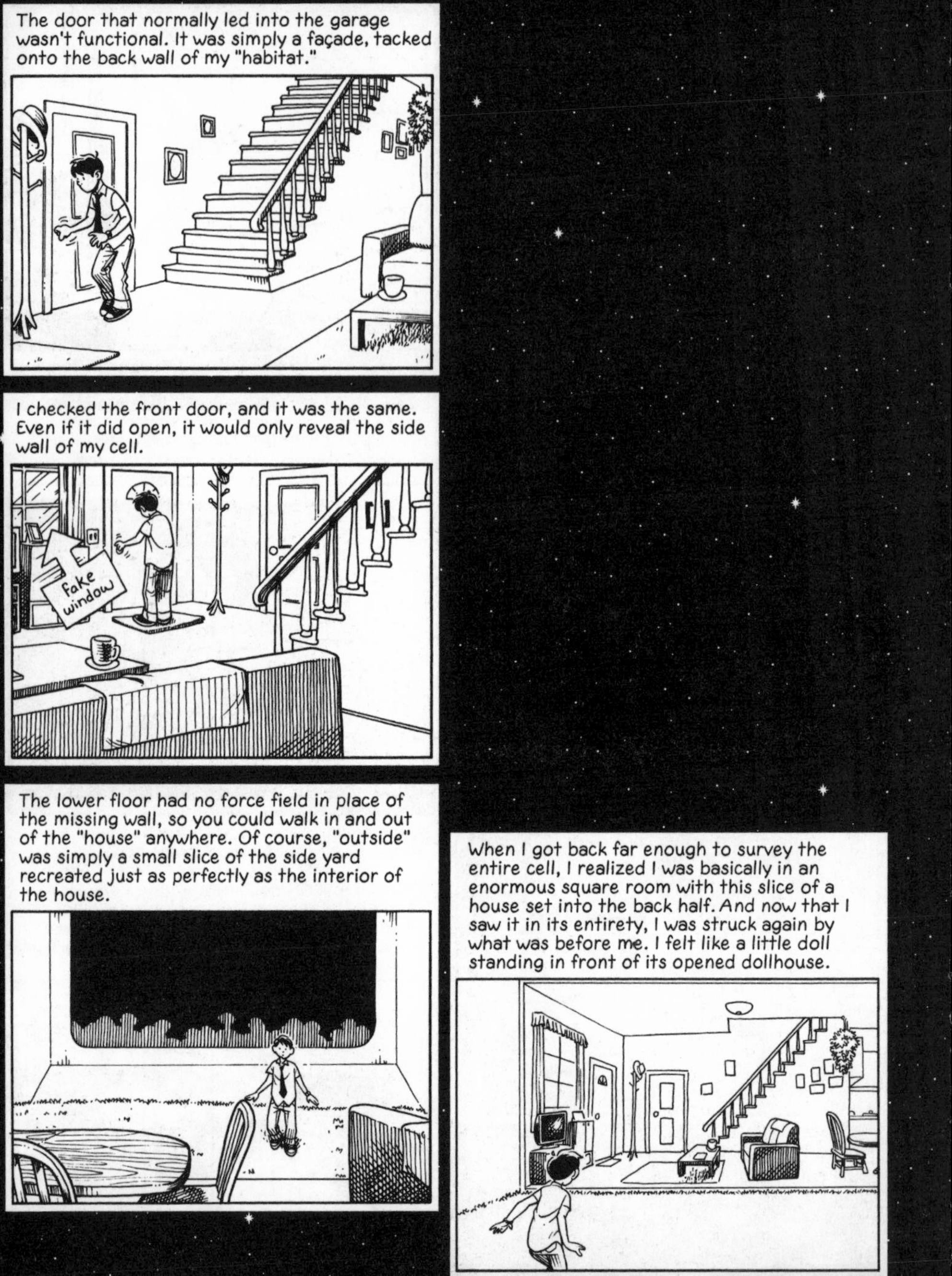
The door that normally led into the garage wasn't functional. It was simply a façade, tacked onto the back wall of my "habitat."
I checked the front door, and it was the same. Even if it did open, it would only reveal the side wall of my cell.
fake window
The lower floor had no force field in place of the missing wall, so you could walk in and out of the "house" anywhere. Of course, "outside" was simply a small slice of the side yard recreated just as perfectly as the interior of the house.
When I got back far enough to survey the entire cell, I realized I was basically in an enormous square room with this slice of a house set into the back half. And now that I saw it in its entirety, I was struck again by what was before me. I felt like a little doll standing in front of its opened dollhouse.

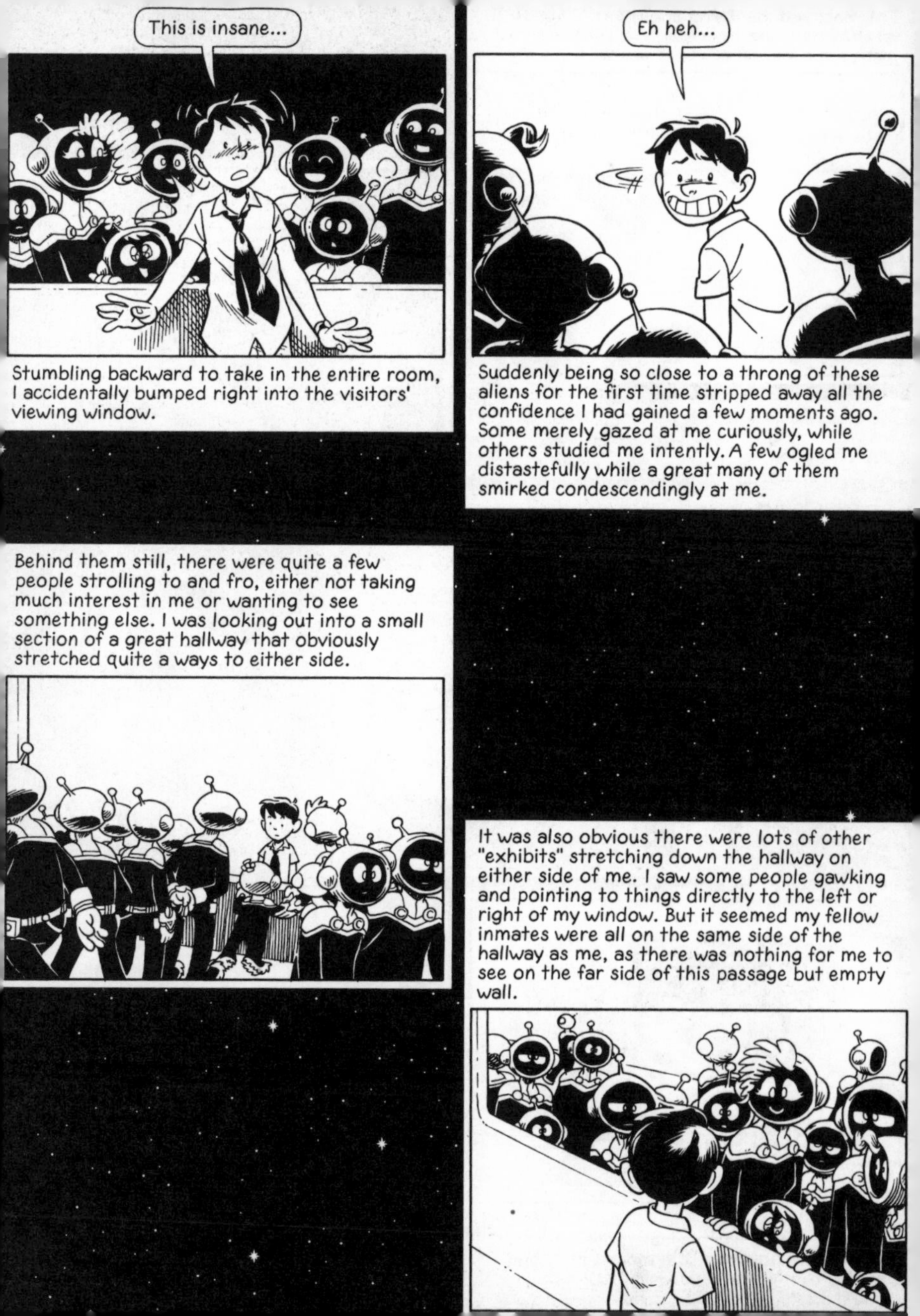
This is insane...
Stumbling backward to take in the entire room, I accidentally bumped right into the visitors' viewing window.
Eh heh...
Suddenly being so close to a throng of these aliens for the first time stripped away all the confidence I had gained a few moments ago. Some merely gazed at me curiously, while others studied me intently. A few ogled me distastefully while a great many of them smirked condescendingly at me.
Behind them still, there were quite a few people strolling to and fro, either not taking much interest in me or wanting to see something else. I was looking out into a small section of a great hallway that obviously stretched quite a ways to either side.
It was also obvious there were lots of other "exhibits" stretching down the hallway on either side of me. I saw some people gawking and pointing to things directly to the left or right of my window. But it seemed my fellow inmates were all on the same side of the hallway as me, as there was nothing for me to see on the far side of this passage but empty wall.

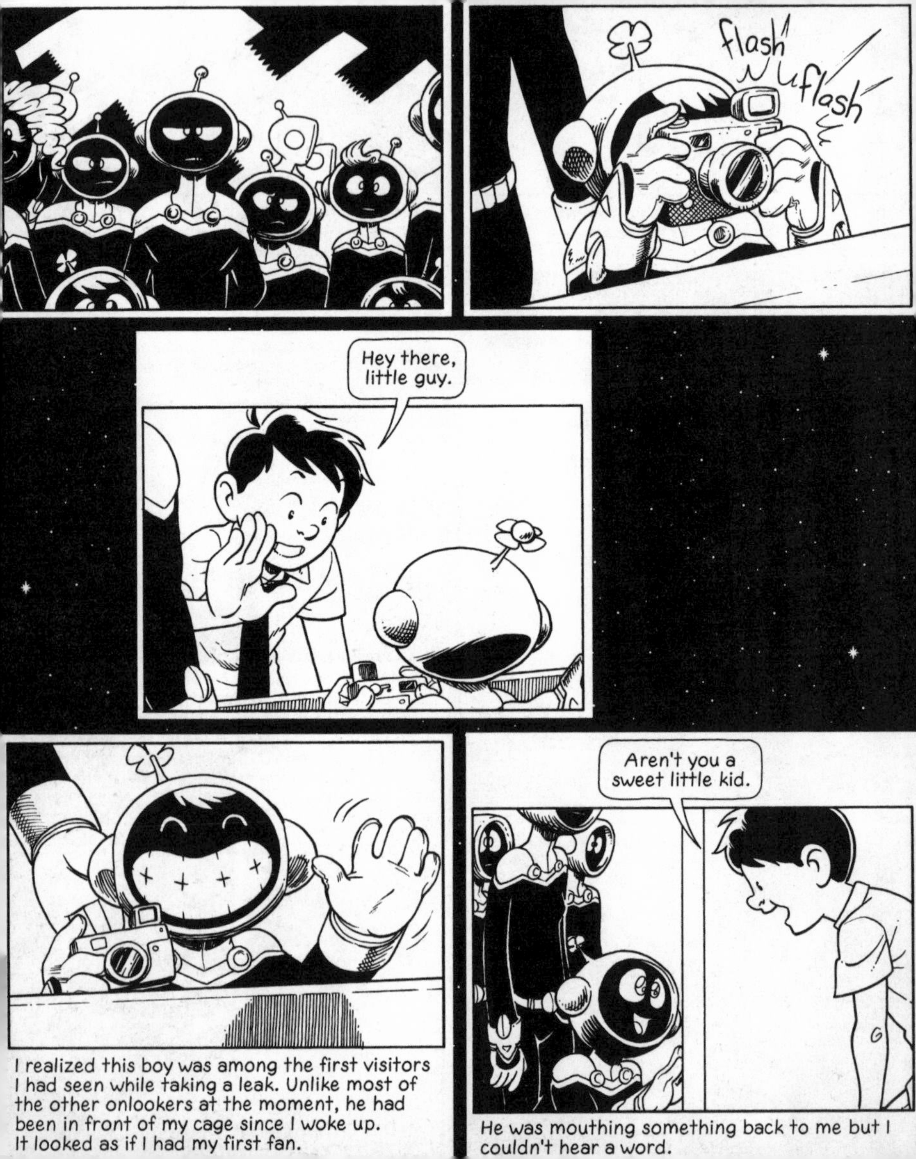
flash
flash
Hey there, little guy.
I realized this boy was among the first visitors I had seen while taking a leak. Unlike most of the other onlookers at the moment, he had been in front of my cage since I woke up. It looked as if I had my first fan.
Aren't you a sweet little kid.
He was mouthing something back to me but I couldn't hear a word.

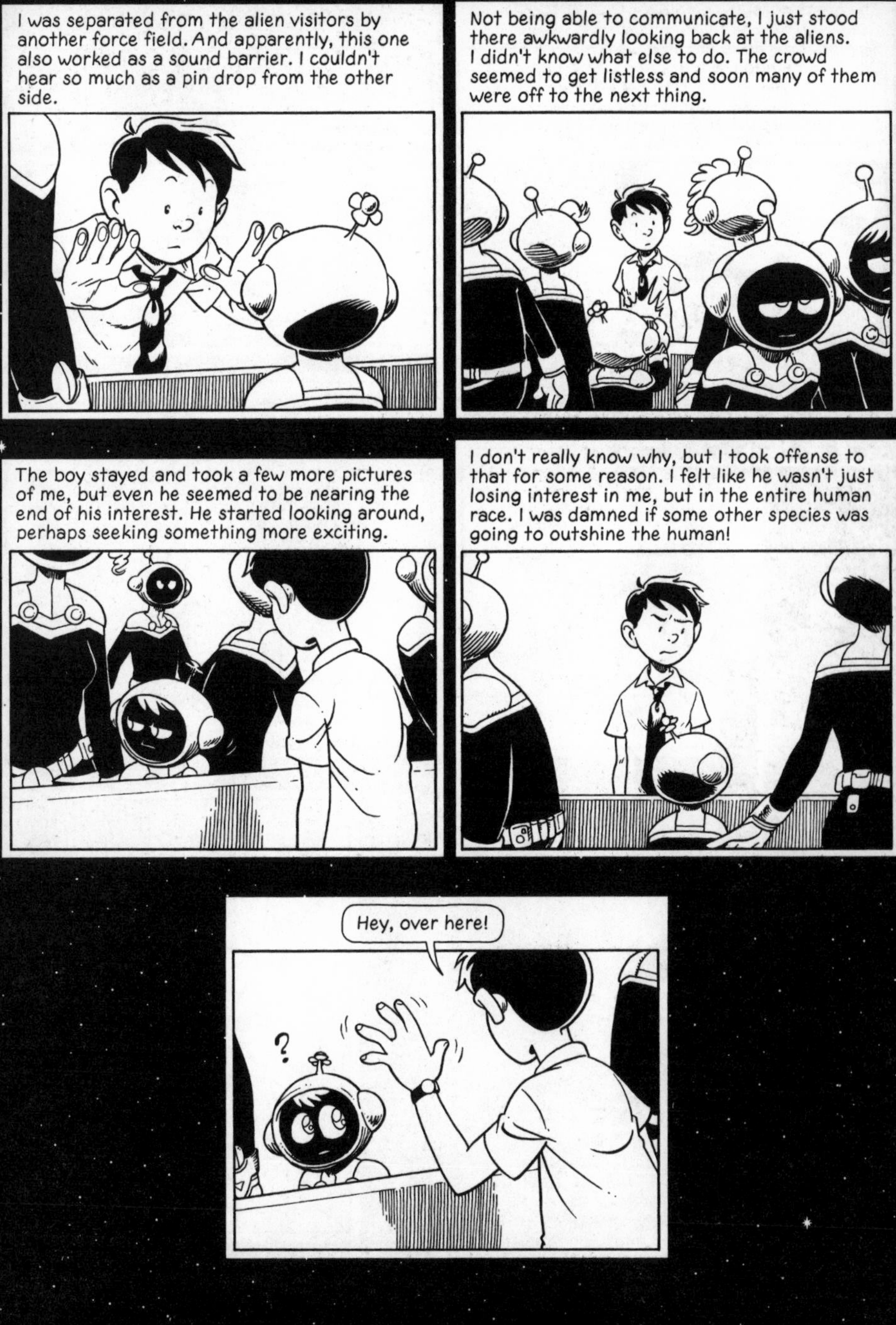
I was separated from the alien visitors by another force field. And apparently, this one also worked as a sound barrier. I couldn't hear so much as a pin drop from the other side.
Not being able to communicate, I just stood there awkwardly looking back at the aliens. I didn't know what else to do. The crowd seemed to get listless and soon many of them were off to the next thing.
The boy stayed and took a few more pictures of me, but even he seemed to be nearing the end of his interest. He started looking around, perhaps seeking something more exciting.
I don't really know why, but I took offense to that for some reason. I felt like he wasn't just losing interest in me, but in the entire human race. I was damned if some other species was going to outshine the human!
Hey, over here!
?

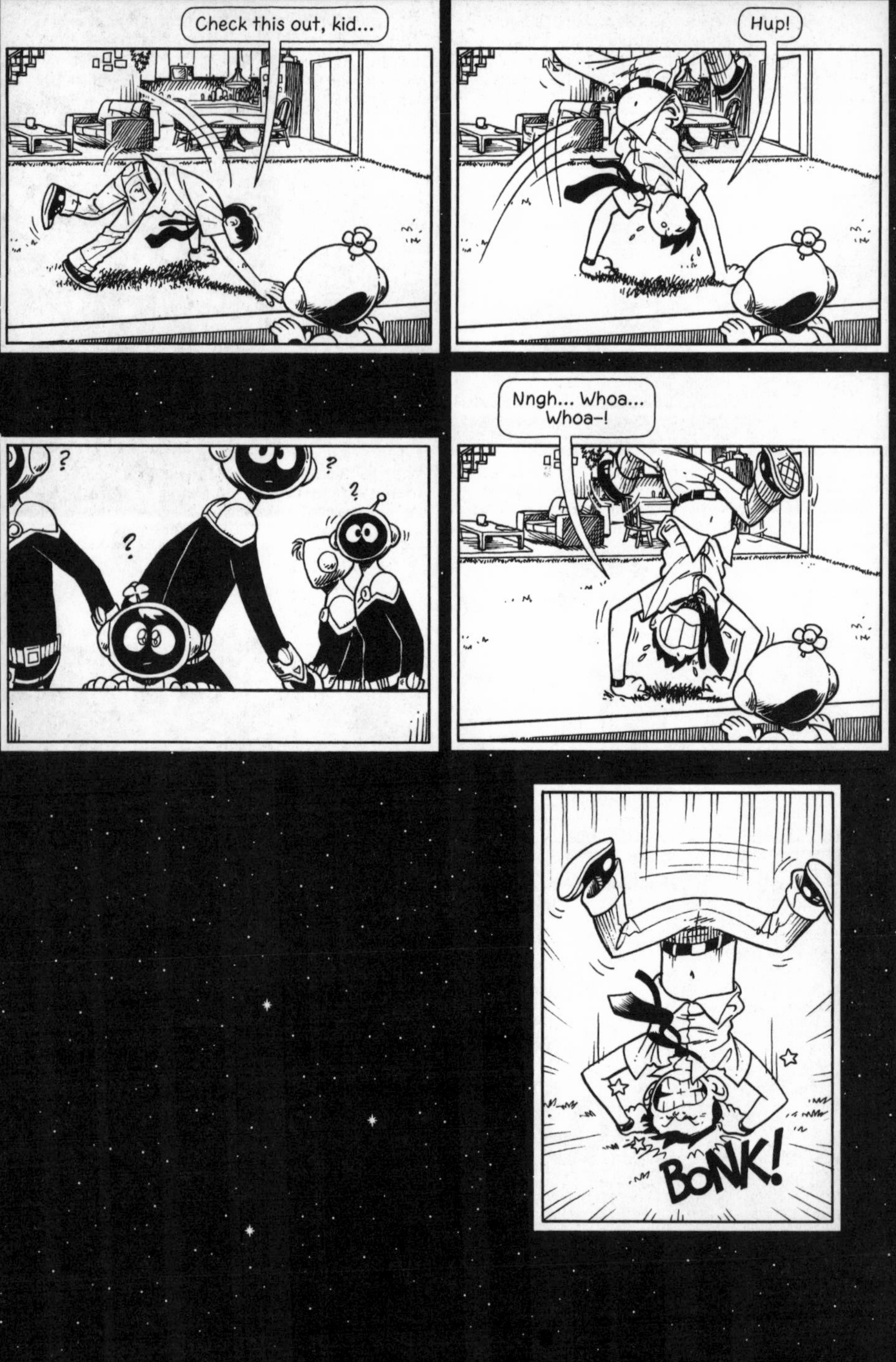
Check this out, kid...
Hup!
?
?
?
?
Nngh... Whoa... Whoa-!
BONK!

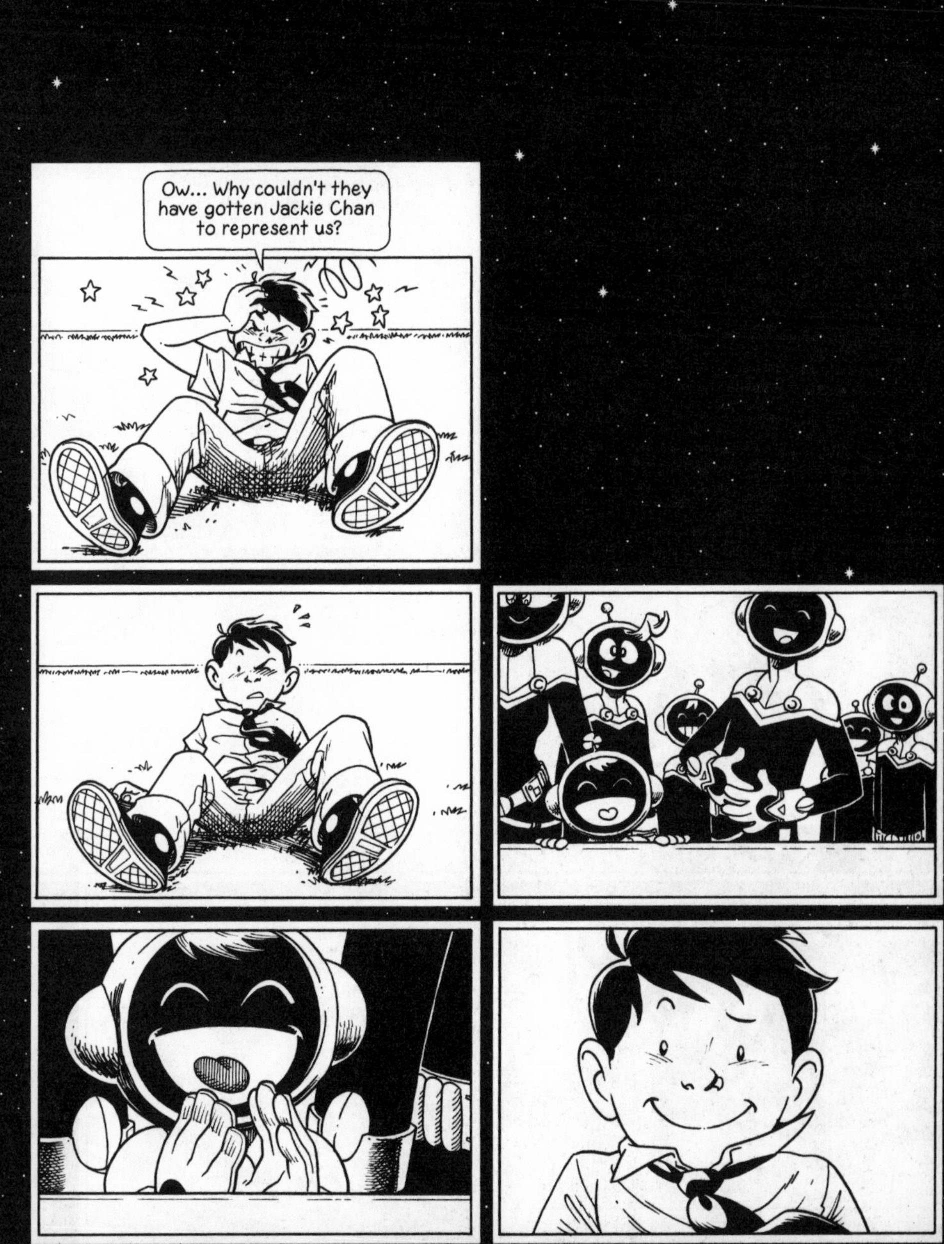
Ow... Why couldn't they have gotten Jackie Chan to represent us?

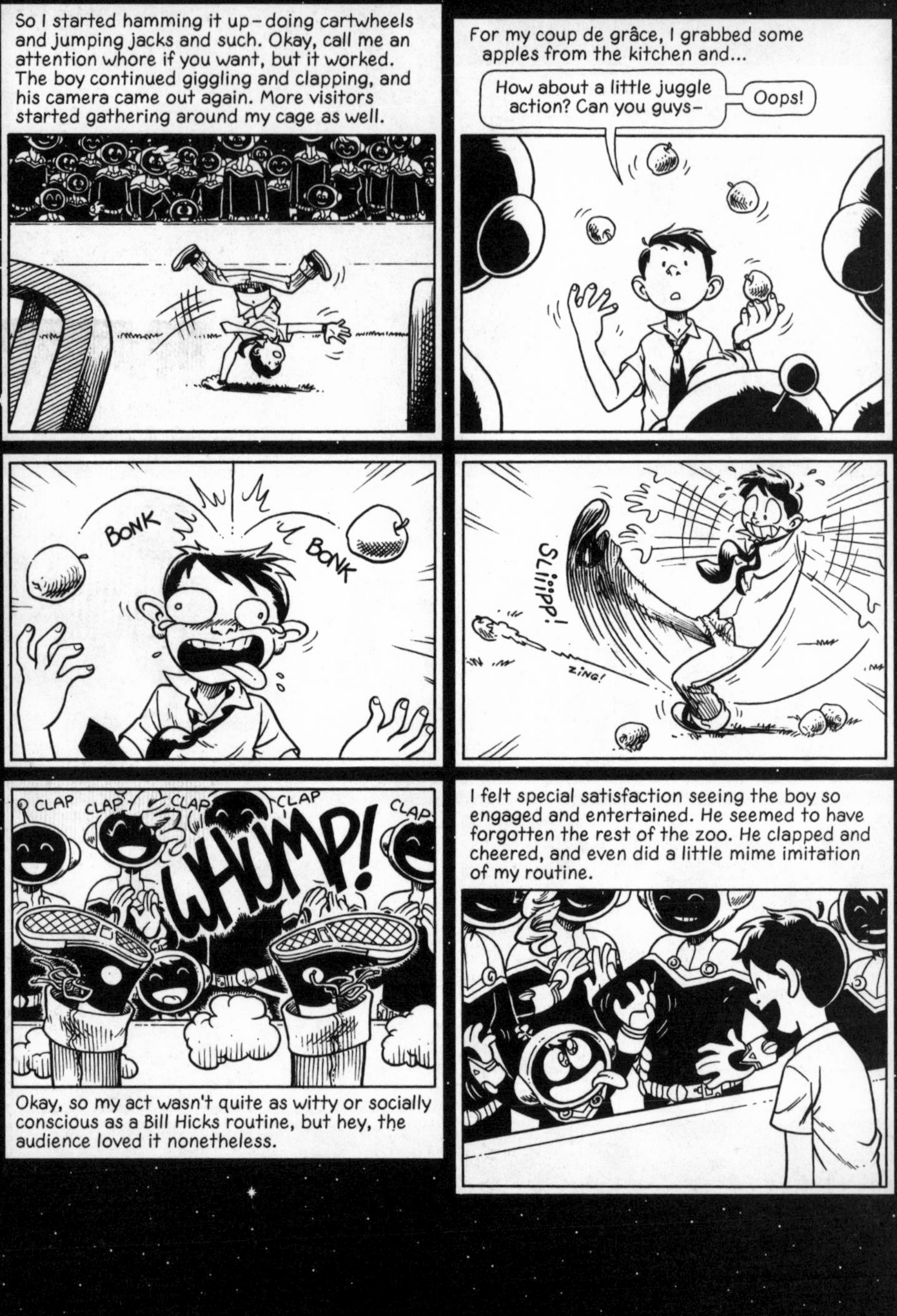
So I started hamming it up–doing cartwheels and jumping jacks and such. Okay, call me an attention whore if you want, but it worked. The boy continued giggling and clapping, and his camera came out again. More visitors started gathering around my cage as well.
For my coup de grâce, I grabbed some apples from the kitchen and...
How about a little juggle action? Can you guys–
Oops!
BONK
BONK
SLIiiPP!
ZING!
CLAP
CLAP
CLAP
CLAP
CLAP
WHUMP!
Okay, so my act wasn't quite as witty or socially conscious as a Bill Hicks routine, but hey, the audience loved it nonetheless.
I felt special satisfaction seeing the boy so engaged and entertained. He seemed to have forgotten the rest of the zoo. He clapped and cheered, and even did a little mime imitation of my routine.

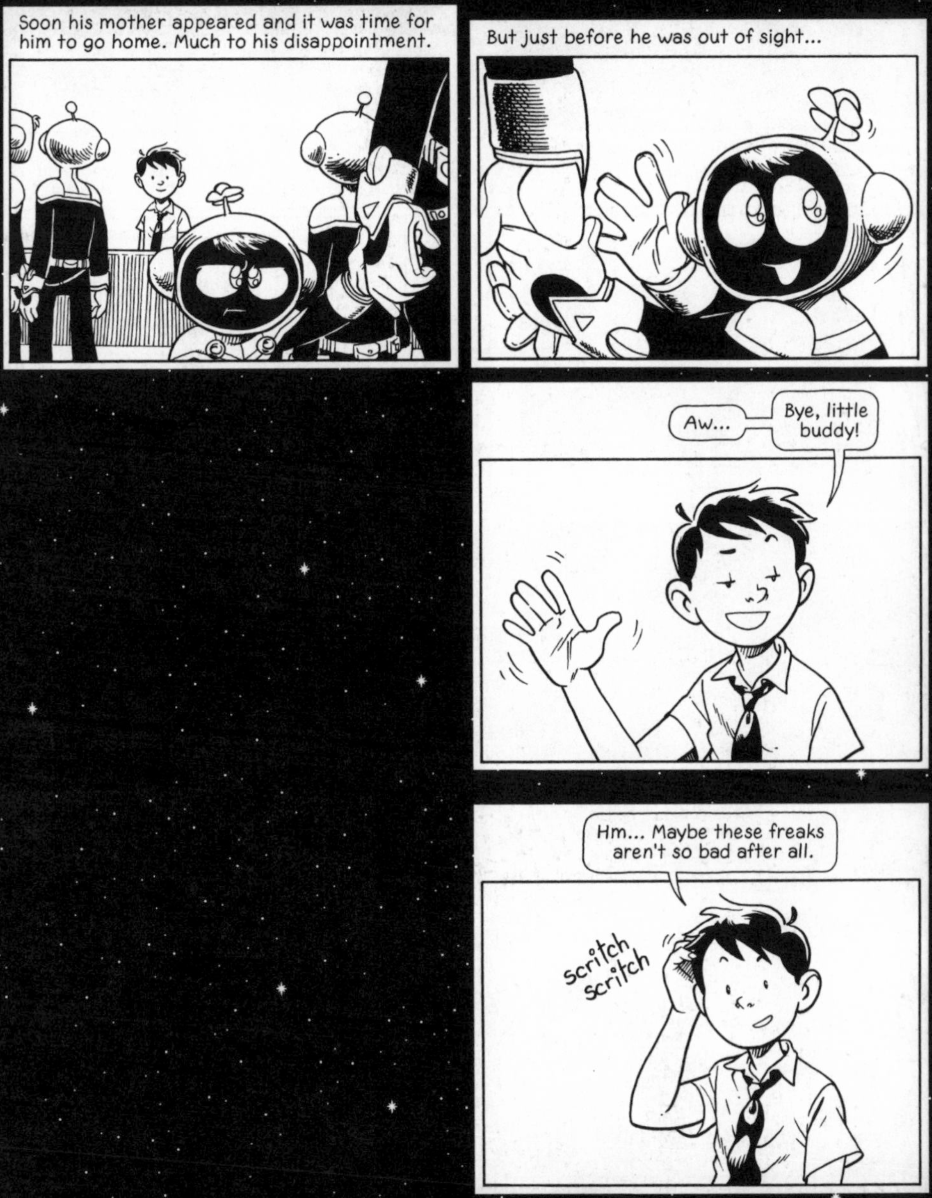
Soon his mother appeared and it was time for him to go home. Much to his disappointment.
But just before he was out of sight...
Aw...
Bye, little buddy!
Hm... Maybe these freaks aren't so bad after all.
scritch scritch

Beat from my miniature vaudeville impression, I went back "into" the living room and plopped down on the couch.

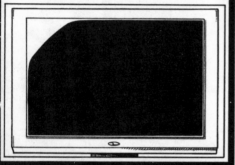

The joy in the boy's face lingered in my mind. An unfamiliar feeling of contentment and calm delight crept into me at the thought of how happy I had made him. It's a feeling I never really experienced before. It seemed there was actually some good to be mined in my new occupation after all. Perhaps I had been a bit hasty in my brash dismissal of it.

click!

...and if you order now, you'll get two Shamwows for the price of one!

But quicker than I'd like to admit, my thoughts simply drifted back to Yumi again. No matter how great this job turned out to be, it still didn't change the fact that for an entire year, I could only see Yumi on the weekends.

I really hope that doesn't stop her from pursuing a relationship with you.

Well, I figure she's extremely busy this coming year anyway considering it's her last year in school and stuff. Who knows, maybe the weekends are the only free time she has herself. I'd be lucky if she could make room for me in any capacity.

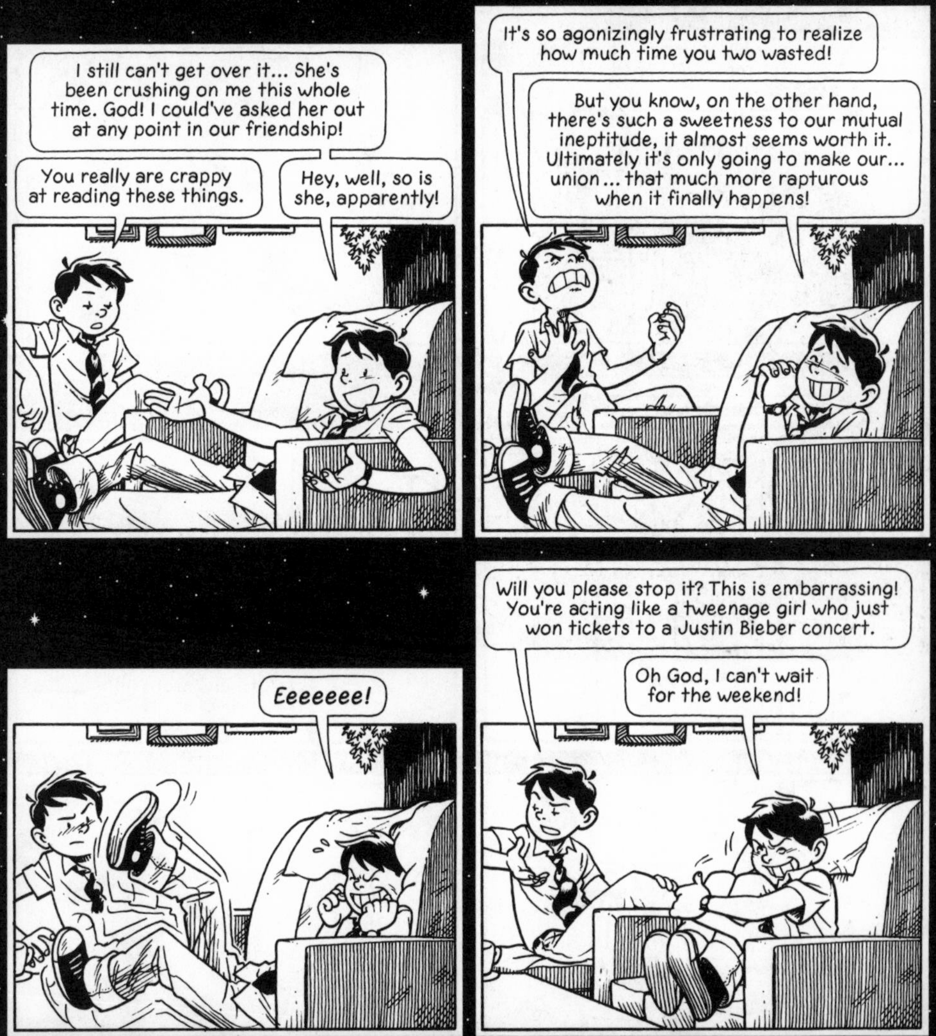

I still can't get over it... She's been crushing on me this whole time. God! I could've asked her out at any point in our friendship!
You really are crappy at reading these things.
Hey, well, so is she, apparently!
It's so agonizingly frustrating to realize how much time you two wasted!
But you know, on the other hand, there's such a sweetness to our mutual ineptitude, it almost seems worth it. Ultimately it's only going to make our... union... that much more rapturous when it finally happens!
Eeeeeee!
Will you please stop it? This is embarrassing! You're acting like a tweenage girl who just won tickets to a Justin Bieber concert.
Oh God, I can't wait for the weekend!

Where should I take her on our first date? What should I wear? How should I go in for our first kiss? Should I do the ol' yawn'n'stretch routine? No no, that would cheapen it. After all, she just might be the love of my life! I mean, what more could I want in a woman?
I was so excited and terrified at the same time. It was awesome! I couldn't remember the last time things had worked out for me like that.
Oh, Yumi!!
SPROING!
Poof!

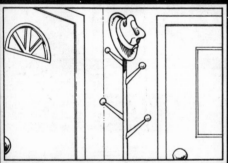

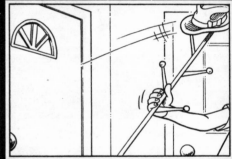

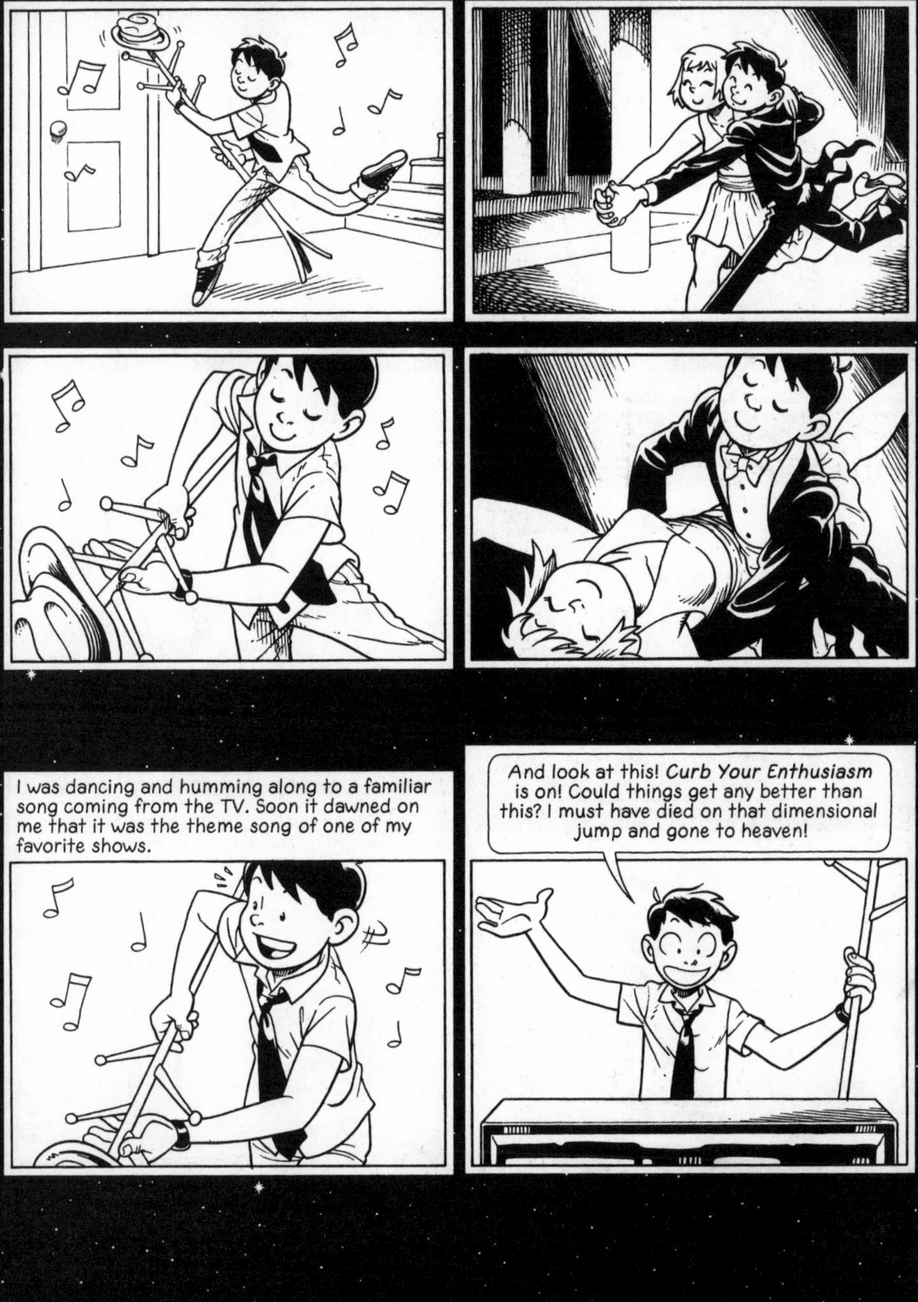
I was dancing and humming along to a familiar song coming from the TV. Soon it dawned on me that it was the theme song of one of my favorite shows.
And look at this! *Curb Your Enthusiasm* is on! Could things get any better than this? I must have died on that dimensional jump and gone to heaven!

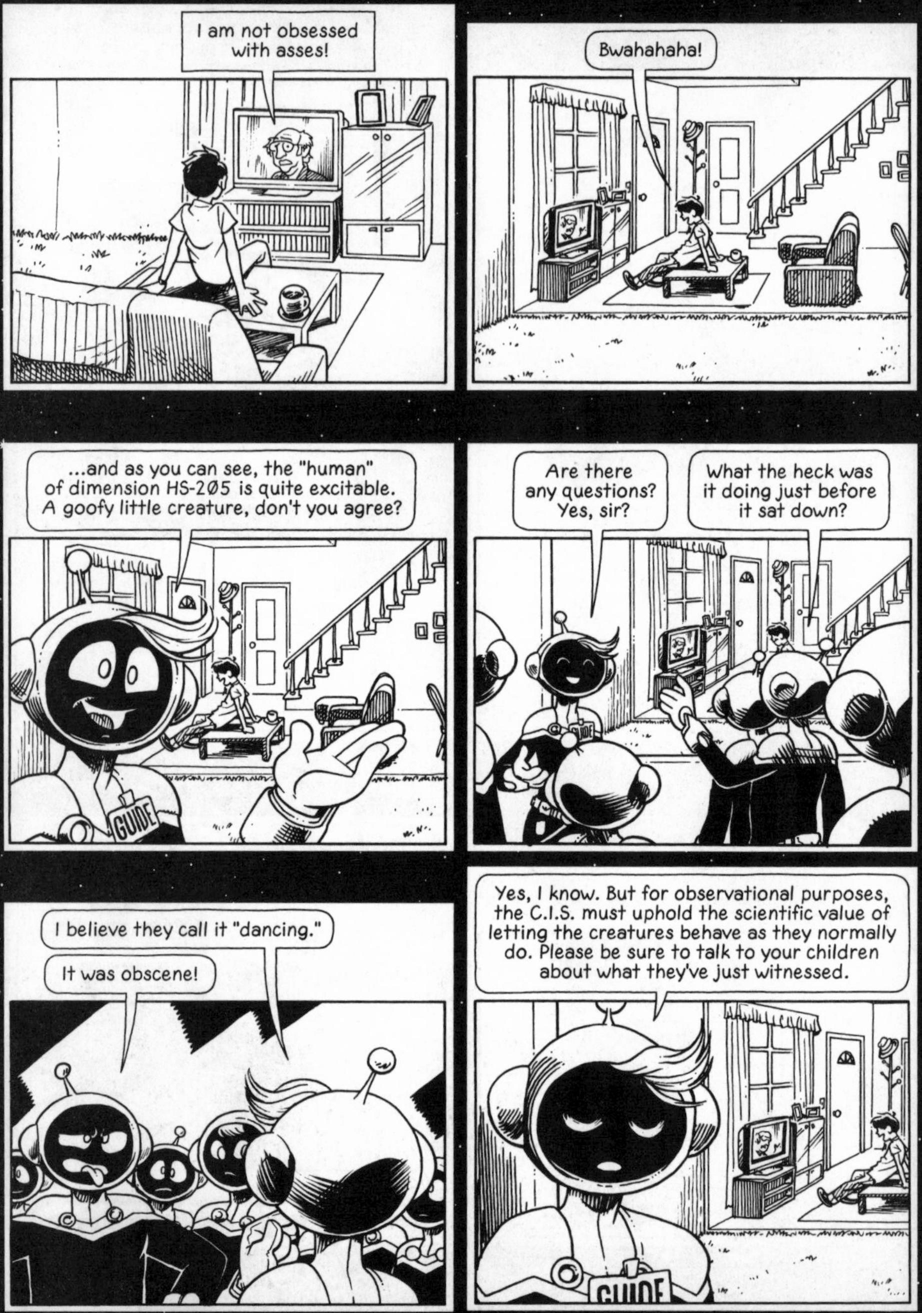
I am not obsessed with asses!
Bwahahaha!
...and as you can see, the "human" of dimension HS-2Ø5 is quite excitable. A goofy little creature, don't you agree?
GUIDE
Are there any questions? Yes, sir?
What the heck was it doing just before it sat down?
I believe they call it "dancing."
It was obscene!
Yes, I know. But for observational purposes, the C.I.S. must uphold the scientific value of letting the creatures behave as they normally do. Please be sure to talk to your children about what they've just witnessed.

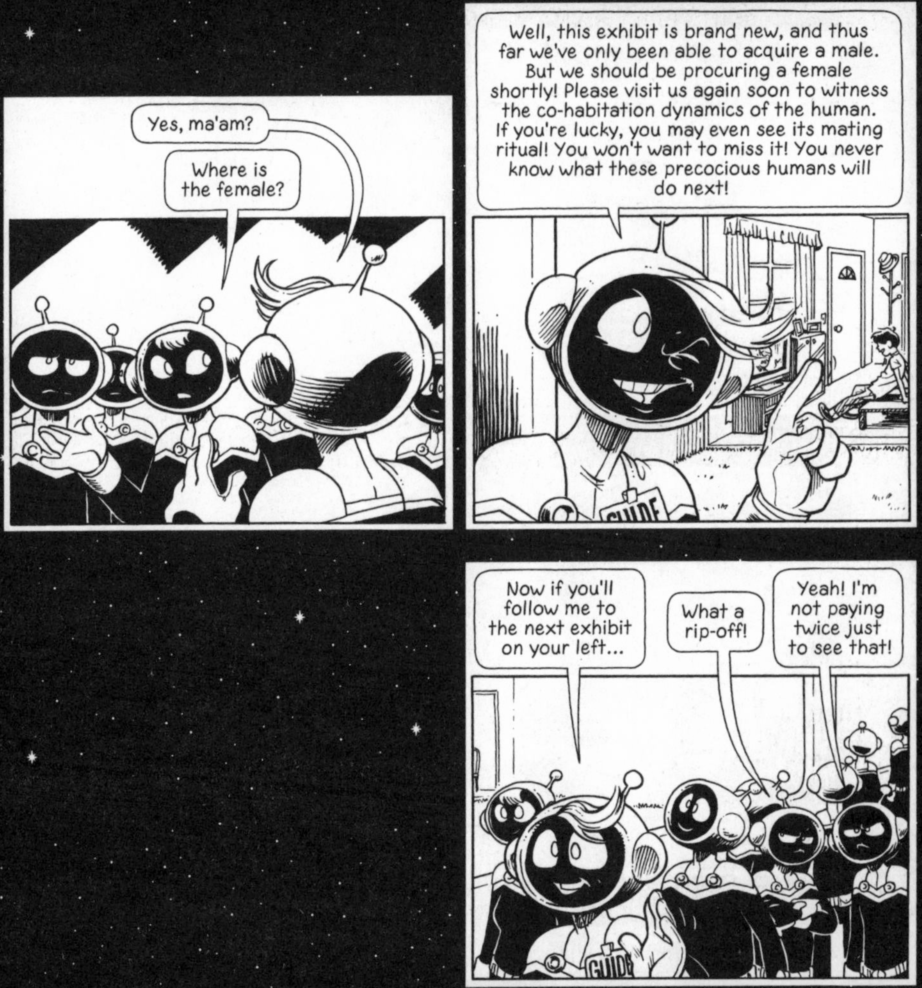
Where is the female?
Yes, ma'am?
Well, this exhibit is brand new, and thus far we've only been able to acquire a male. But we should be procuring a female shortly! Please visit us again soon to witness the co-habitation dynamics of the human. If you're lucky, you may even see its mating ritual! You won't want to miss it! You never know what these precocious humans will do next!
GUIDE
Now if you'll follow me to the next exhibit on your left...
What a rip-off!
Yeah! I'm not paying twice just to see that!
GUIDE

CHAPTER
12

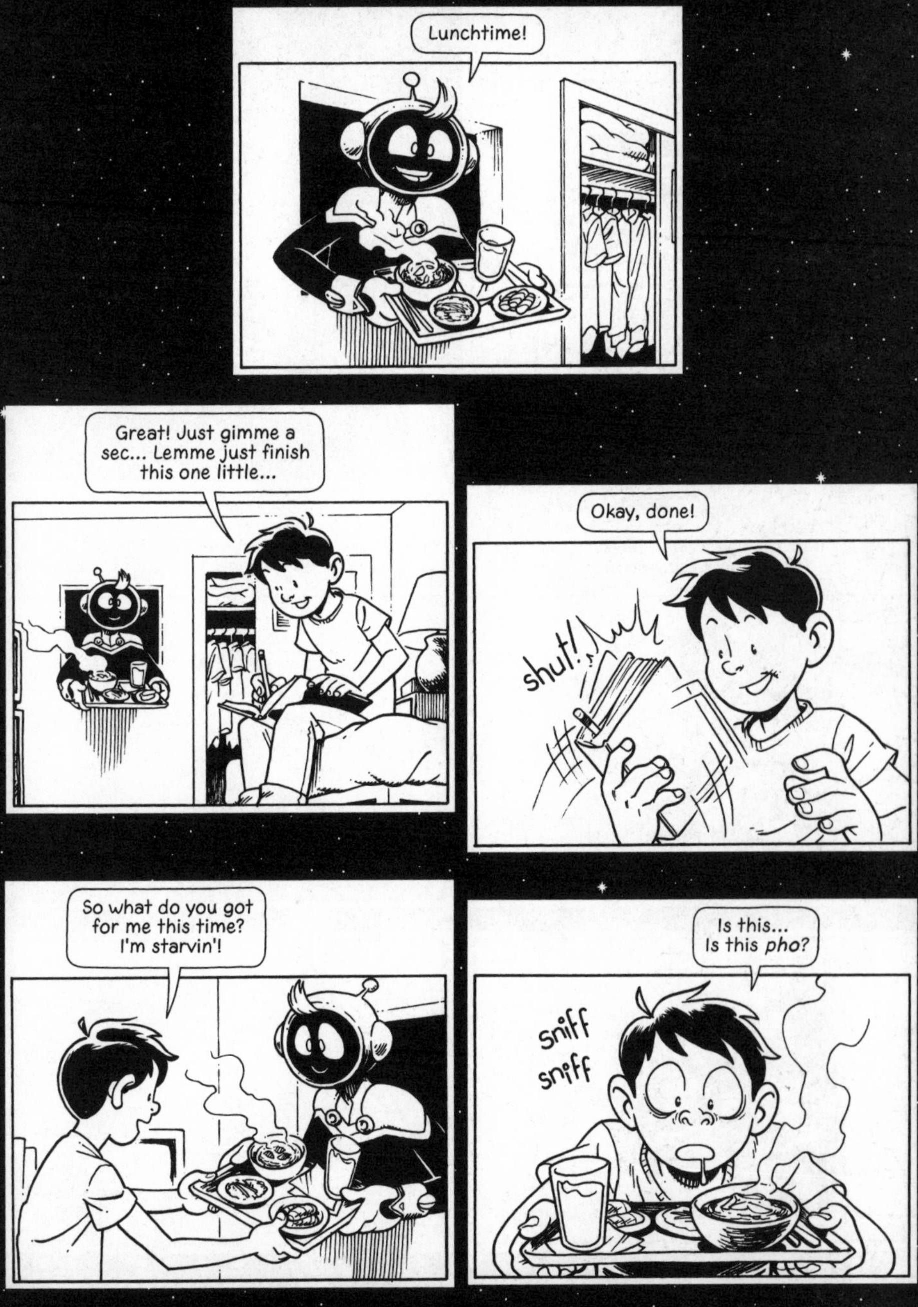
Lunchtime!
Great! Just gimme a sec... Lemme just finish this one little...
Okay, done!
shut!
So what do you got for me this time? I'm starvin'!
Is this... Is this *pho?*
sniff sniff

Oh, bless you!
What were you doing just now, Andy Go?
Hm? Oh, I was just sketching.
I have to tell you... I haven't drawn for pleasure in months. Both art school and my total failure to break into the illustration biz killed all the joy out of drawing for me.
But this whole experience has rejuvenated me! It's really inspired me to document all this craziness through my art.
Wanna see?
TOSS!
SLURP

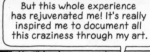

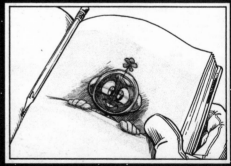

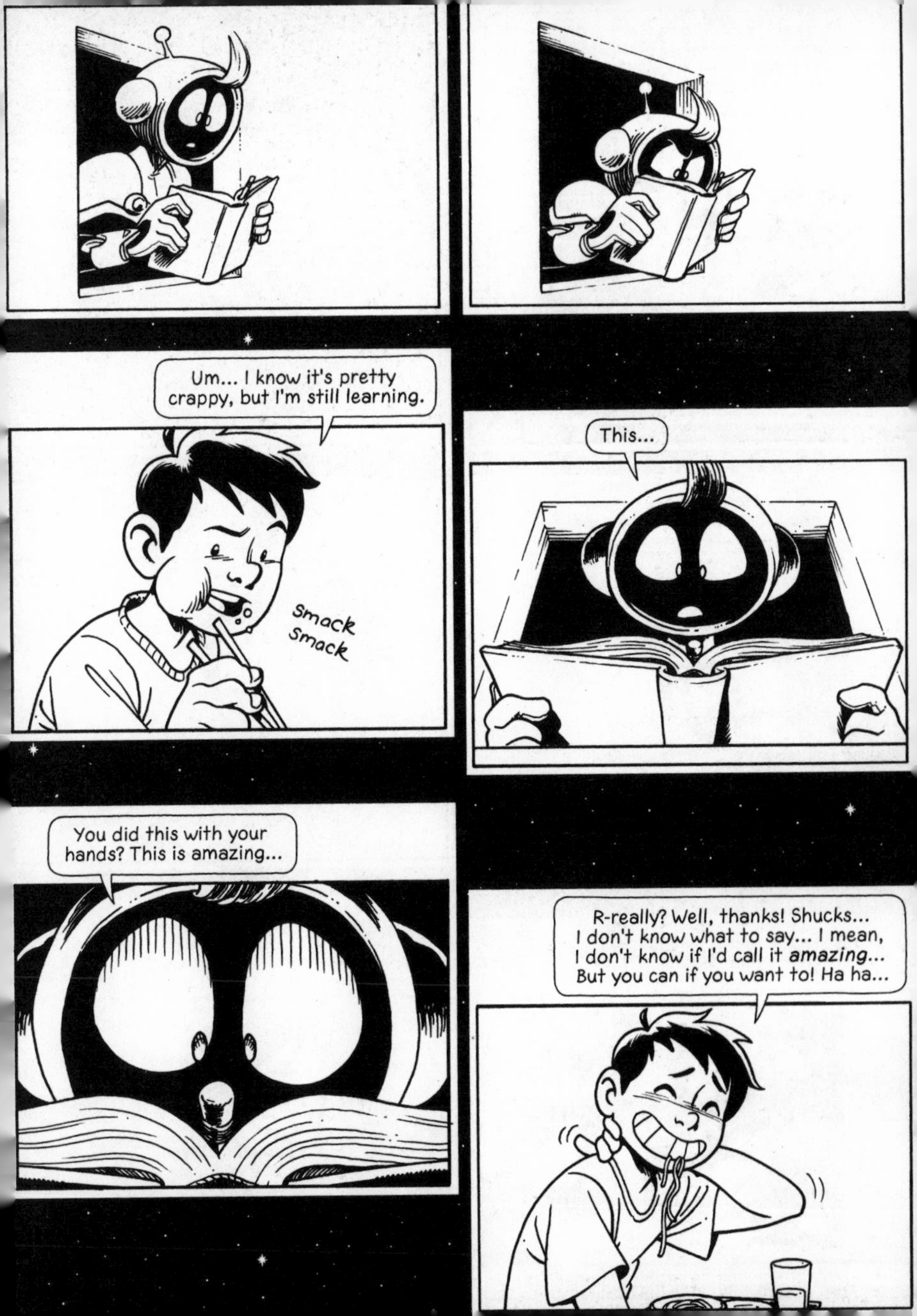
Um... I know it's pretty crappy, but I'm still learning.
Smack Smack
This...
You did this with your hands? This is amazing...
R-really? Well, thanks! Shucks... I don't know what to say... I mean, I don't know if I'd call it *amazing*... But you can if you want to! Ha ha...

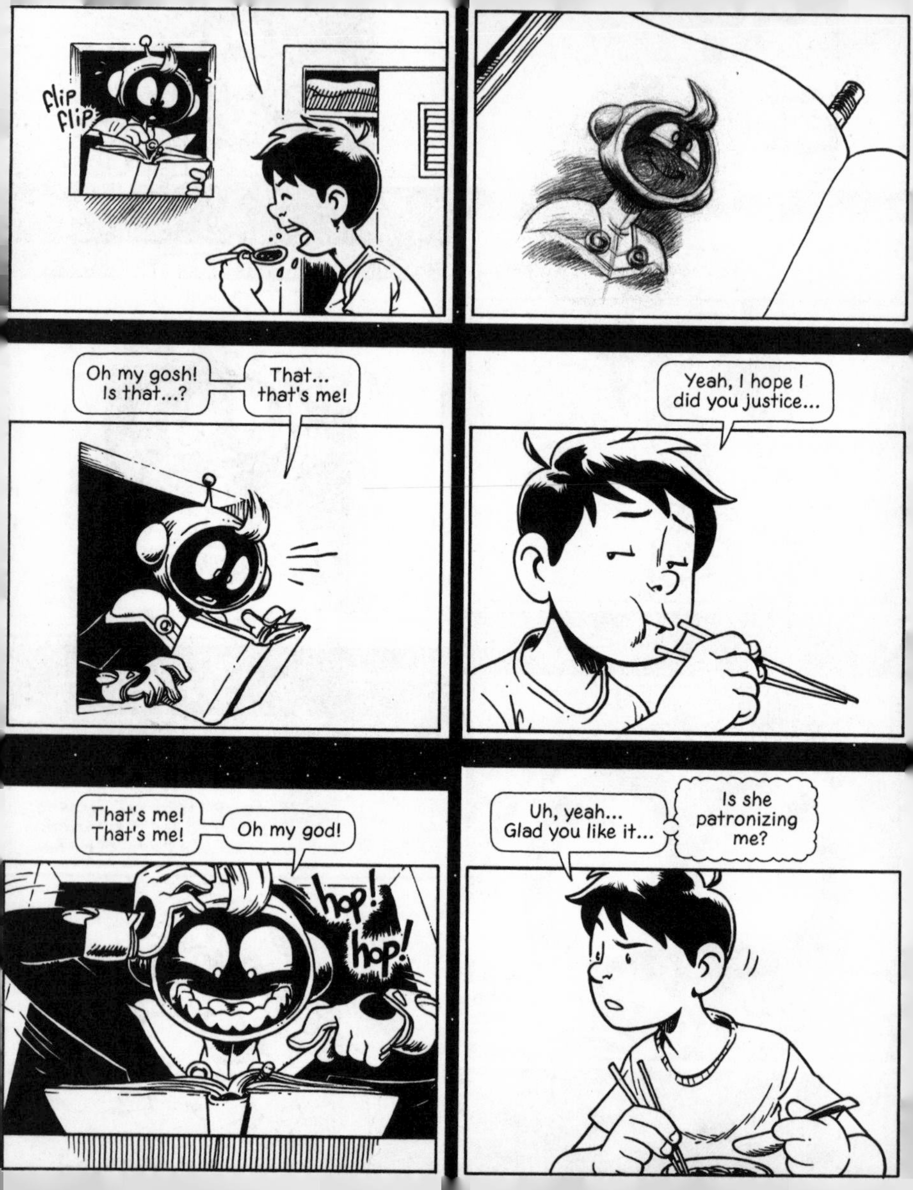
flip flip
Oh my gosh! Is that...?
That... that's me!
Yeah, I hope I did you justice...
That's me! That's me!
Oh my god!
hop! hop!
Uh, yeah... Glad you like it...
Is she patronizing me?

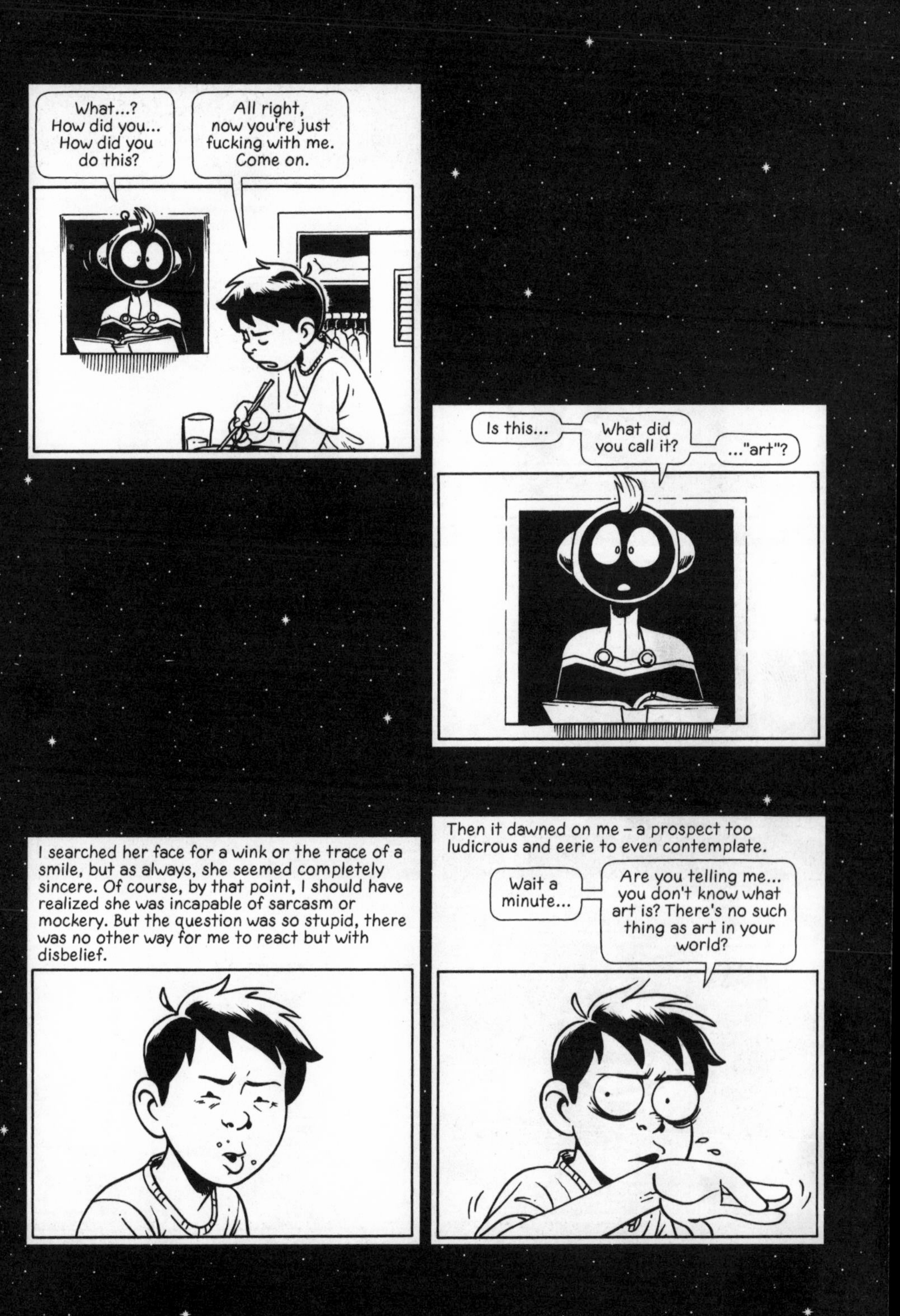
What...?
How did you...
How did you
do this?
All right,
now you're just
fucking with me.
Come on.
Is this...
What did
you call it?
..."art"?
I searched her face for a wink or the trace of a smile, but as always, she seemed completely sincere. Of course, by that point, I should have realized she was incapable of sarcasm or mockery. But the question was so stupid, there was no other way for me to react but with disbelief.
Then it dawned on me – a prospect too ludicrous and eerie to even contemplate.
Wait a
minute...
Are you telling me...
you don't know what
art is? There's no such
thing as art in your
world?

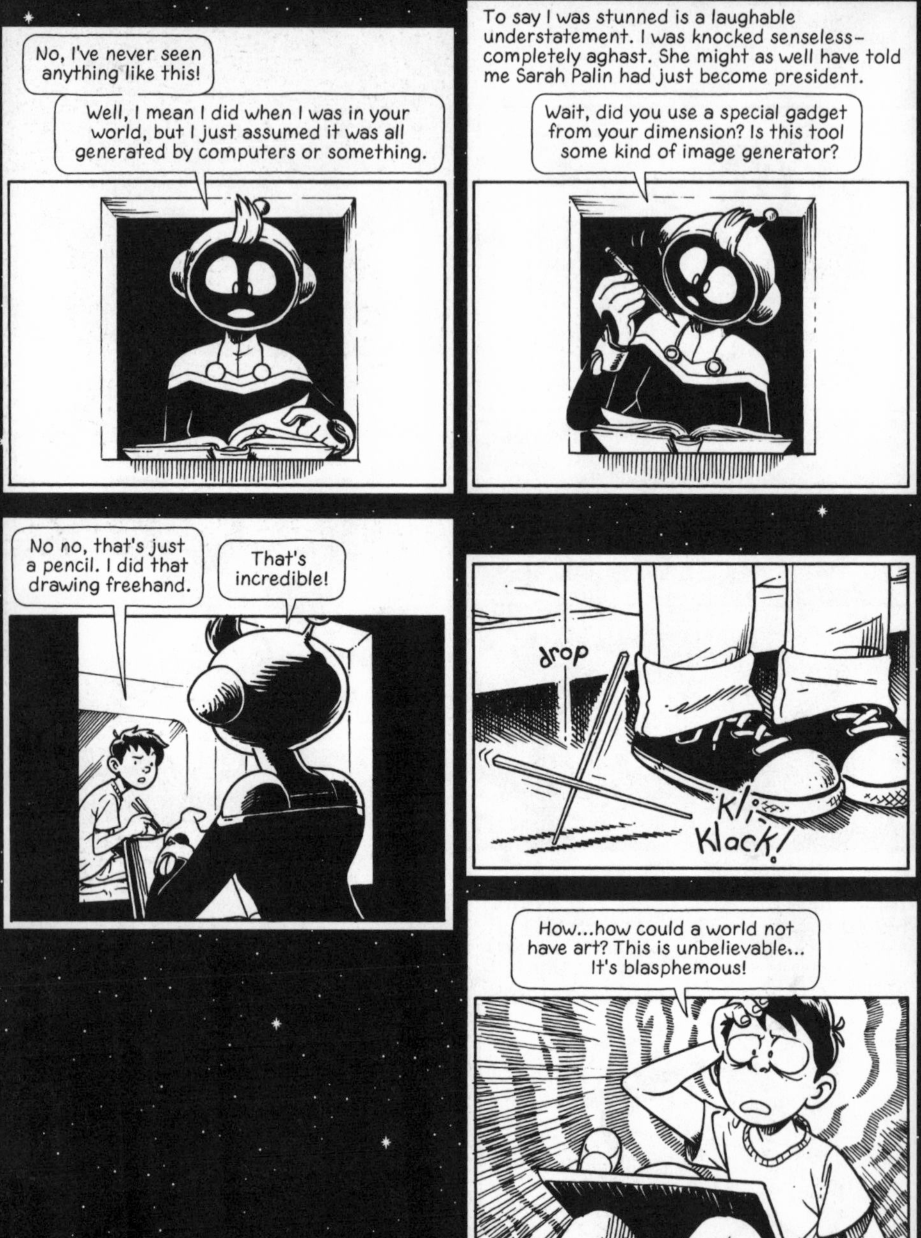
No, I've never seen anything like this!
Well, I mean I did when I was in your world, but I just assumed it was all generated by computers or something.
To say I was stunned is a laughable understatement. I was knocked senseless- completely aghast. She might as well have told me Sarah Palin had just become president.
Wait, did you use a special gadget from your dimension? Is this tool some kind of image generator?
No no, that's just a pencil. I did that drawing freehand.
That's incredible!
drop
Kli-Klack!
How...how could a world not have art? This is unbelievable... It's blasphemous!

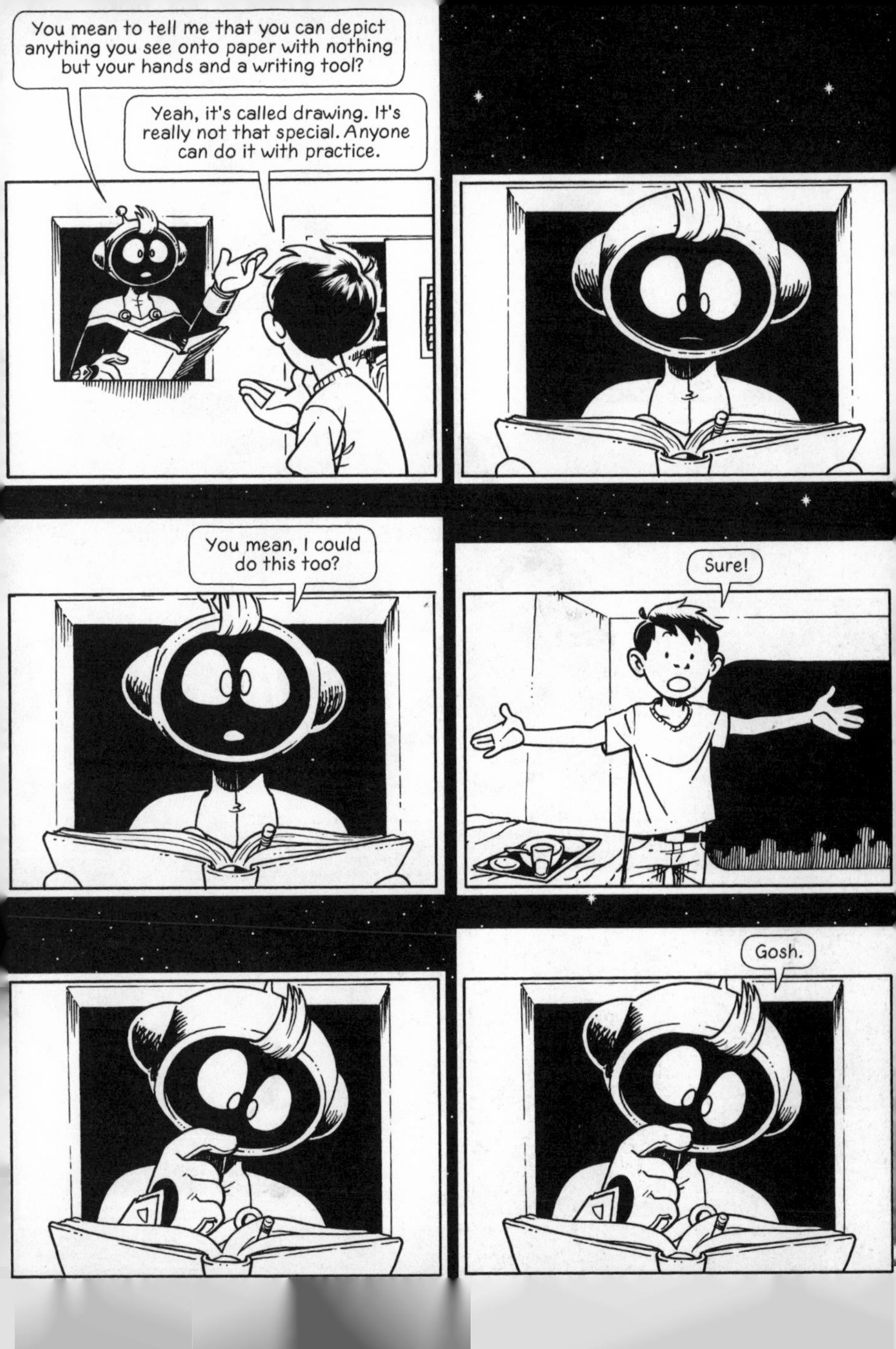
You mean to tell me that you can depict anything you see onto paper with nothing but your hands and a writing tool?
Yeah, it's called drawing. It's really not that special. Anyone can do it with practice.
You mean, I could do this too?
Sure!
Gosh.

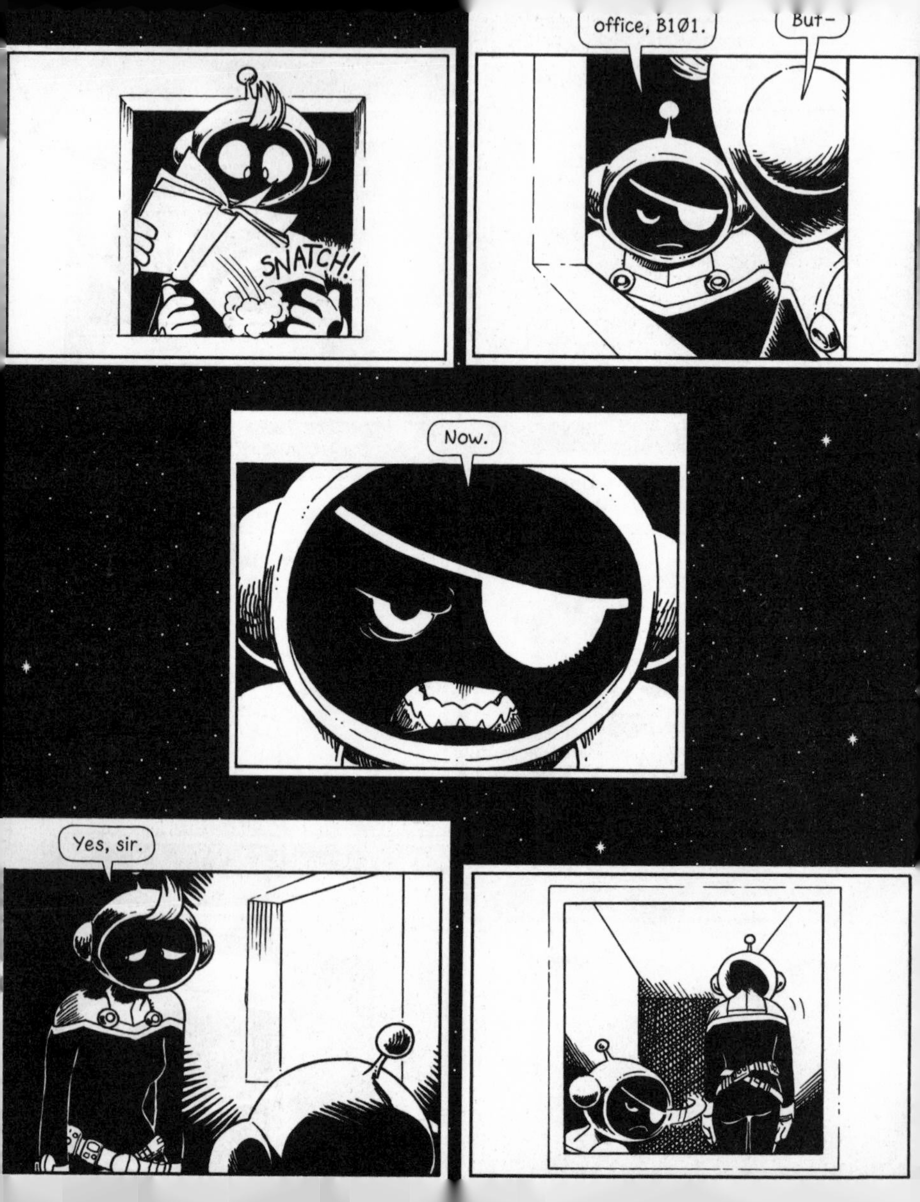
SNATCH!
office, B1Ø1.
But-
Now.
Yes, sir.

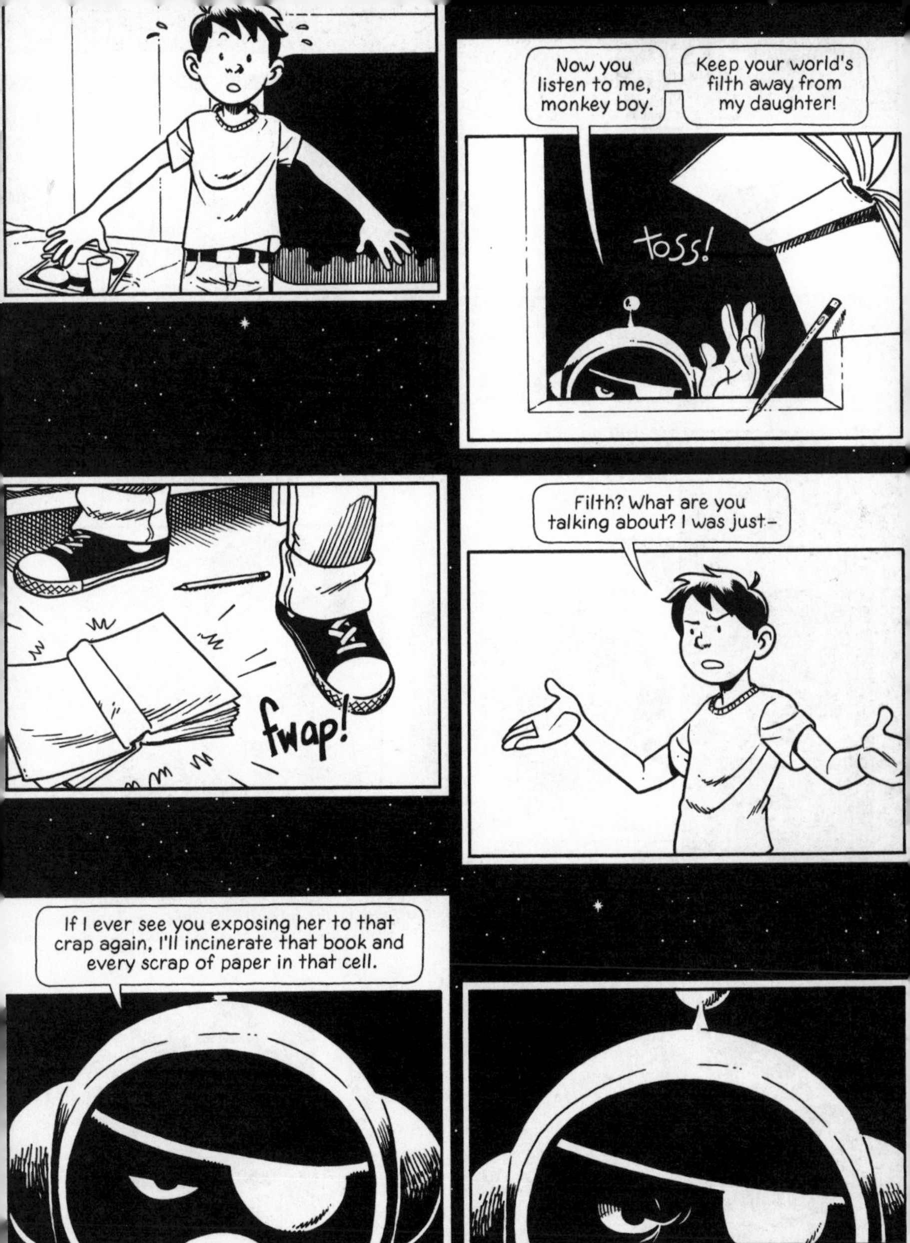
Now you listen to me, monkey boy.
Keep your world's filth away from my daughter!
toss!
fwap!
Filth? What are you talking about? I was just–
If I ever see you exposing her to that crap again, I'll incinerate that book and every scrap of paper in that cell.

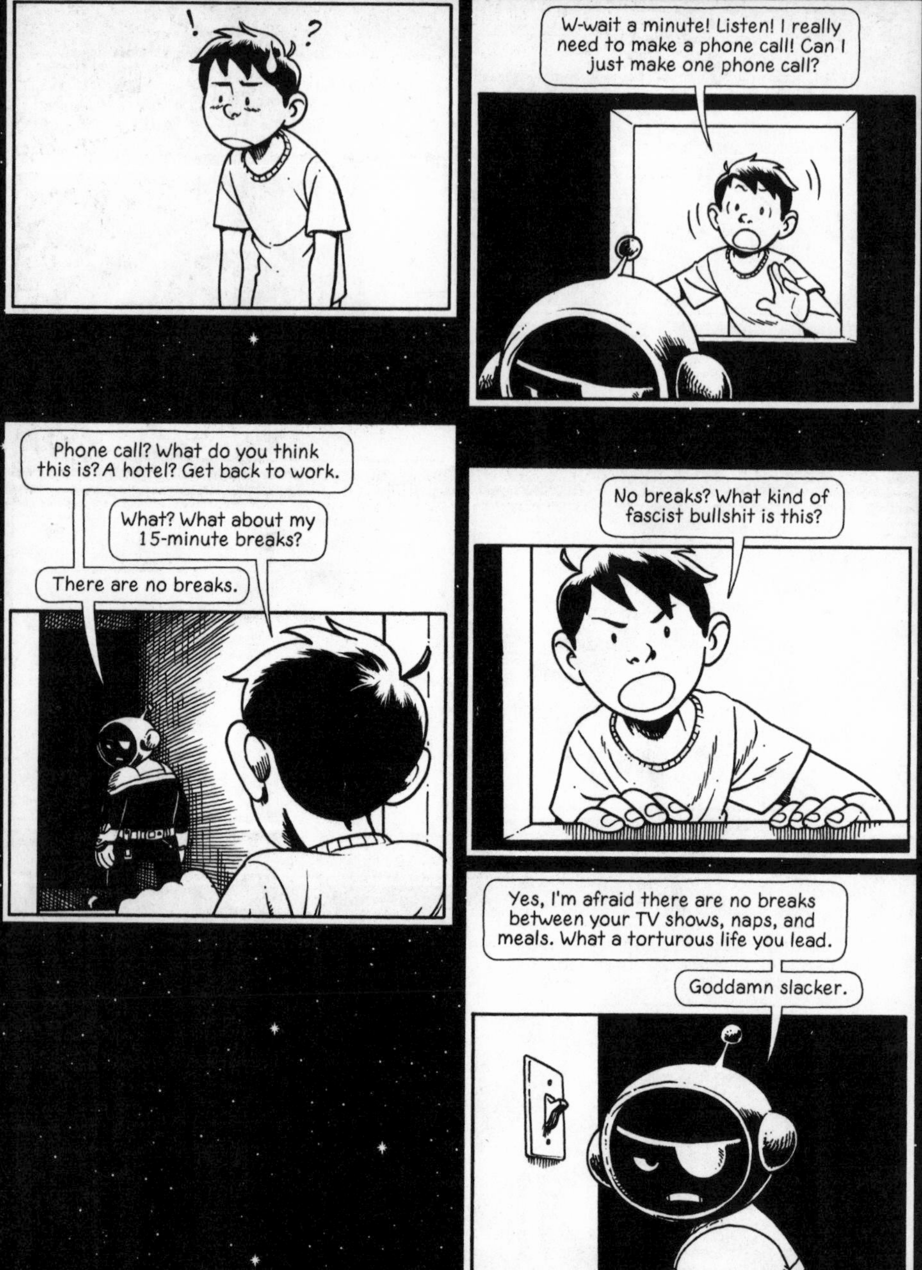
!
?
W-wait a minute! Listen! I really need to make a phone call! Can I just make one phone call?
Phone call? What do you think this is? A hotel? Get back to work.
What? What about my 15-minute breaks?
There are no breaks.
No breaks? What kind of fascist bullshit is this?
Yes, I'm afraid there are no breaks between your TV shows, naps, and meals. What a torturous life you lead.
Goddamn slacker.

Okay, fine. But when the museum closes tonight and I'm off the clock, that phone better be ready for me.
click
Man, what is that guy's problem?
He's a douchebag, that's his problem.

help himself. He is a Praxian after all.
Wh-who said that?
Look down. At your air vent.
Beanbag
Air Vent
?
As I mentioned before, every little detail of my parents' house was recreated and the heater vent was no exception.
H-hello?
Howdy.
Who is this?
This is God.

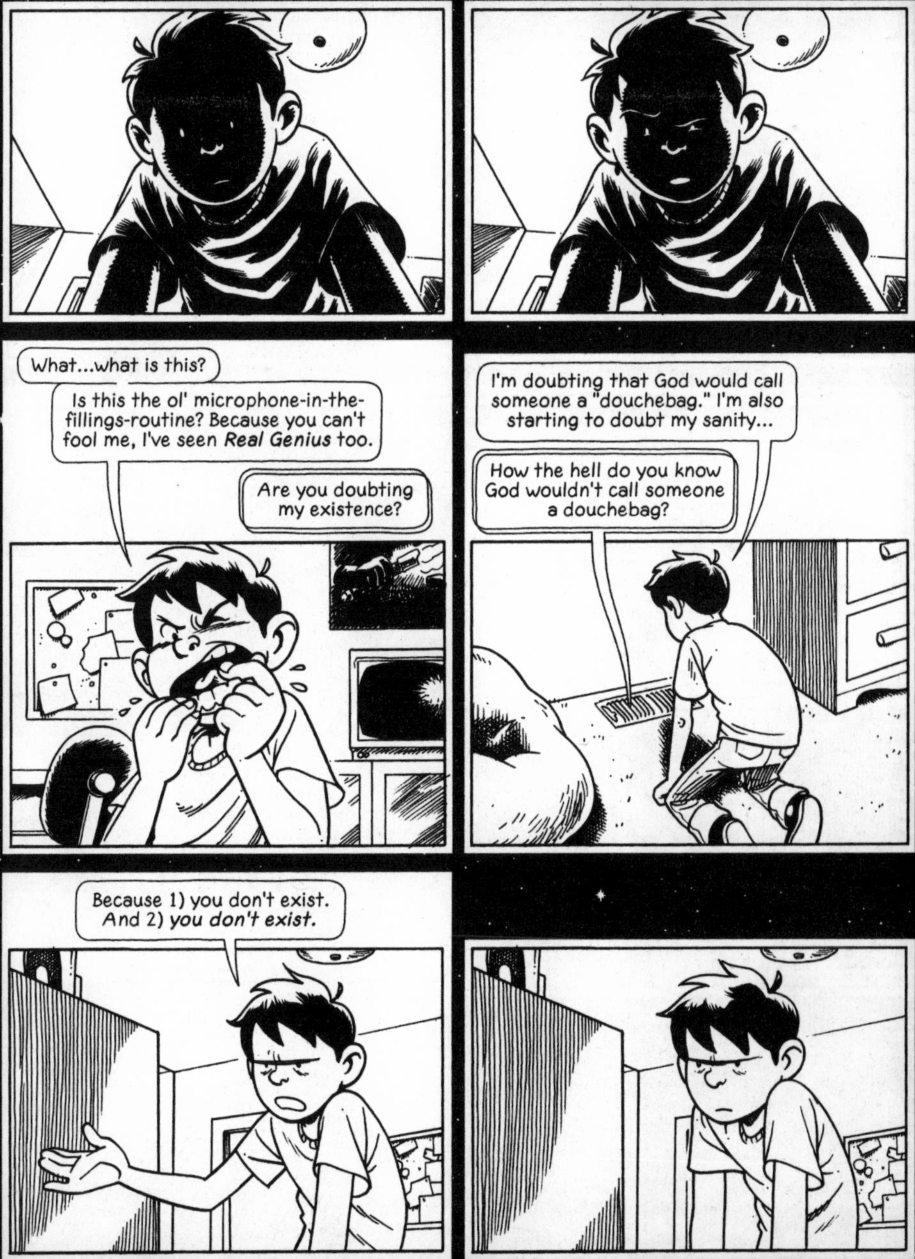
What...what is this?
Is this the ol' microphone-in-the-fillings-routine? Because you can't fool me, I've seen *Real Genius* too.
Are you doubting my existence?
I'm doubting that God would call someone a "douchebag." I'm also starting to doubt my sanity...
How the hell do you know God wouldn't call someone a douchebag?
Because 1) you don't exist. And 2) *you don't exist.*

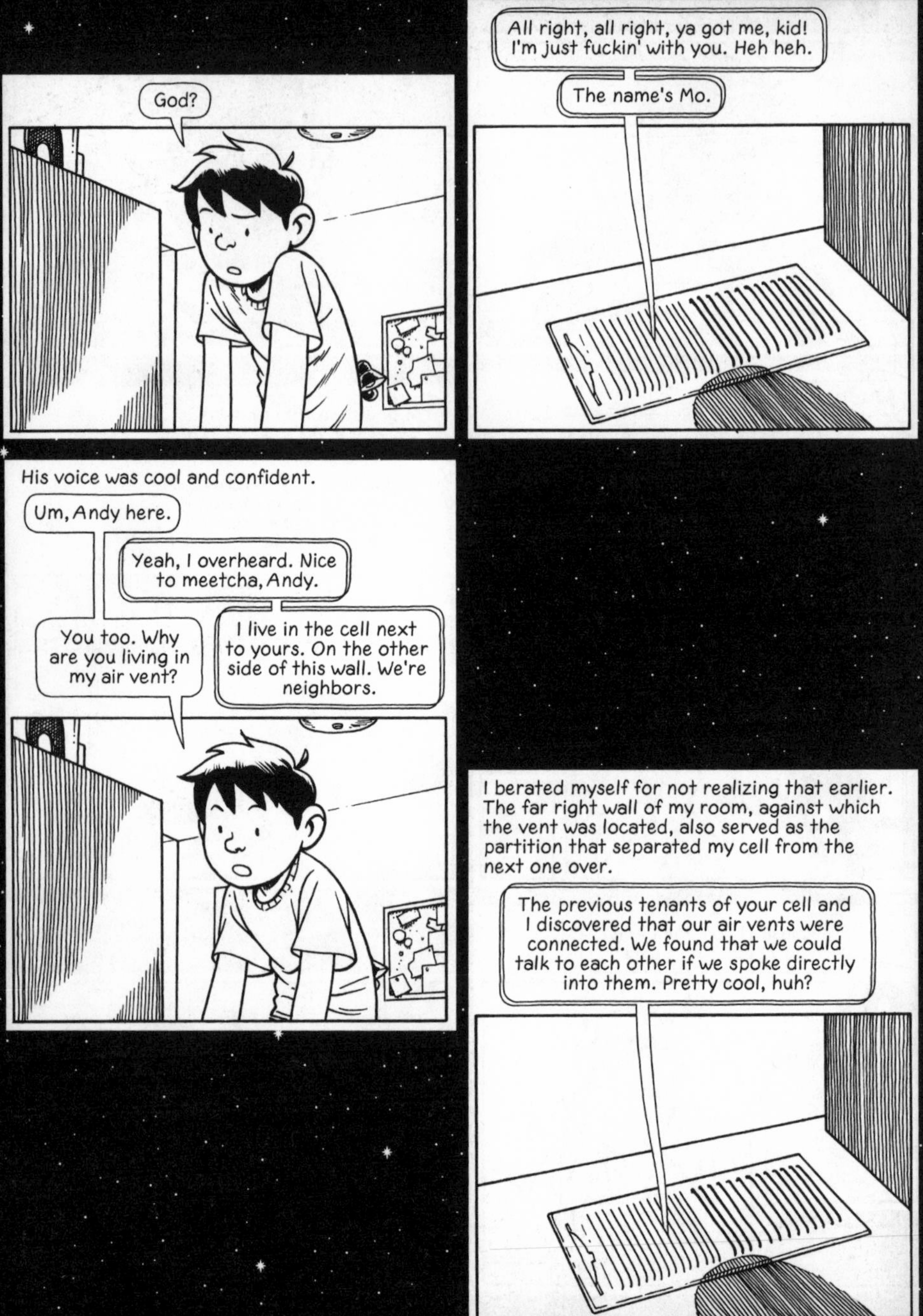
God?
All right, all right, ya got me, kid! I'm just fuckin' with you. Heh heh.
The name's Mo.
His voice was cool and confident.
Um, Andy here.
Yeah, I overheard. Nice to meetcha, Andy.
You too. Why are you living in my air vent?
I live in the cell next to yours. On the other side of this wall. We're neighbors.
I berated myself for not realizing that earlier. The far right wall of my room, against which the vent was located, also served as the partition that separated my cell from the next one over.
The previous tenants of your cell and I discovered that our air vents were connected. We found that we could talk to each other if we spoke directly into them. Pretty cool, huh?

Although he was a complete stranger, and I couldn't even see his face, I felt surprising comfort upon hearing his voice. It was reassuring somehow to talk to someone who was in the same situation. I guess the way two *Star Trek* fans might clump together at a *Star Wars* convention, despite whatever differences they may have as individuals.

What happened to the people that were in here before me?

They killed themselves.

Oh...

It was awful...

Yeah, that's really–

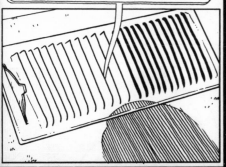

They were stinkin' up the whole damn museum! I could smell their rotting carcasses right through the vent. I tell you, I'll never forget it... Do me a favor, Andy, if you're gonna kill yourself, do it bright and early during a work day so they find you right away, all right? None of this killing yourself right before the weekend business. Have some consideration for your neighbors.

Duly noted.

Images of what my neighbor might look like flickered around in my head. He didn't sound that much older than me. I'd say maybe early to mid-30s. And despite his flippant remarks, he dripped with charisma. My initial picture of him was someone like Jack Black. But I quickly realized how limited that thinking was, considering he was from an entirely different universe. He could have been a talking Jell-O mold for all I knew.

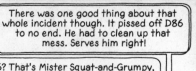

There was one good thing about that whole incident though. It pissed off D86 to no end. He had to clean up that mess. Serves him right!

D86? That's Mister Squat-and-Grumpy, right? I have to admit, he does have one seriously stiff stick up his butt.

Well, like I said, he is a Praxian. What do you expect? They're all like that. He's just the epitome.

Hey, is it true that they don't have any kind of art in this world?!

Are you kidding me? They don't even know what it is. They have no concept of it! Just like a mouse has no concept of algebra.

fwump!

I have no concept of algebra.

Apparently, all the arts—painting, music, dance, theater, fiction, you name it—were outlawed centuries ago on this world. Consequently, most of these people have lost all concept of art over the centuries. In fact, creativity itself is virtually unknown here.

Look at their names! You know 503(4)-0717.04.23.B101? 503(4)—or 4,503—is the year of her birth, 0717 is the month and date of her birth, 04 is the hour of her birth, 23 the minute, and B101 is the order in which she born during that minute.

The Praxians decided that coming up with actual names was considered too creative and banned it!

You're kidding me...!

Why do you think they all wear the same clothes? They have no other design agenda in their clothing other than functionality. All their buildings are the same way. Look at that hallway outside your cell's viewing window. Just barren.

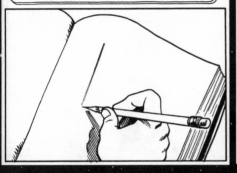

Any design that you do see–whether it be architectural, industrial, or fashion– it's all laid out by computers, extrapolated from designs the Praxians created before the ban on art. These days, they consider it a waste of time to apply their intelligence to something so frivolous.

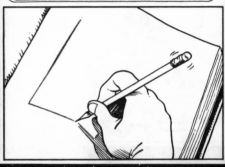

The Praxians believe that art is *the* main drag on a civilization's development. And their discovery of alternate dimensions like yours and mine is the ultimate proof to them.

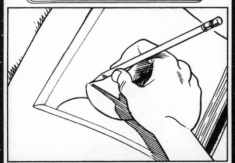

They're zipping through the galaxy at light speed, while we can barely crawl across our art-plastered planets. To them, we're as sophisticated as dogs are to us.

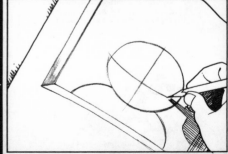

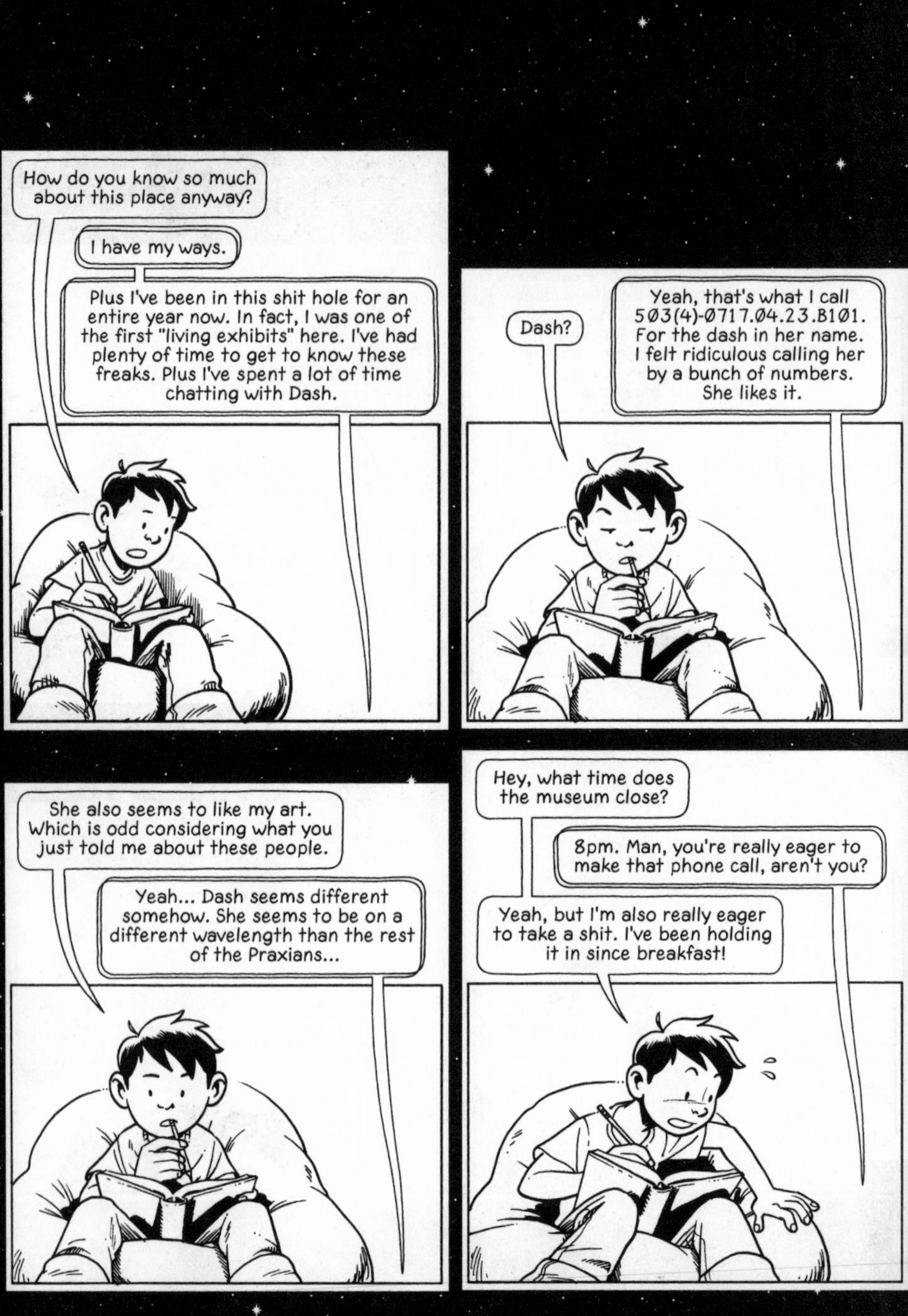
How do you know so much about this place anyway?
I have my ways.
Plus I've been in this shit hole for an entire year now. In fact, I was one of the first "living exhibits" here. I've had plenty of time to get to know these freaks. Plus I've spent a lot of time chatting with Dash.
Dash?
Yeah, that's what I call 5Ø3(4)-Ø717.Ø4.23.B1Ø1. For the dash in her name. I felt ridiculous calling her by a bunch of numbers. She likes it.
She also seems to like my art. Which is odd considering what you just told me about these people.
Yeah... Dash seems different somehow. She seems to be on a different wavelength than the rest of the Praxians...
Hey, what time does the museum close?
8pm. Man, you're really eager to make that phone call, aren't you?
Yeah, but I'm also really eager to take a shit. I've been holding it in since breakfast!

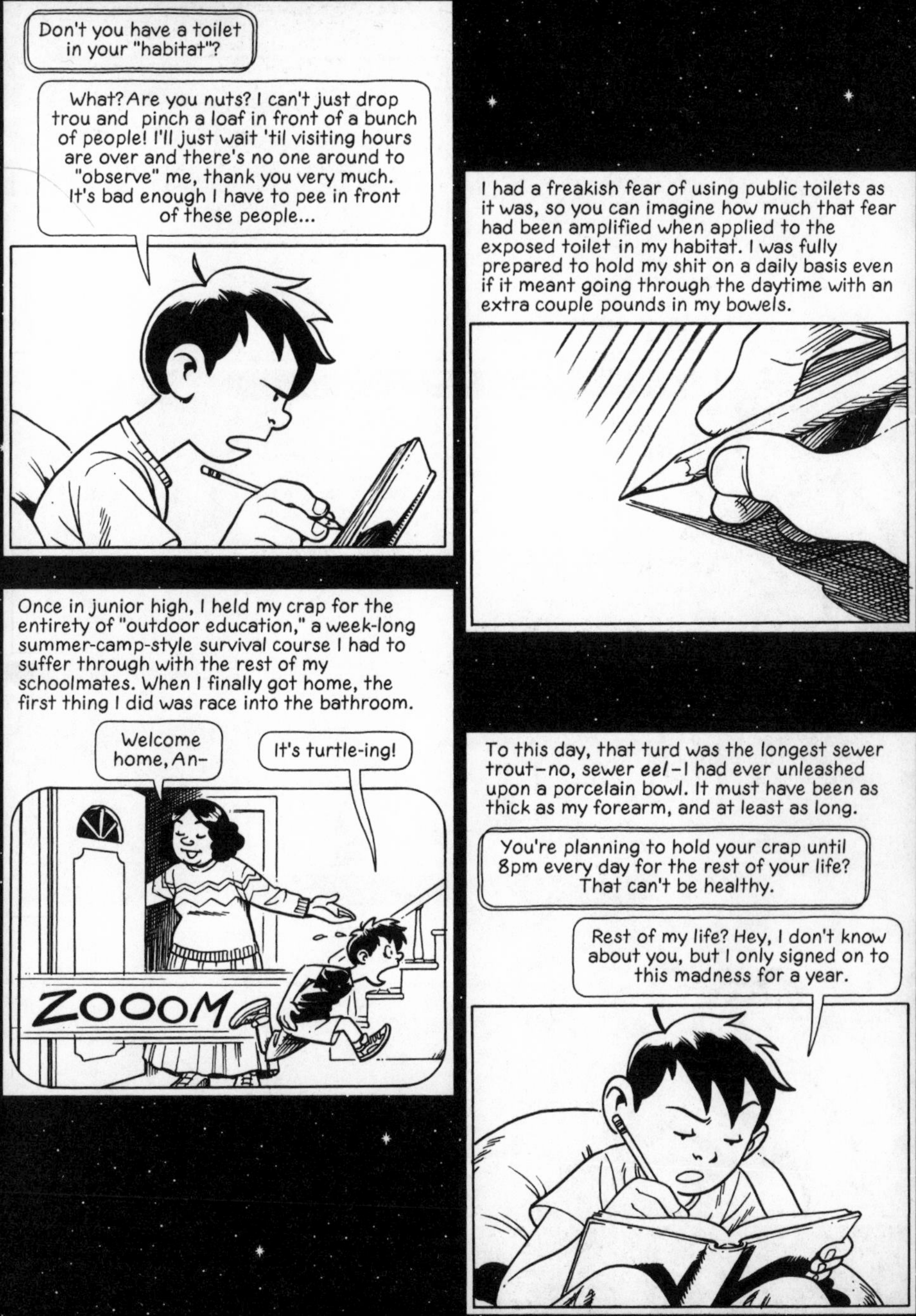

Don't you have a toilet in your "habitat"?
What? Are you nuts? I can't just drop trou and pinch a loaf in front of a bunch of people! I'll just wait 'til visiting hours are over and there's no one around to "observe" me, thank you very much. It's bad enough I have to pee in front of these people...
I had a freakish fear of using public toilets as it was, so you can imagine how much that fear had been amplified when applied to the exposed toilet in my habitat. I was fully prepared to hold my shit on a daily basis even if it meant going through the daytime with an extra couple pounds in my bowels.
Once in junior high, I held my crap for the entirety of "outdoor education," a week-long summer-camp-style survival course I had to suffer through with the rest of my schoolmates. When I finally got home, the first thing I did was race into the bathroom.
Welcome home, An-
It's turtle-ing!
ZOOOM
To this day, that turd was the longest sewer trout–no, sewer *eel*–I had ever unleashed upon a porcelain bowl. It must have been as thick as my forearm, and at least as long.
You're planning to hold your crap until 8pm every day for the rest of your life? That can't be healthy.
Rest of my life? Hey, I don't know about you, but I only signed on to this madness for a year.

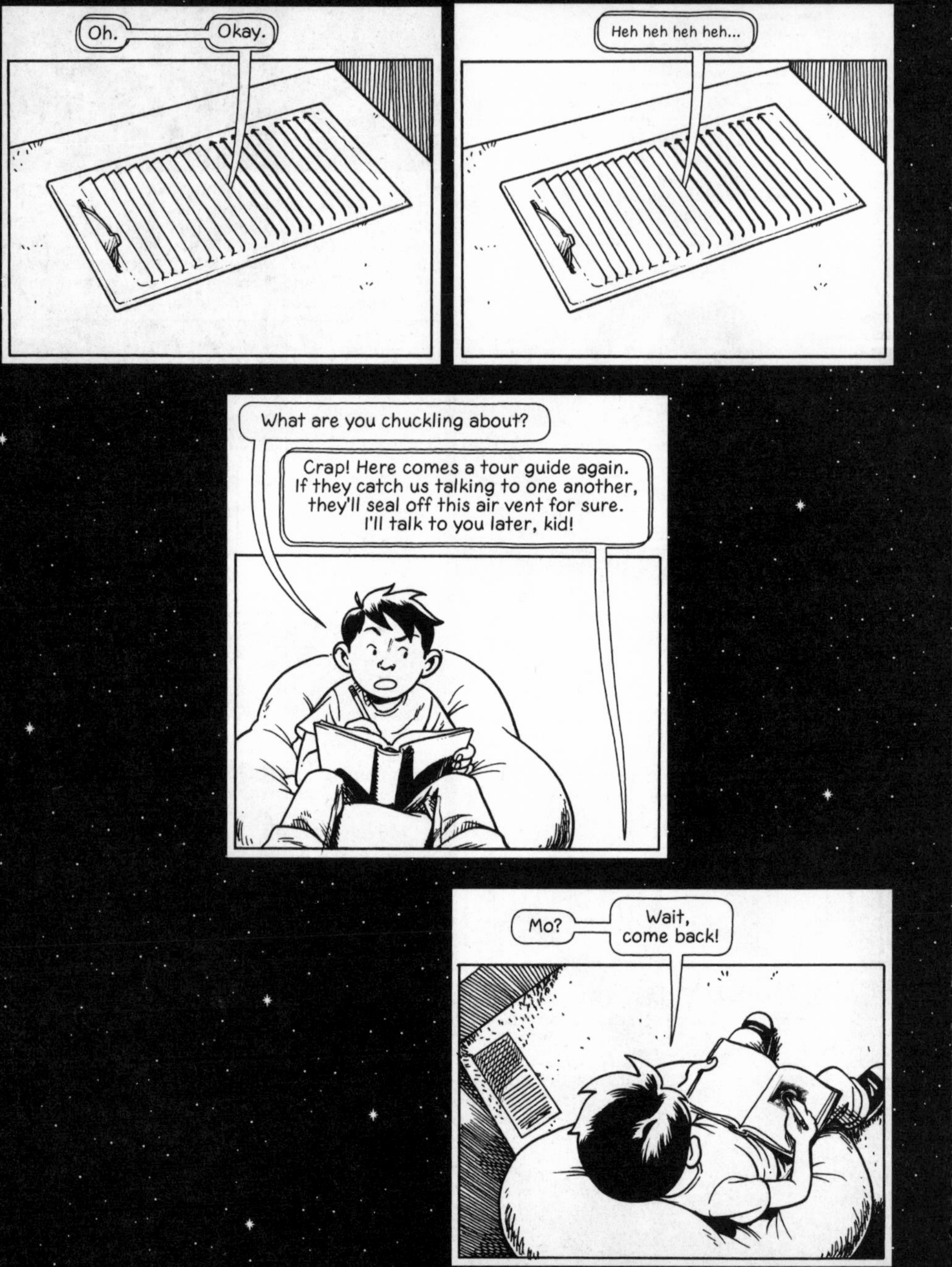
Oh.
Okay.
Heh heh heh heh...
What are you chuckling about?
Crap! Here comes a tour guide again. If they catch us talking to one another, they'll seal off this air vent for sure. I'll talk to you later, kid!
Mo?
Wait, come back!

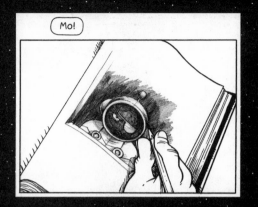

Mo!

CHAPTER 13

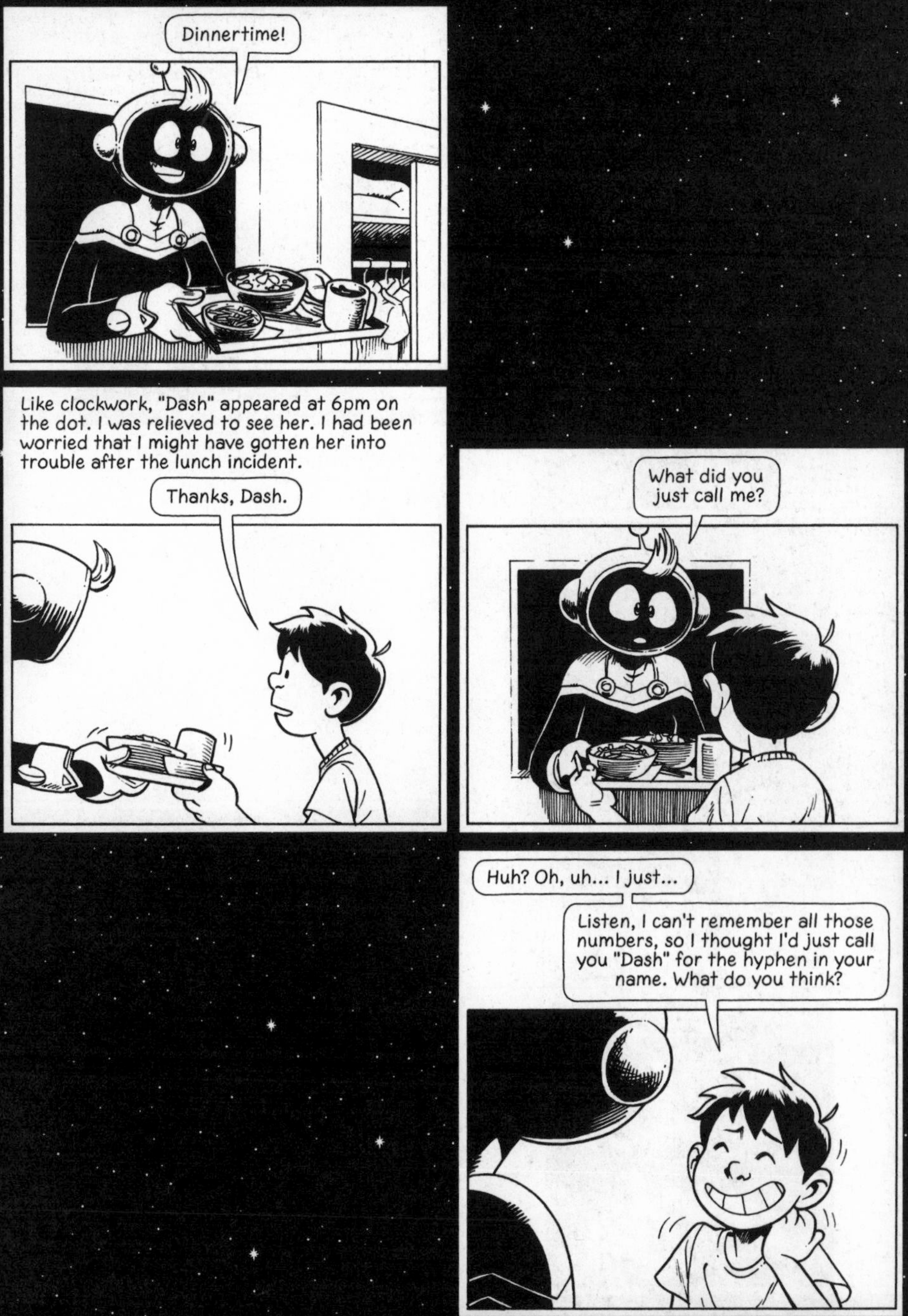
Dinnertime!
Like clockwork, "Dash" appeared at 6pm on the dot. I was relieved to see her. I had been worried that I might have gotten her into trouble after the lunch incident.
Thanks, Dash.
What did you just call me?
Huh? Oh, uh... I just...
Listen, I can't remember all those numbers, so I thought I'd just call you "Dash" for the hyphen in your name. What do you think?

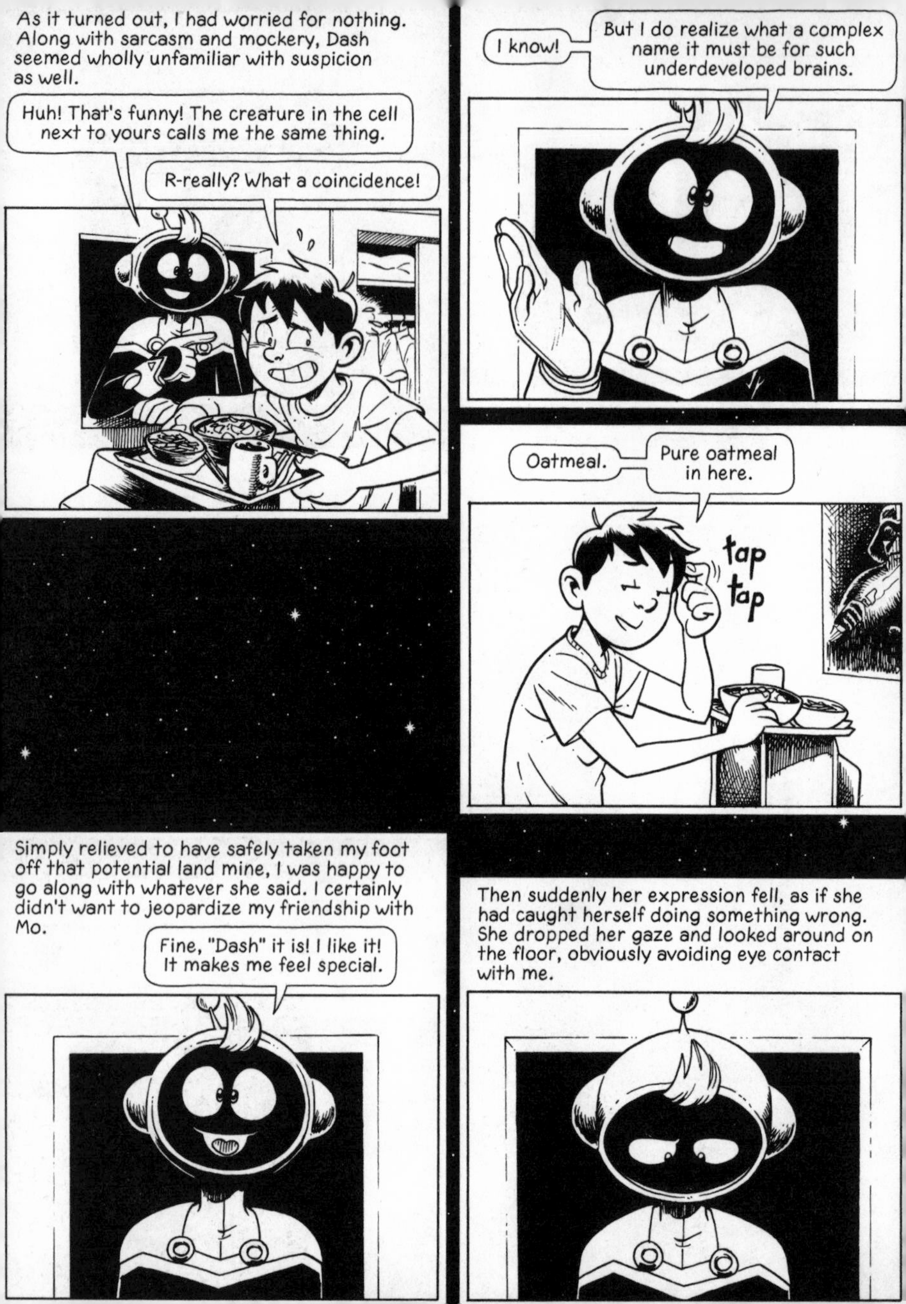
As it turned out, I had worried for nothing. Along with sarcasm and mockery, Dash seemed wholly unfamiliar with suspicion as well.
Huh! That's funny! The creature in the cell next to yours calls me the same thing.
R-really? What a coincidence!
I know!
But I do realize what a complex name it must be for such underdeveloped brains.
Oatmeal.
Pure oatmeal in here.
tap tap
Simply relieved to have safely taken my foot off that potential land mine, I was happy to go along with whatever she said. I certainly didn't want to jeopardize my friendship with Mo.
Fine, "Dash" it is! I like it! It makes me feel special.
Then suddenly her expression fell, as if she had caught herself doing something wrong. She dropped her gaze and looked around on the floor, obviously avoiding eye contact with me.

Okay, well, I gotta go, Andy Go.

Enjoy your dinner.

Hey, wait!

Listen, Dash. I just wanted to say I'm sorry about what happened earlier. I had no idea that–

Don't talk about it!

I've never seen my dad so furious! And that's saying something. If he hears us so much as even mention that incident again, I'll lose my job. It took a lot of begging and pleading for me to keep it as it is.

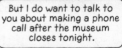

Okay, fine. I understand.

But I do want to talk to you about making a phone call after the museum closes tonight.

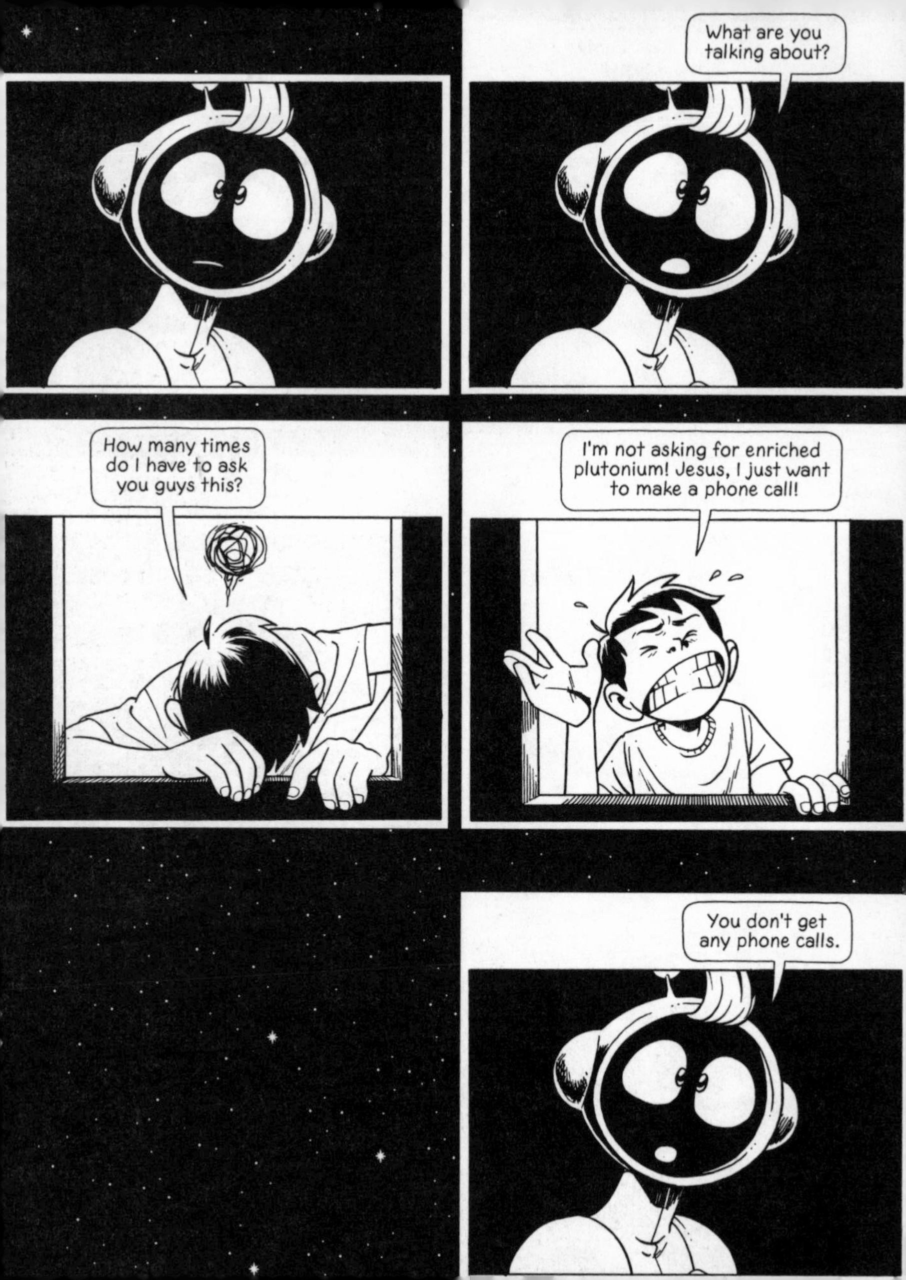
What are you talking about?
How many times do I have to ask you guys this?
I'm not asking for enriched plutonium! Jesus, I just want to make a phone call!
You don't get any phone calls.

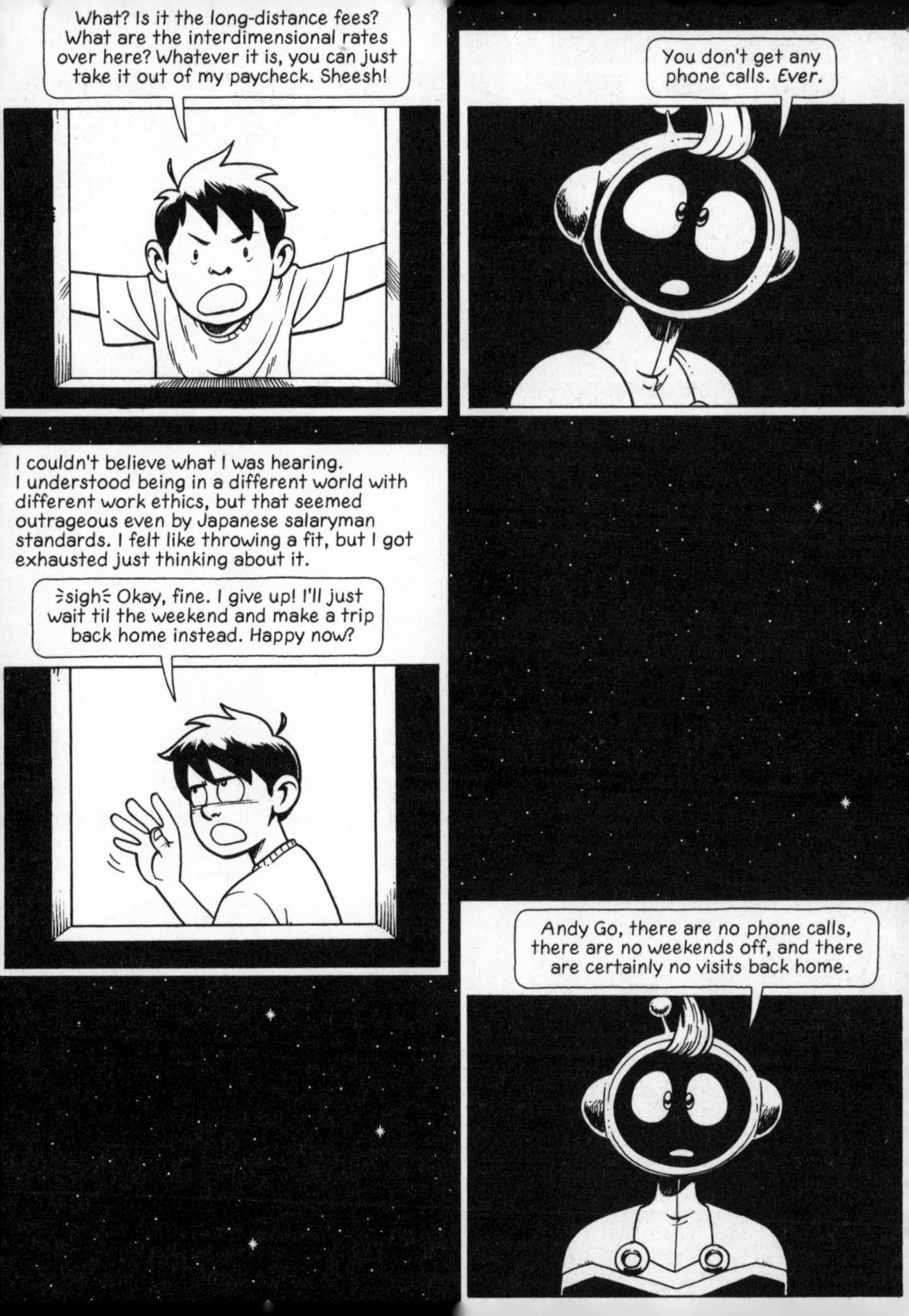
What? Is it the long-distance fees? What are the interdimensional rates over here? Whatever it is, you can just take it out of my paycheck. Sheesh!
You don't get any phone calls. *Ever.*
I couldn't believe what I was hearing. I understood being in a different world with different work ethics, but that seemed outrageous even by Japanese salaryman standards. I felt like throwing a fit, but I got exhausted just thinking about it.
≋sigh≋ Okay, fine. I give up! I'll just wait til the weekend and make a trip back home instead. Happy now?
Andy Go, there are no phone calls, there are no weekends off, and there are certainly no visits back home.

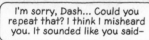

I'm sorry, Dash... Could you repeat that? I think I misheard you. It sounded like you said–

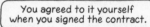

You agreed to it yourself when you signed the contract.

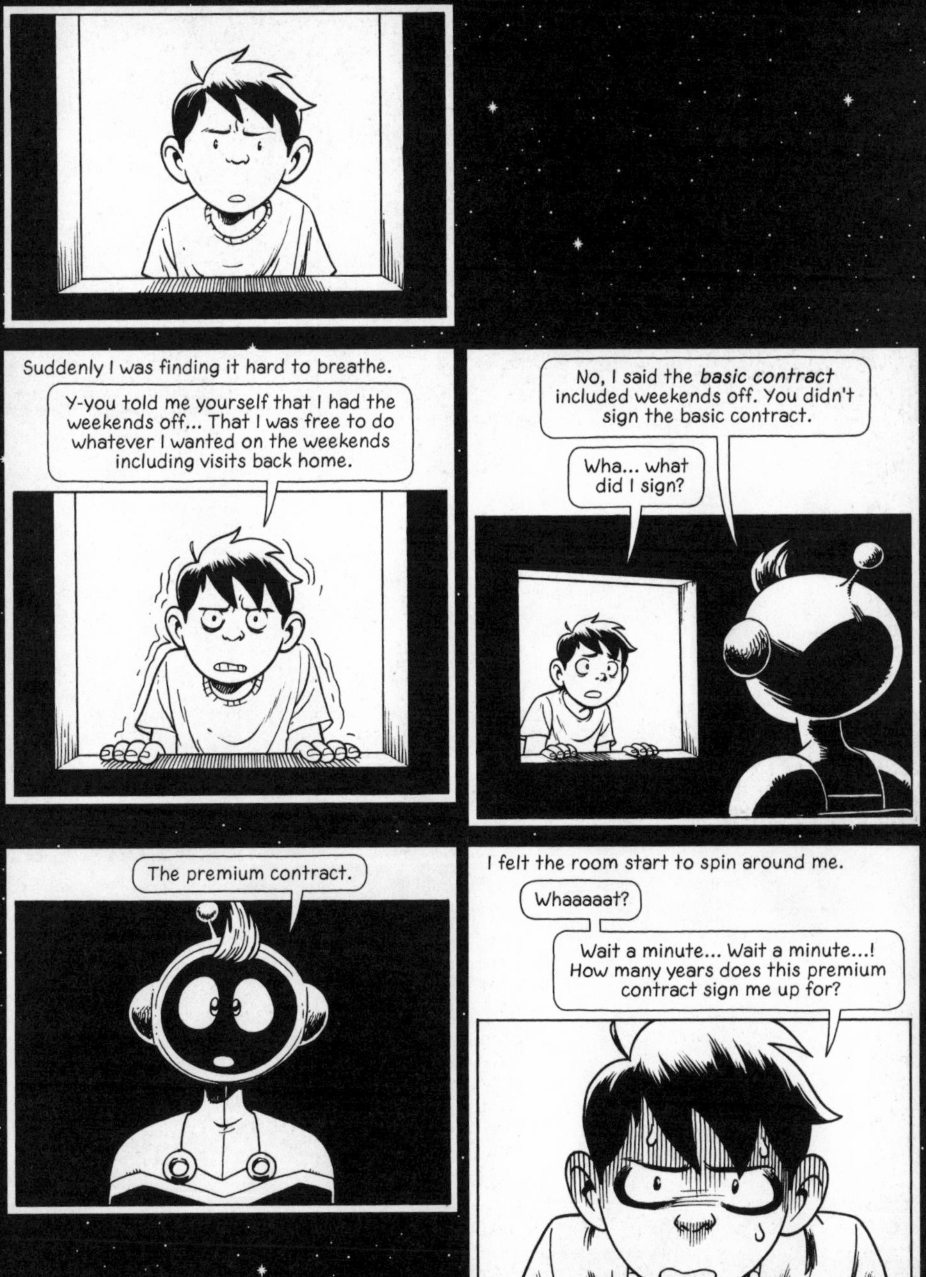
Suddenly I was finding it hard to breathe.
Y-you told me yourself that I had the weekends off... That I was free to do whatever I wanted on the weekends including visits back home.
No, I said the *basic contract* included weekends off. You didn't sign the basic contract.
Wha... what did I sign?
The premium contract.
I felt the room start to spin around me.
Whaaaaat?
Wait a minute... Wait a minute...! How many years does this premium contract sign me up for?

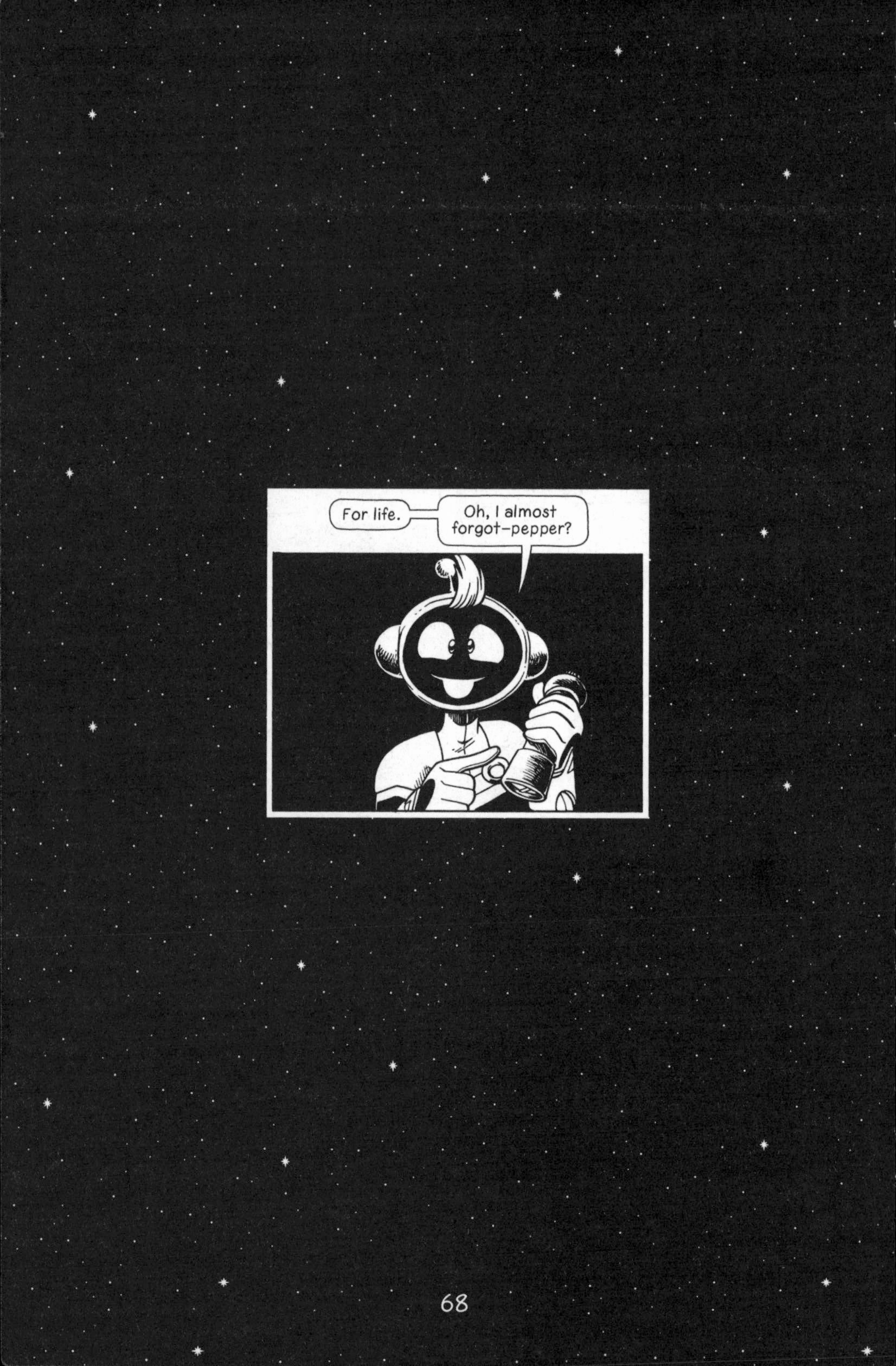
For life.
Oh, I almost forgot—pepper?

CHAPTER 14

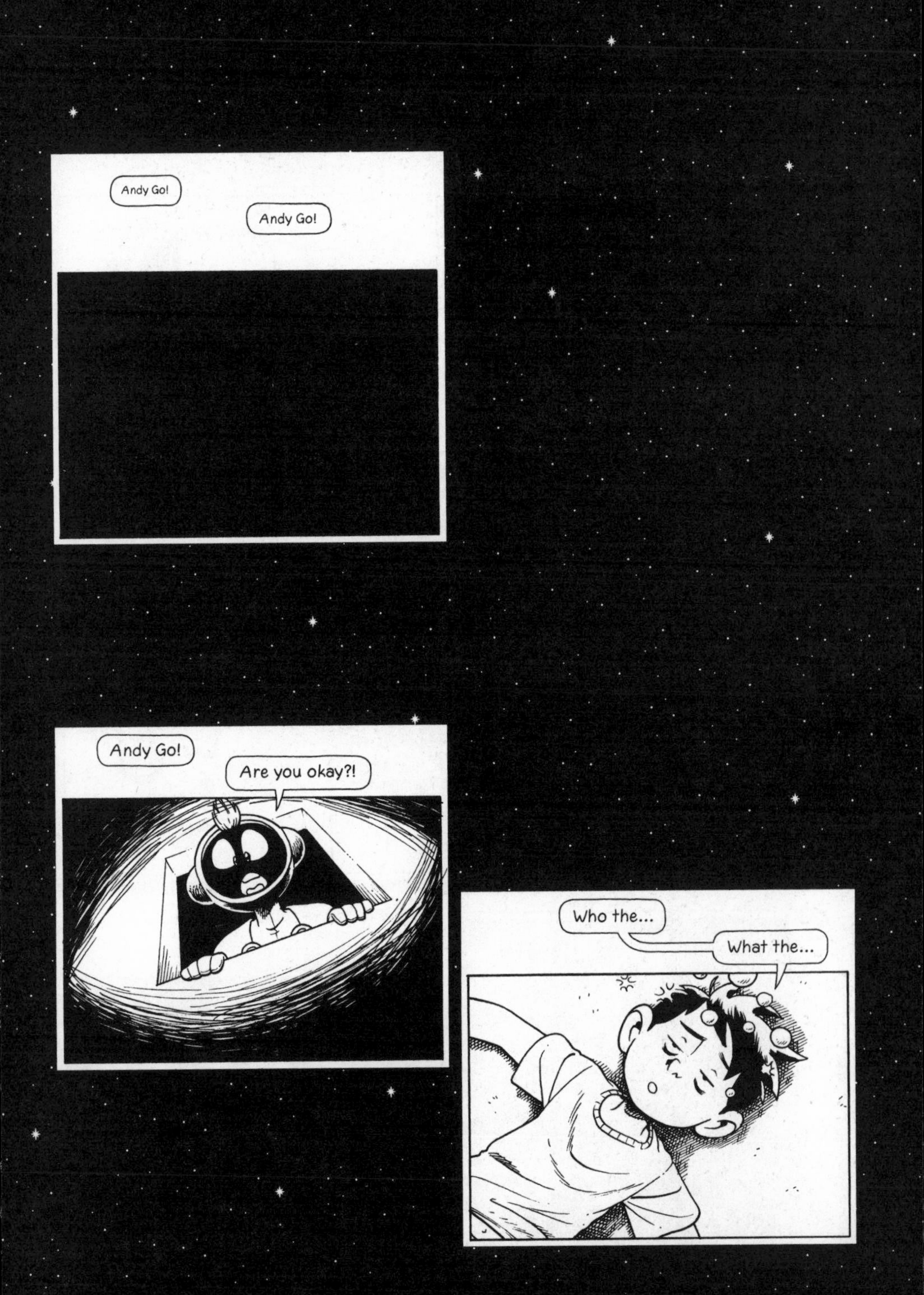
Andy Go!
Andy Go!
Andy Go!
Are you okay?!
Who the...
What the...

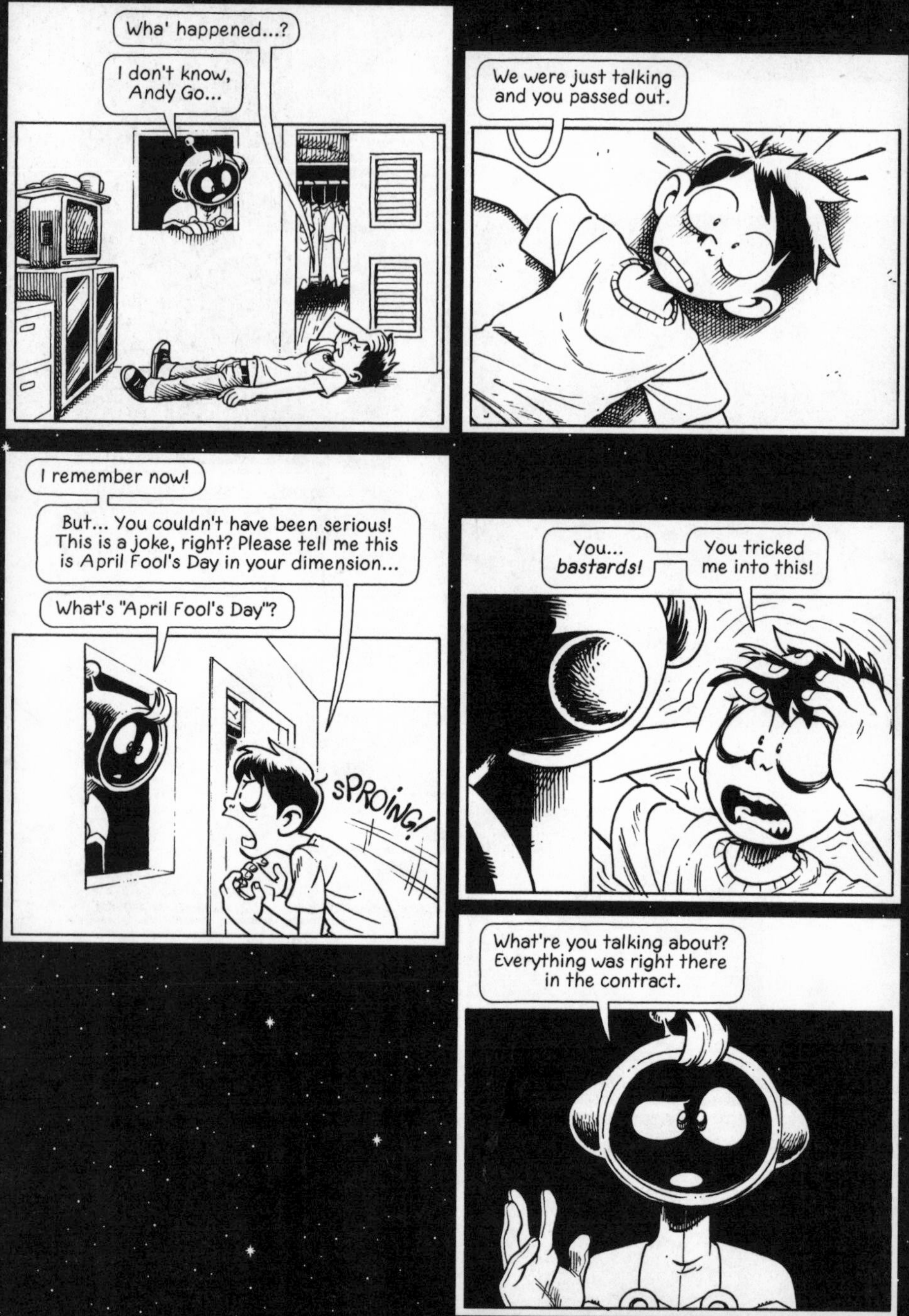
Wha' happened...?
I don't know, Andy Go...
We were just talking and you passed out.
I remember now!
But... You couldn't have been serious! This is a joke, right? Please tell me this is April Fool's Day in your dimension...
What's "April Fool's Day"?
SPROING!
You... *bastards!*
You tricked me into this!
What're you talking about? Everything was right there in the contract.

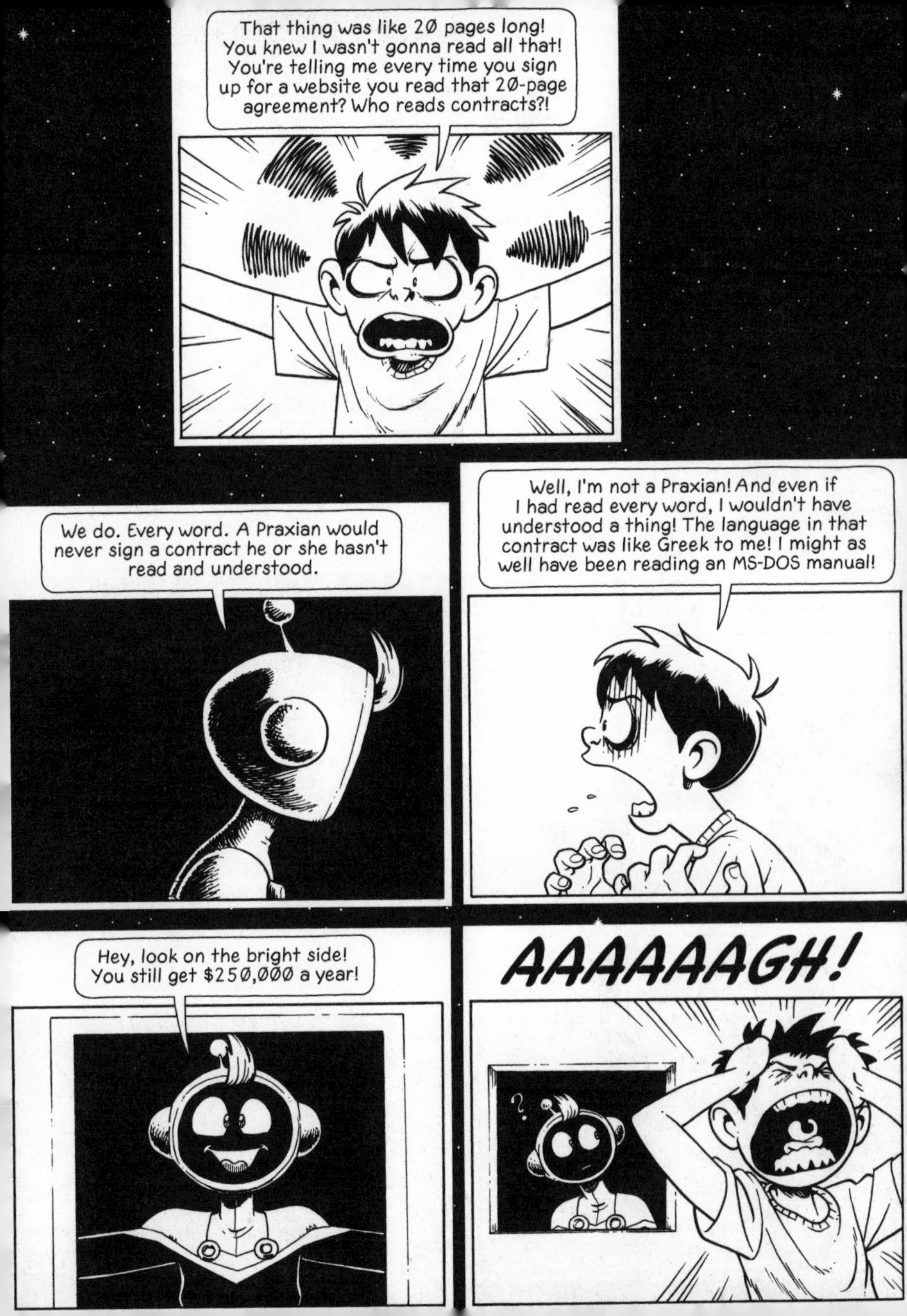
That thing was like 2Ø pages long! You knew I wasn't gonna read all that! You're telling me every time you sign up for a website you read that 2Ø-page agreement? Who reads contracts?!
We do. Every word. A Praxian would never sign a contract he or she hasn't read and understood.
Well, I'm not a Praxian! And even if I had read every word, I wouldn't have understood a thing! The language in that contract was like Greek to me! I might as well have been reading an MS-DOS manual!
Hey, look on the bright side! You still get $25Ø,ØØØ a year!
AAAAAAGH!
?

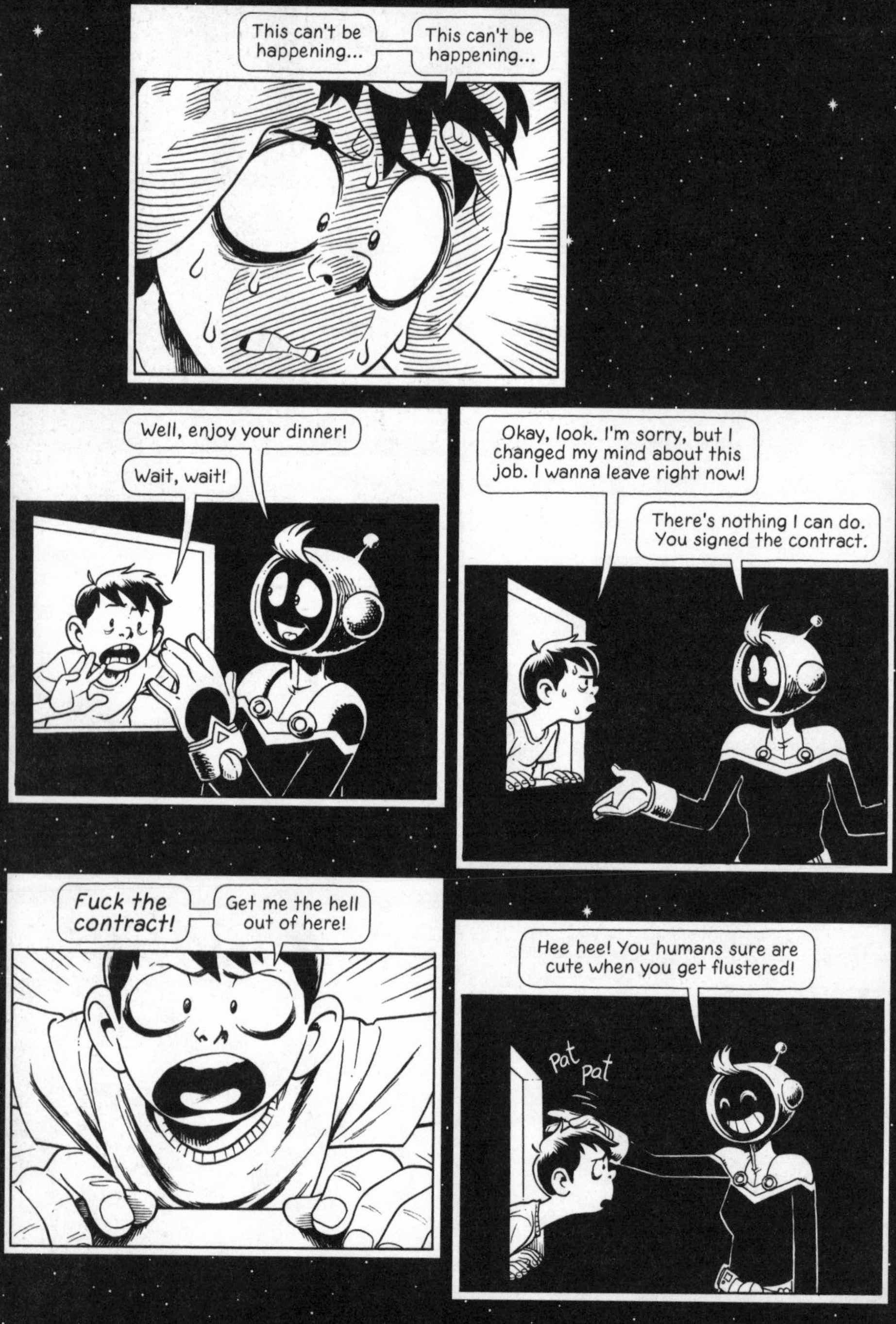
This can't be happening...
This can't be happening...
Well, enjoy your dinner!
Wait, wait!
Okay, look. I'm sorry, but I changed my mind about this job. I wanna leave right now!
There's nothing I can do. You signed the contract.
Fuck the contract!
Get me the hell out of here!
Hee hee! You humans sure are cute when you get flustered!
Pat pat

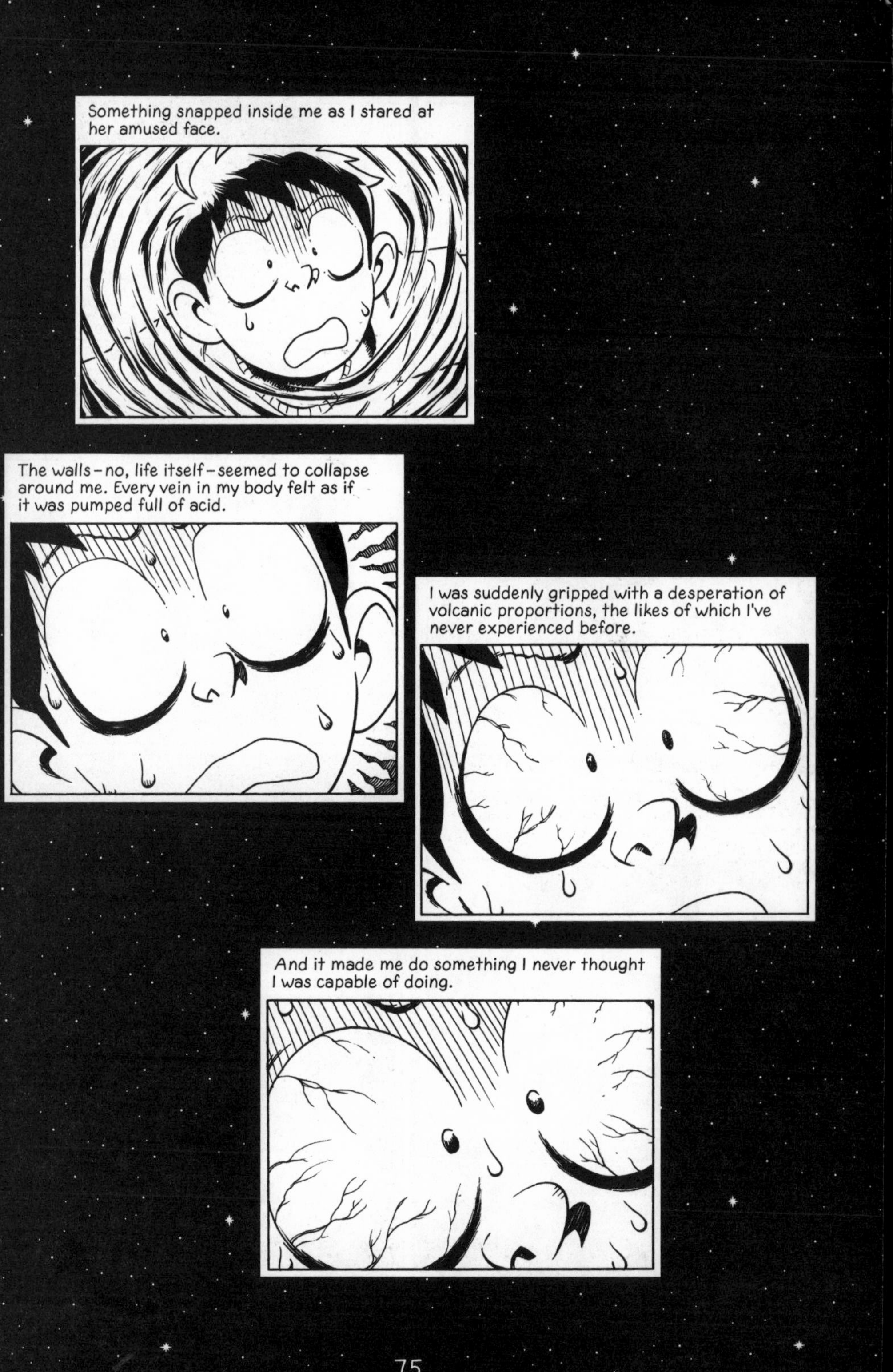
Something snapped inside me as I stared at her amused face.
The walls–no, life itself–seemed to collapse around me. Every vein in my body felt as if it was pumped full of acid.
I was suddenly gripped with a desperation of volcanic proportions, the likes of which I've never experienced before.
And it made me do something I never thought I was capable of doing.

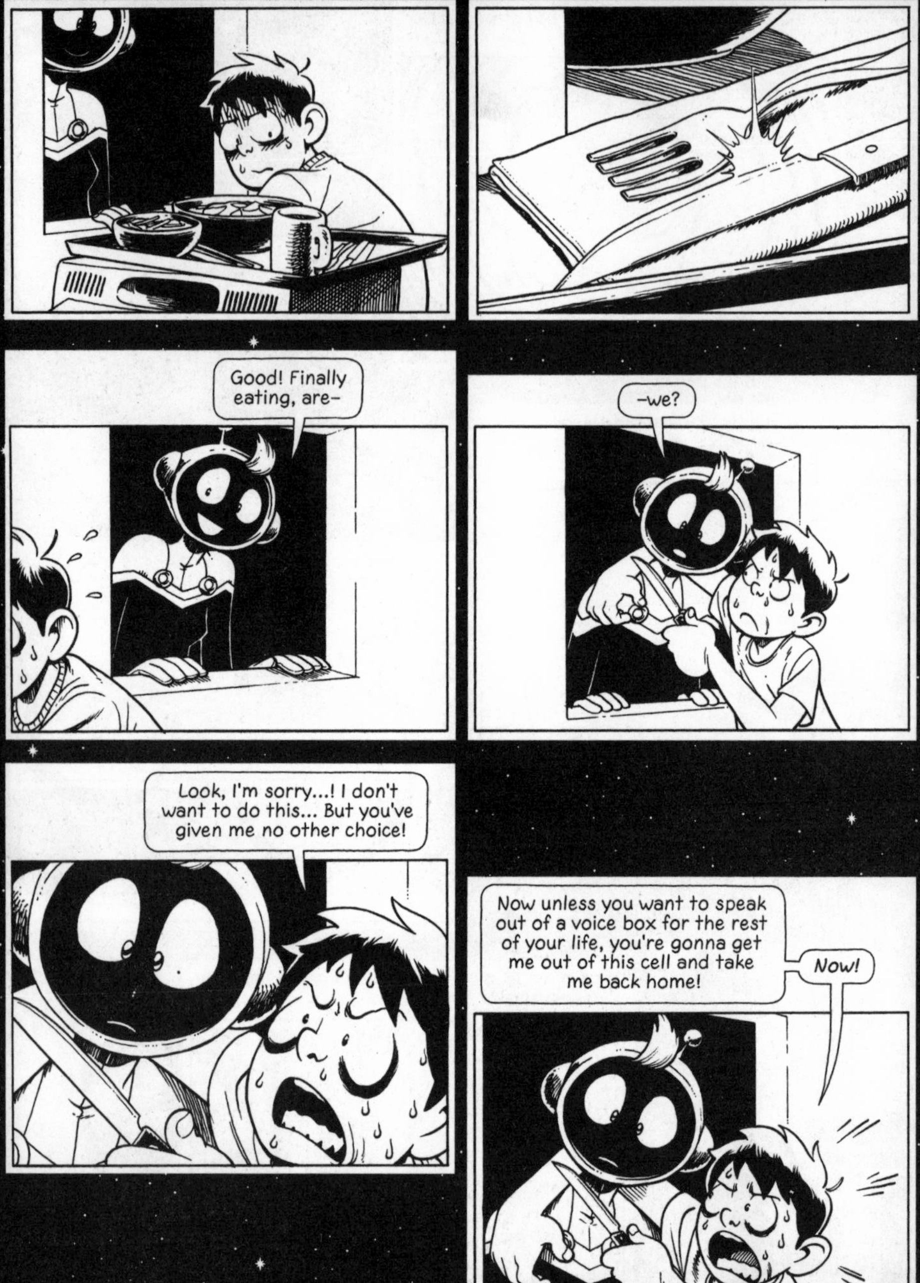
Good! Finally eating, are-
-we?
Look, I'm sorry...! I don't want to do this... But you've given me no other choice!
Now unless you want to speak out of a voice box for the rest of your life, you're gonna get me out of this cell and take me back home!
Now!

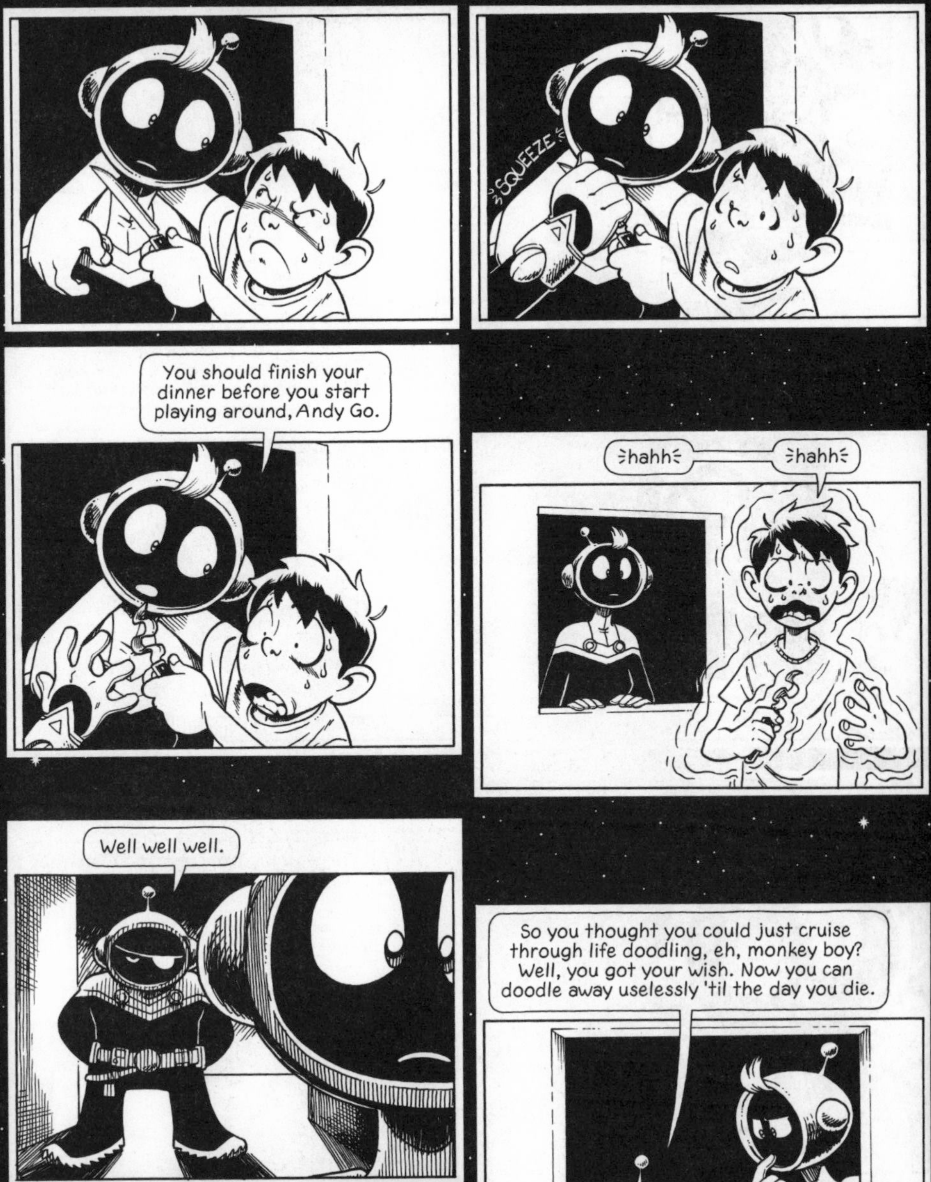
SQUEEZE
You should finish your dinner before you start playing around, Andy Go.
hahh
hahh
Well well well.
So you thought you could just cruise through life doodling, eh, monkey boy? Well, you got your wish. Now you can doodle away uselessly 'til the day you die.

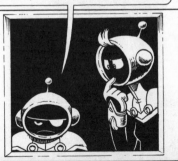

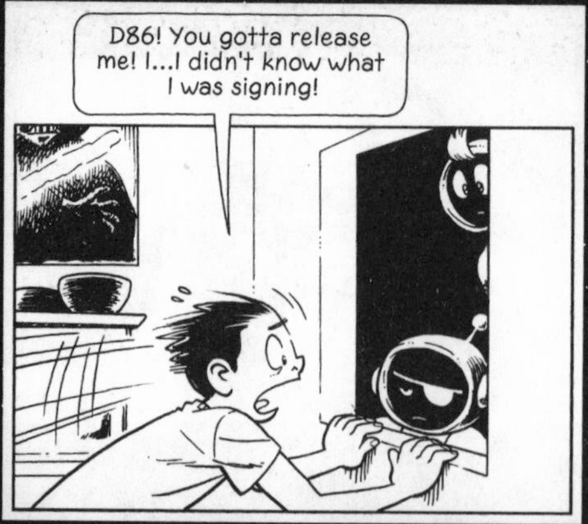
D86! You gotta release me! I...I didn't know what I was signing!

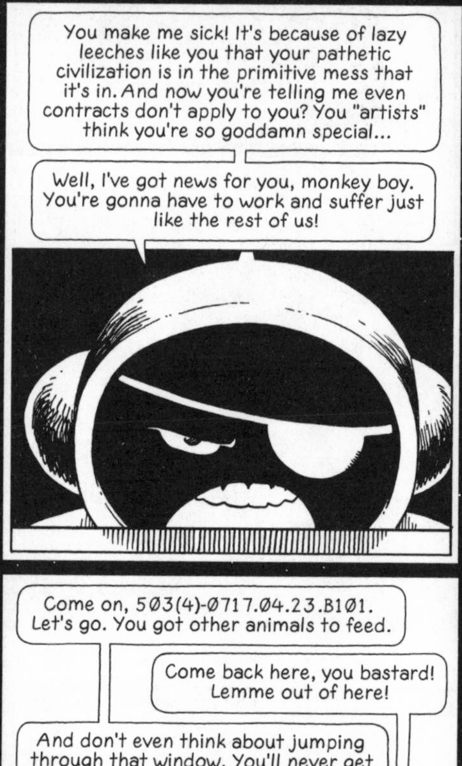
You make me sick! It's because of lazy leeches like you that your pathetic civilization is in the primitive mess that it's in. And now you're telling me even contracts don't apply to you? You "artists" think you're so goddamn special...
Well, I've got news for you, monkey boy. You're gonna have to work and suffer just like the rest of us!

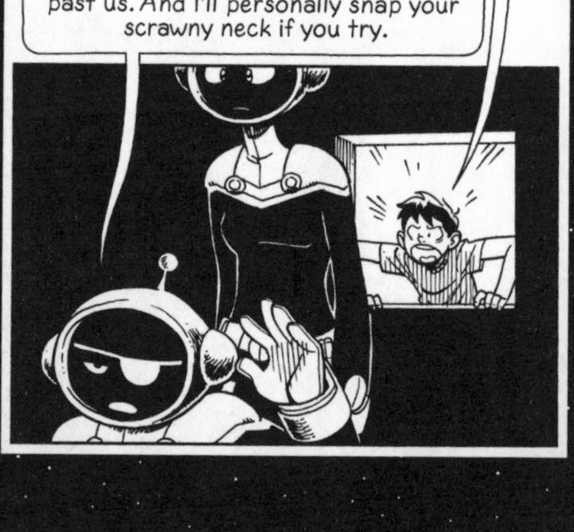
Come on, 5Ø3(4)-Ø717.Ø4.23.B1Ø1. Let's go. You got other animals to feed.
Come back here, you bastard! Lemme out of here!
And don't even think about jumping through that window. You'll never get past us. And I'll personally snap your scrawny neck if you try.

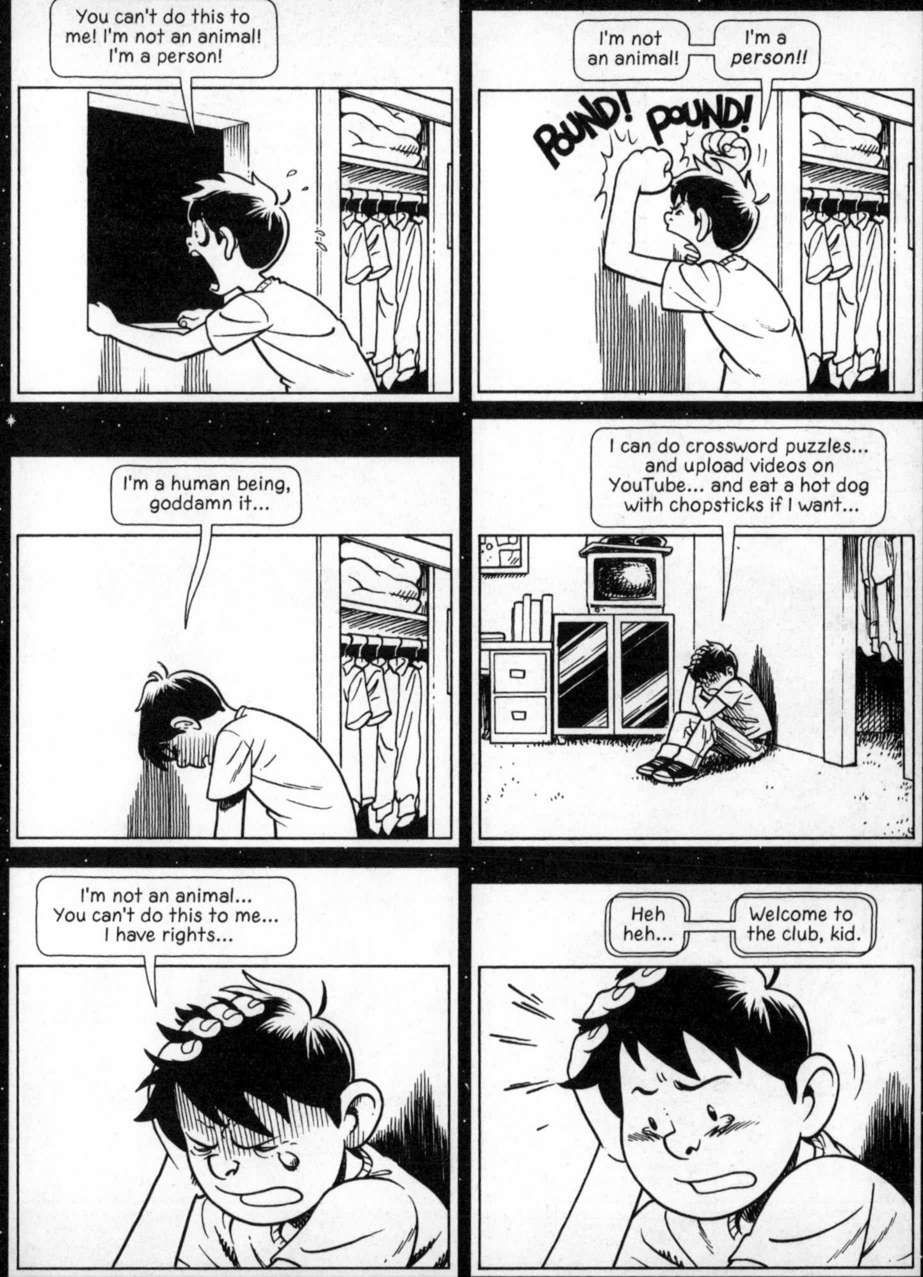
You can't do this to me! I'm not an animal! I'm a person!
I'm not an animal!
I'm a *person!!*
POUND! POUND!
I'm a human being, goddamn it...
I can do crossword puzzles... and upload videos on YouTube... and eat a hot dog with chopsticks if I want...
I'm not an animal... You can't do this to me... I have rights...
Heh heh...
Welcome to the club, kid.

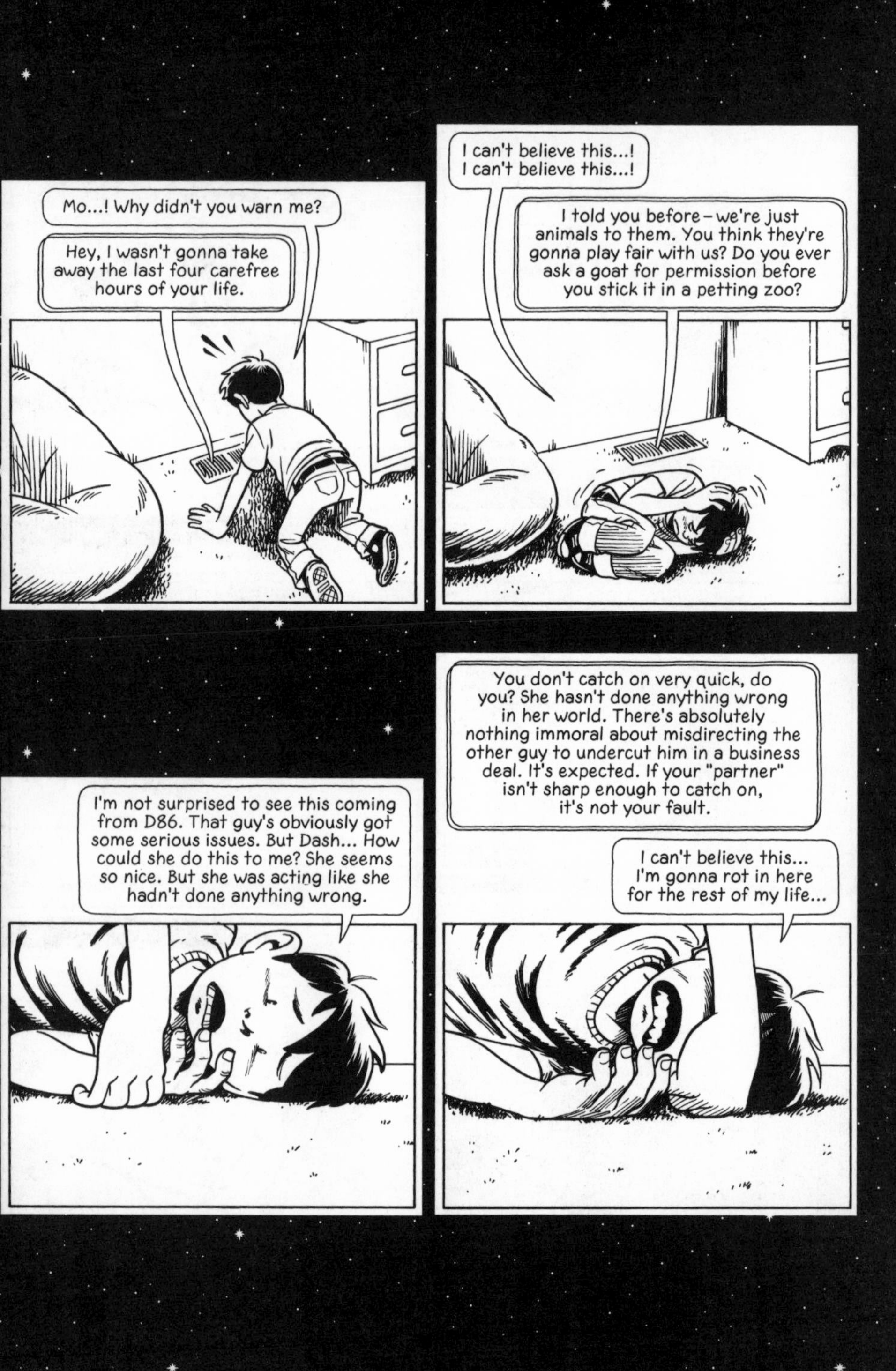
Mo...! Why didn't you warn me?
Hey, I wasn't gonna take away the last four carefree hours of your life.
I can't believe this...! I can't believe this...!
I told you before – we're just animals to them. You think they're gonna play fair with us? Do you ever ask a goat for permission before you stick it in a petting zoo?
I'm not surprised to see this coming from D86. That guy's obviously got some serious issues. But Dash... How could she do this to me? She seems so nice. But she was acting like she hadn't done anything wrong.
You don't catch on very quick, do you? She hasn't done anything wrong in her world. There's absolutely nothing immoral about misdirecting the other guy to undercut him in a business deal. It's expected. If your "partner" isn't sharp enough to catch on, it's not your fault.
I can't believe this... I'm gonna rot in here for the rest of my life...

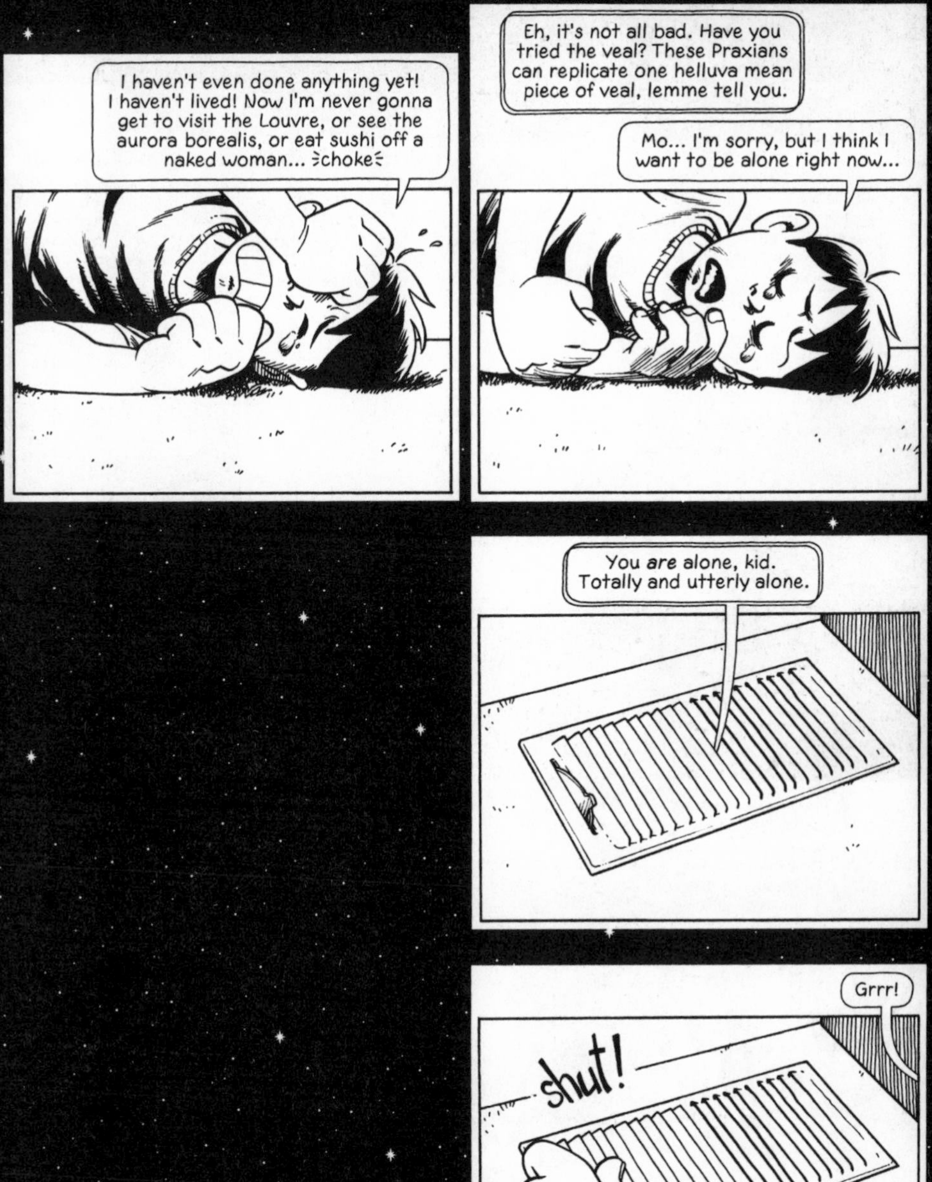
I haven't even done anything yet! I haven't lived! Now I'm never gonna get to visit the Louvre, or see the aurora borealis, or eat sushi off a naked woman... choke
Eh, it's not all bad. Have you tried the veal? These Praxians can replicate one helluva mean piece of veal, lemme tell you.
Mo... I'm sorry, but I think I want to be alone right now...
You *are* alone, kid. Totally and utterly alone.
Grrr!
shut!

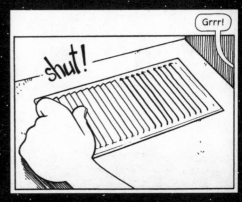

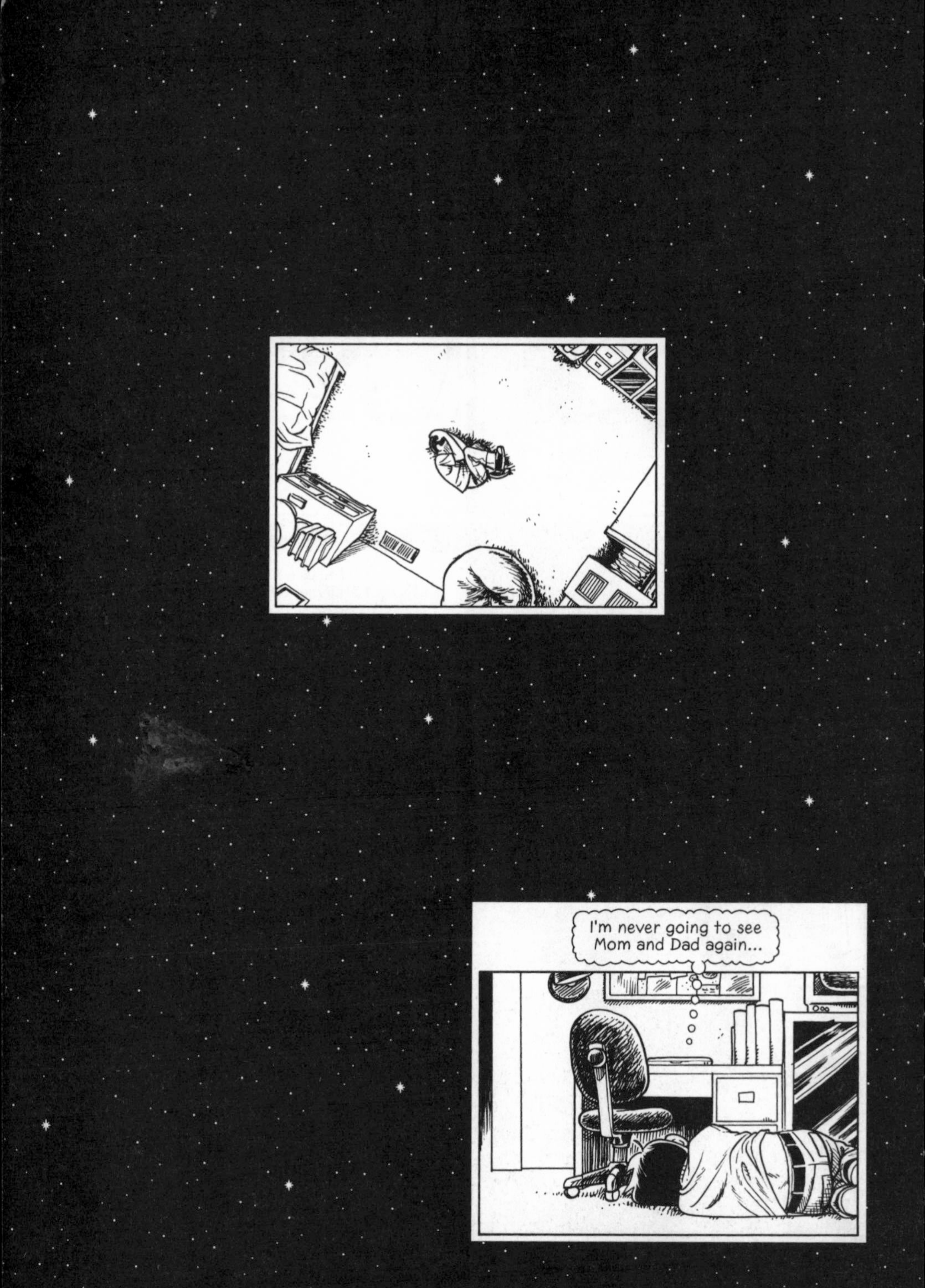
I'm never going to see Mom and Dad again...

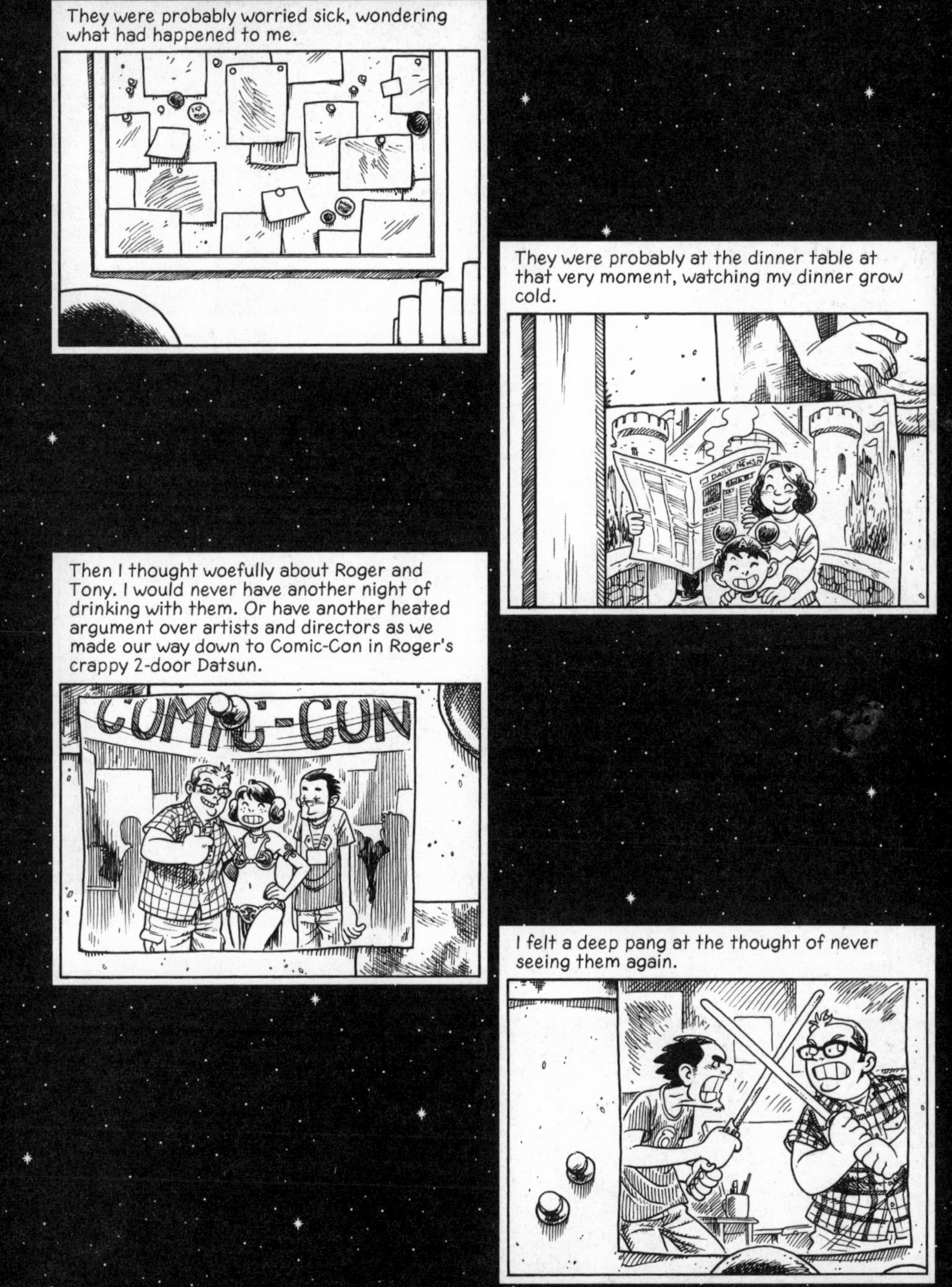
They were probably worried sick, wondering what had happened to me.
They were probably at the dinner table at that very moment, watching my dinner grow cold.
DAILY NEWS
Then I thought woefully about Roger and Tony. I would never have another night of drinking with them. Or have another heated argument over artists and directors as we made our way down to Comic-Con in Roger's crappy 2-door Datsun.
COMIC-CON
I felt a deep pang at the thought of never seeing them again.

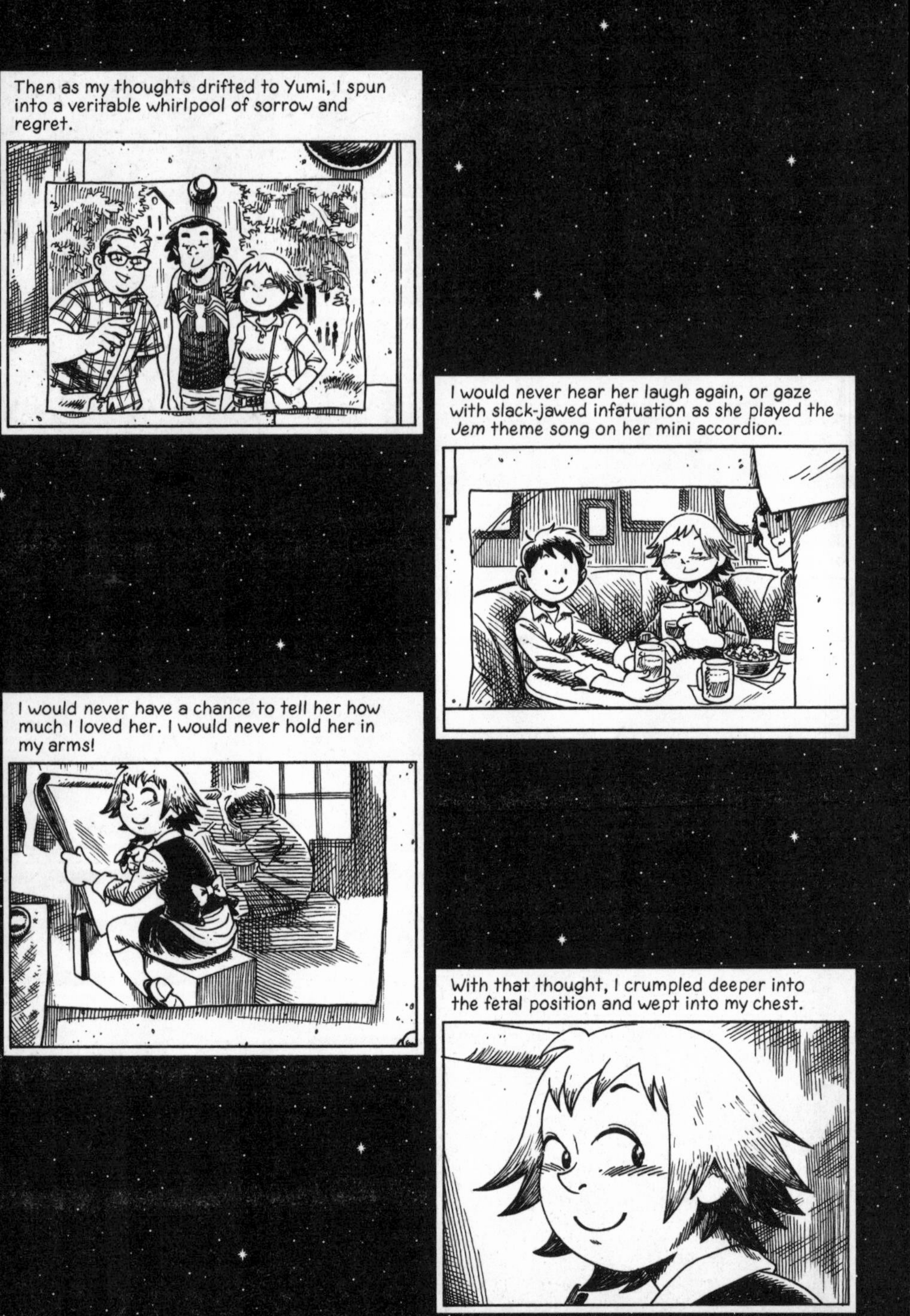
Then as my thoughts drifted to Yumi, I spun into a veritable whirlpool of sorrow and regret.
I would never hear her laugh again, or gaze with slack-jawed infatuation as she played the *Jem* theme song on her mini accordion.
I would never have a chance to tell her how much I loved her. I would never hold her in my arms!
With that thought, I crumpled deeper into the fetal position and wept into my chest.

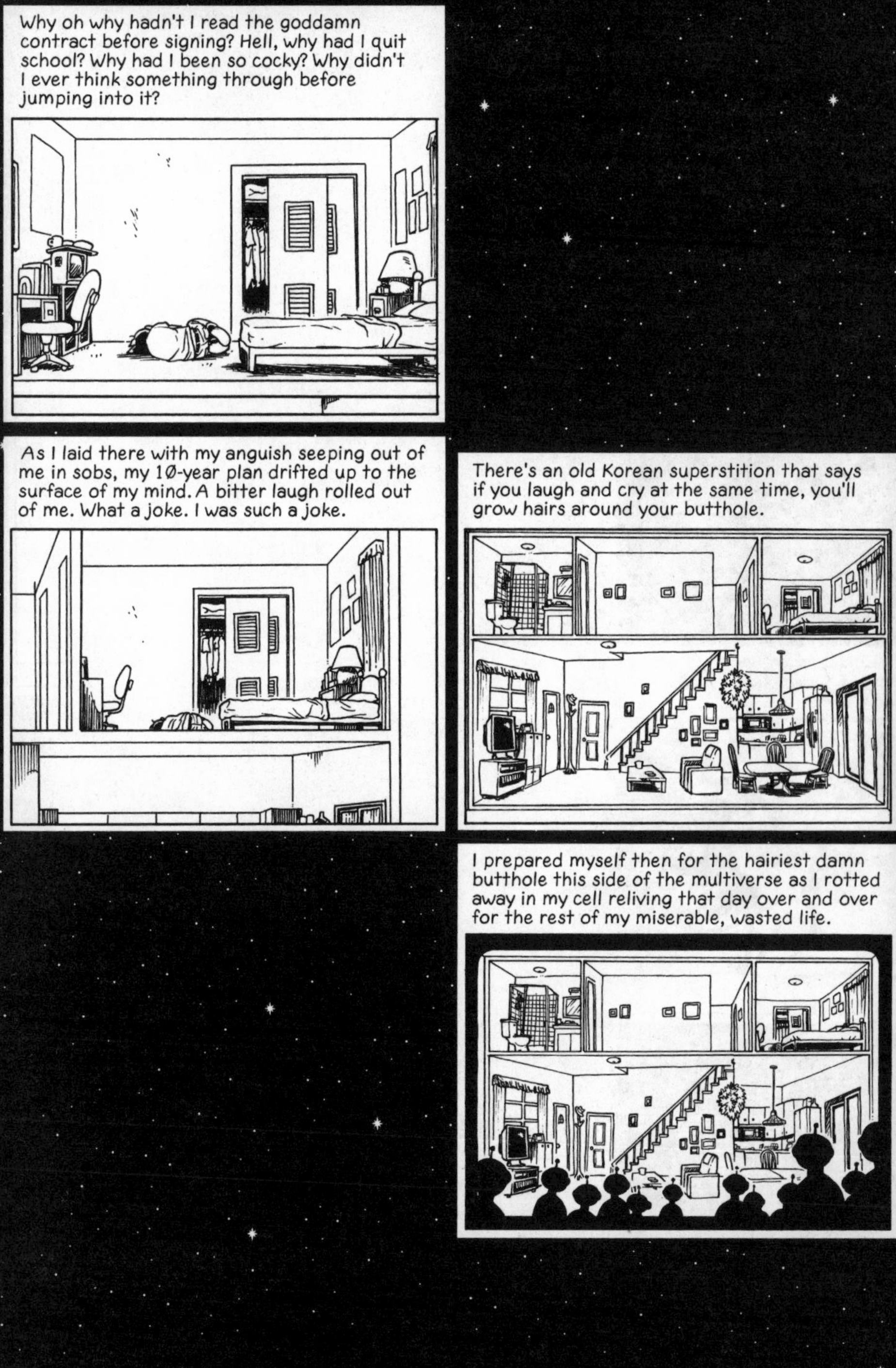
Why oh why hadn't I read the goddamn contract before signing? Hell, why had I quit school? Why had I been so cocky? Why didn't I ever think something through before jumping into it?
As I laid there with my anguish seeping out of me in sobs, my 10-year plan drifted up to the surface of my mind. A bitter laugh rolled out of me. What a joke. I was such a joke.
There's an old Korean superstition that says if you laugh and cry at the same time, you'll grow hairs around your butthole.
I prepared myself then for the hairiest damn butthole this side of the multiverse as I rotted away in my cell reliving that day over and over for the rest of my miserable, wasted life.

CHAPTER 15

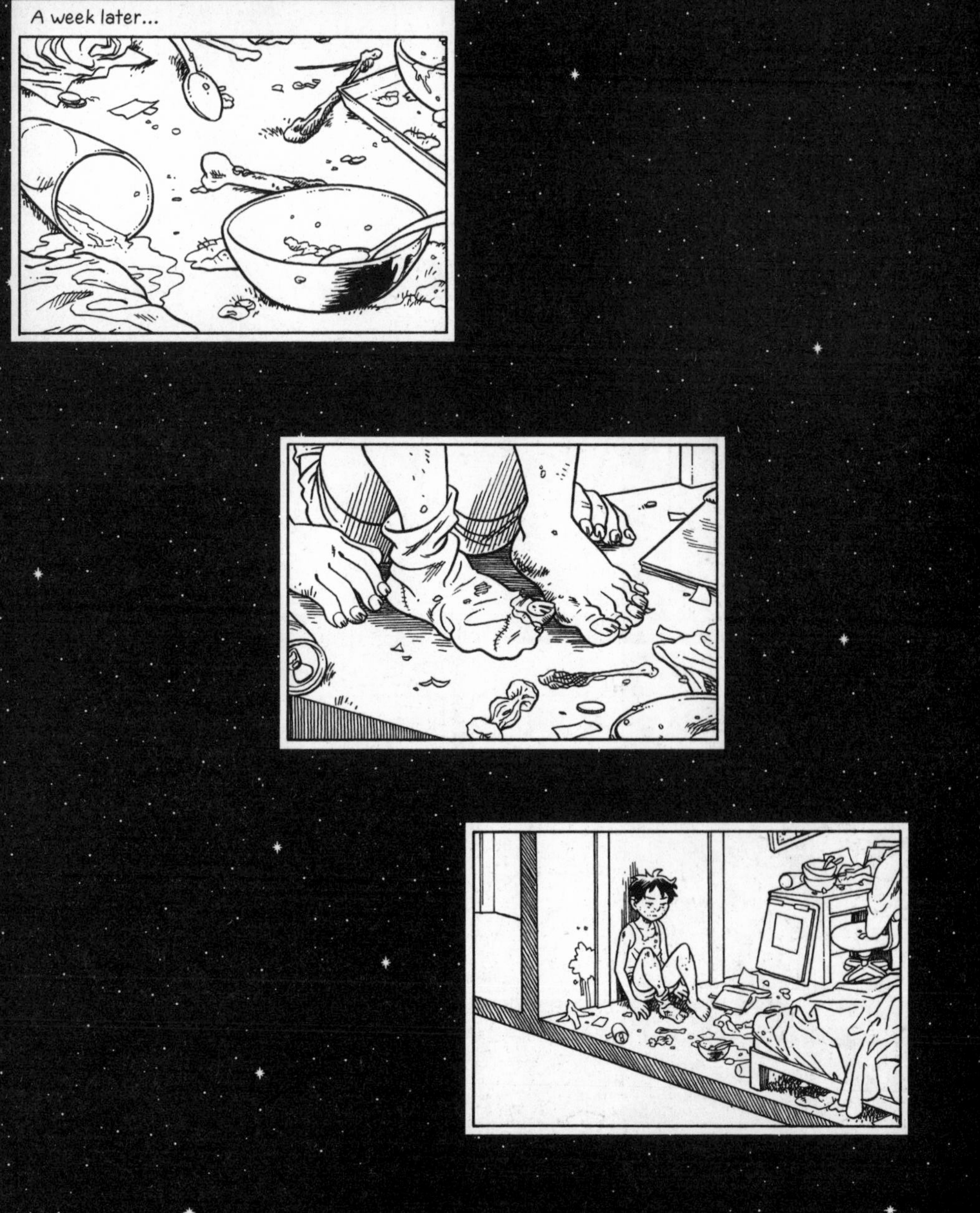
A week later...

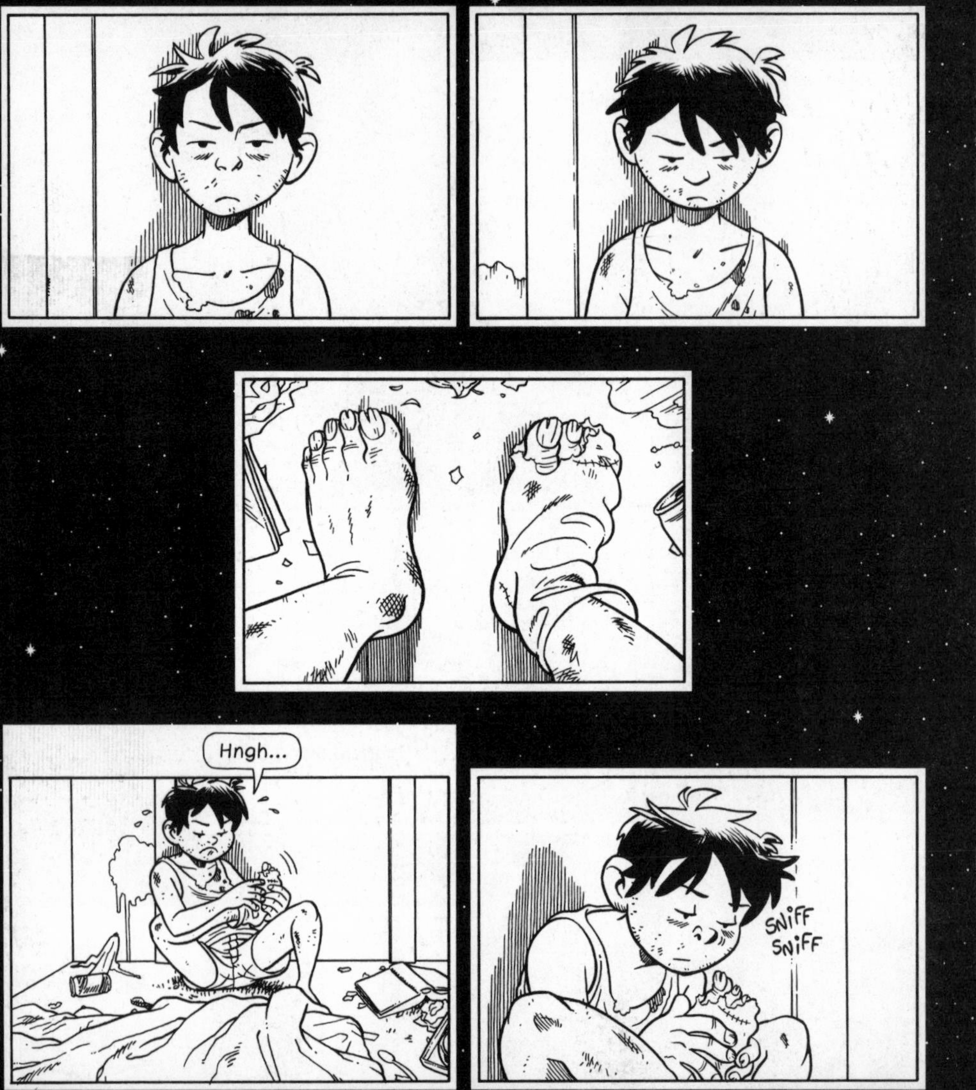
Hngh...
SNIFF
SNIFF

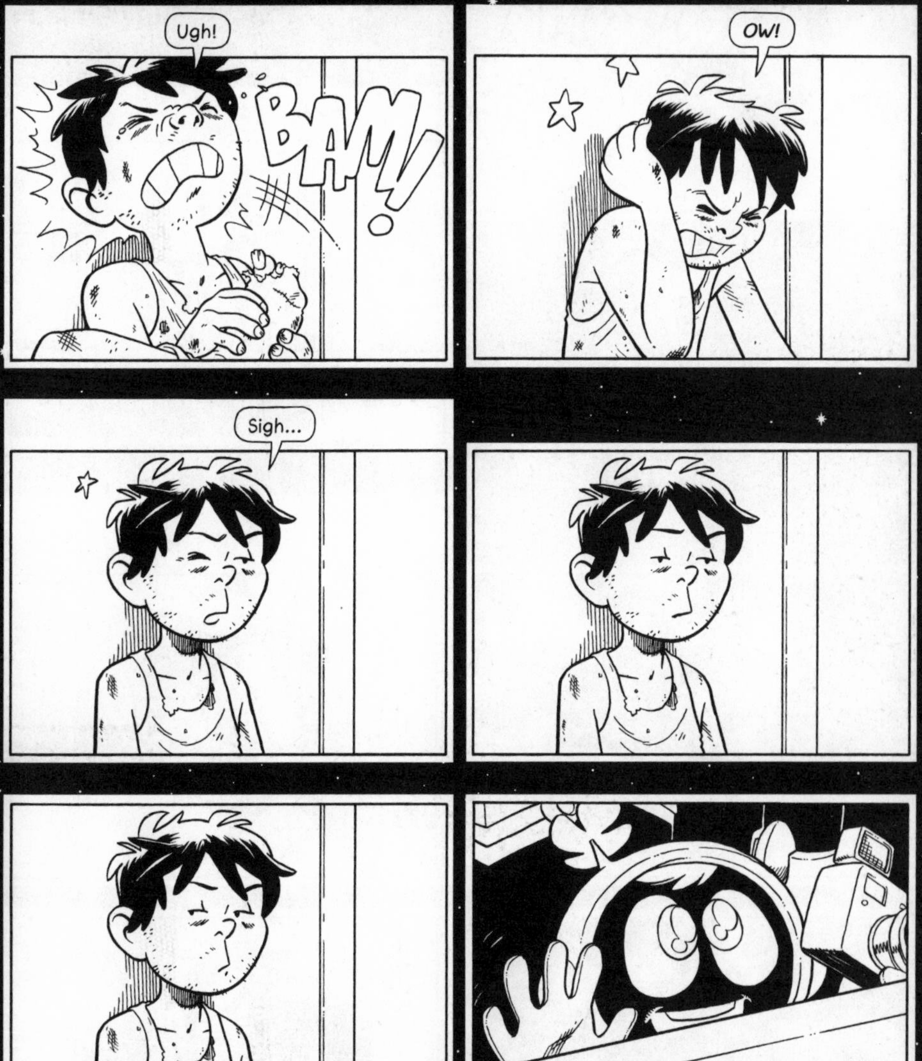
Ugh!
BAM!
OW!
Sigh...

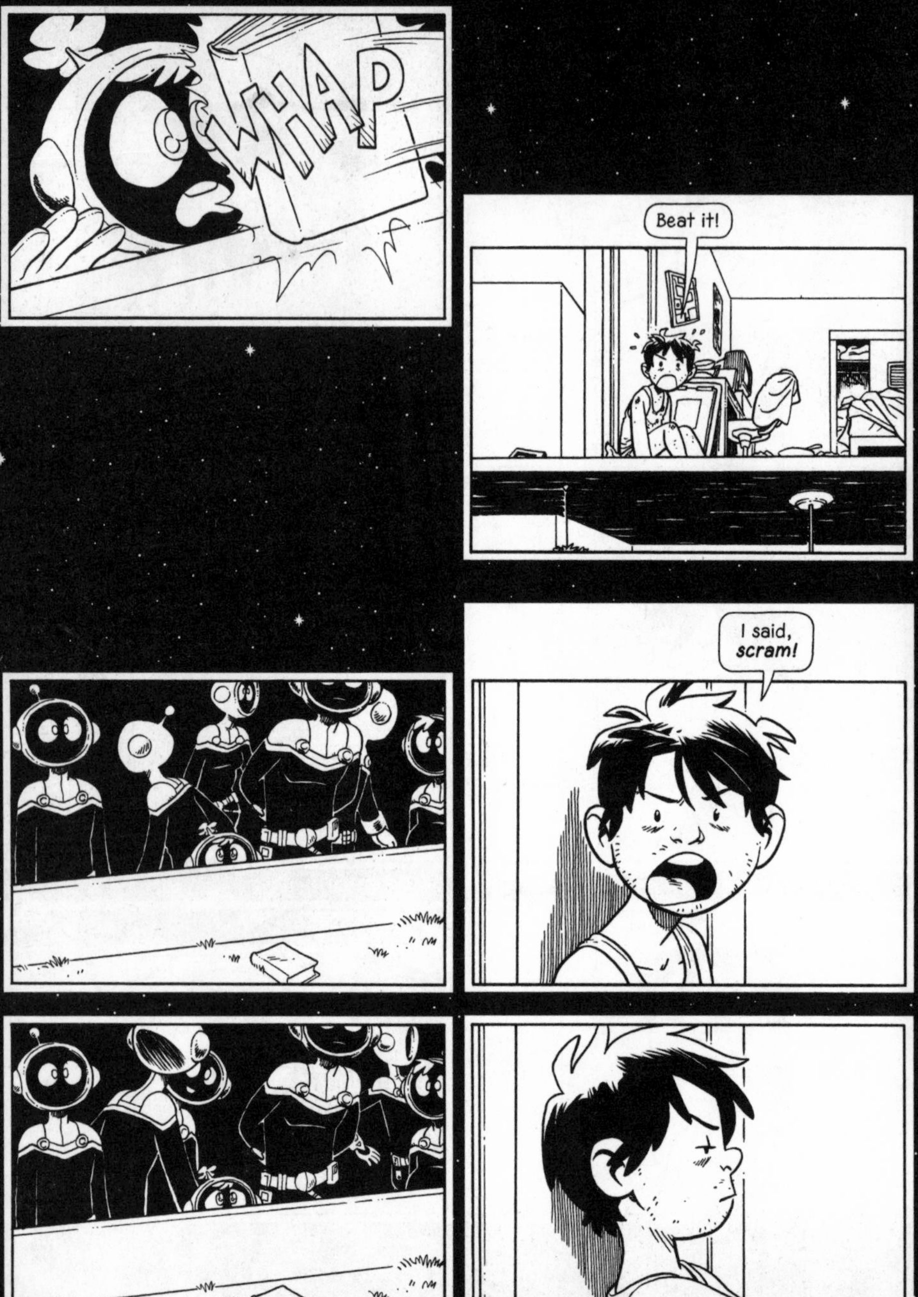
WHAP
Beat it!
I said, *scram!*

Yo, Andy. What did you do to that kid?

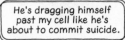

He's dragging himself past my cell like he's about to commit suicide.

She was the one, Mo...

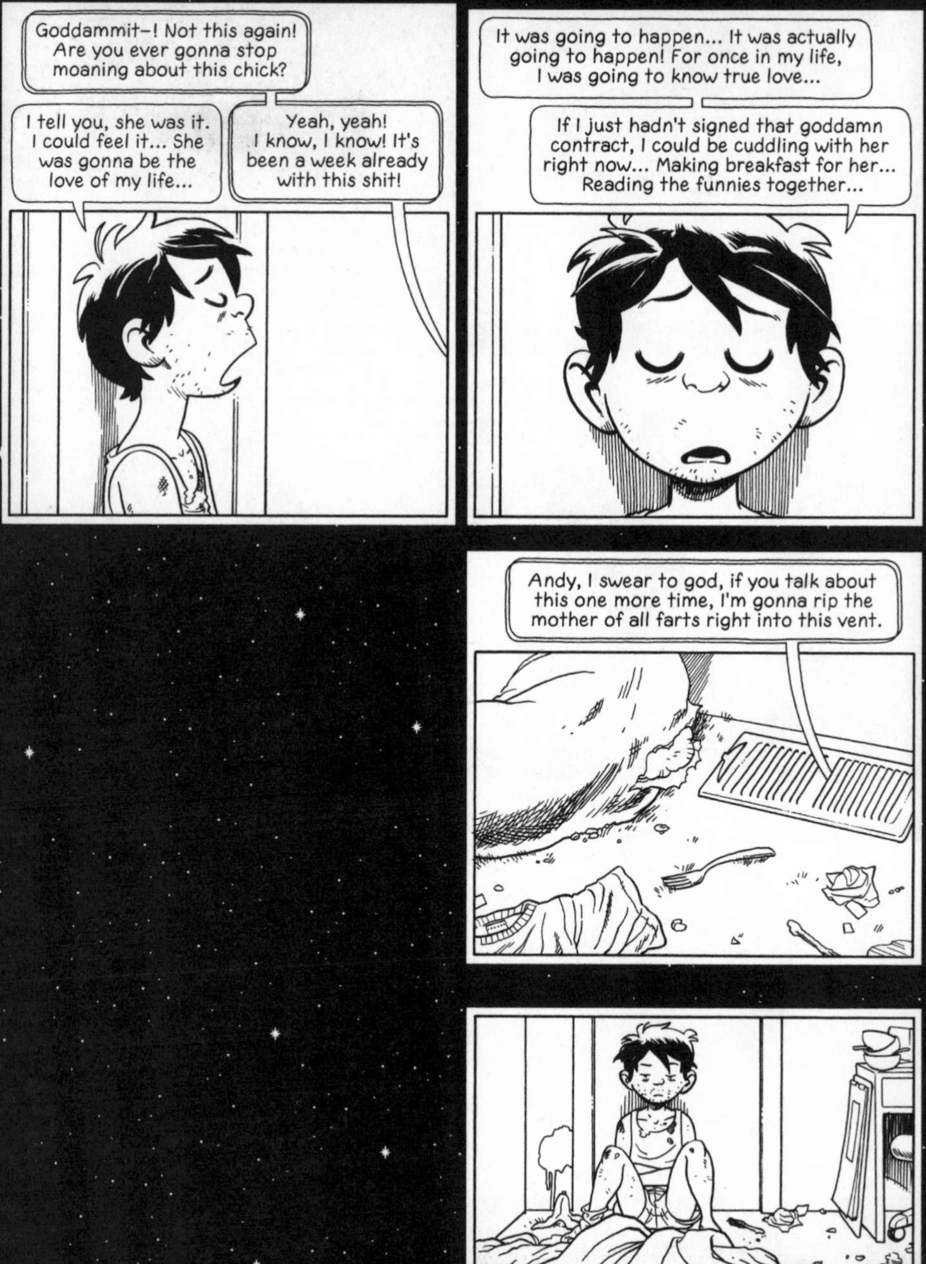
Goddammit-! Not this again! Are you ever gonna stop moaning about this chick?
I tell you, she was it. I could feel it... She was gonna be the love of my life...
Yeah, yeah! I know, I know! It's been a week already with this shit!
It was going to happen... It was actually going to happen! For once in my life, I was going to know true love...
If I just hadn't signed that goddamn contract, I could be cuddling with her right now... Making breakfast for her... Reading the funnies together...
Andy, I swear to god, if you talk about this one more time, I'm gonna rip the mother of all farts right into this vent.

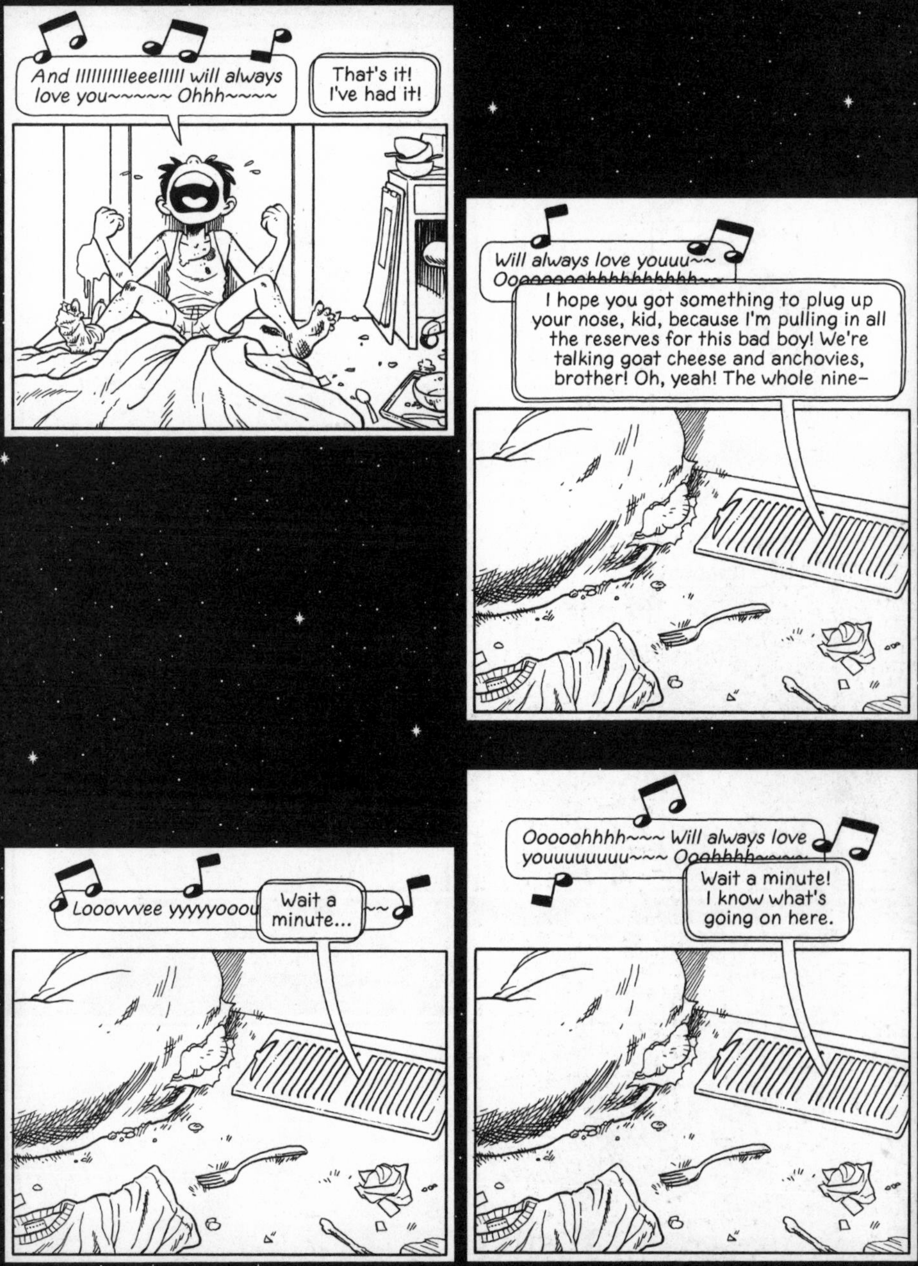
And IIIIIIIIIeeeIIIII will always love you~~~~~ Ohhh~~~~
That's it! I've had it!
Will always love youuu~~ Oooooooohhhhhhhhhh~~
I hope you got something to plug up your nose, kid, because I'm pulling in all the reserves for this bad boy! We're talking goat cheese and anchovies, brother! Oh, yeah! The whole nine-
Looovvvee yyyyoooo
Wait a minute...
Oooohhhh~~~ Will always love youuuuuuuu~~~ Ooohhhh~~~~
Wait a minute! I know what's going on here.

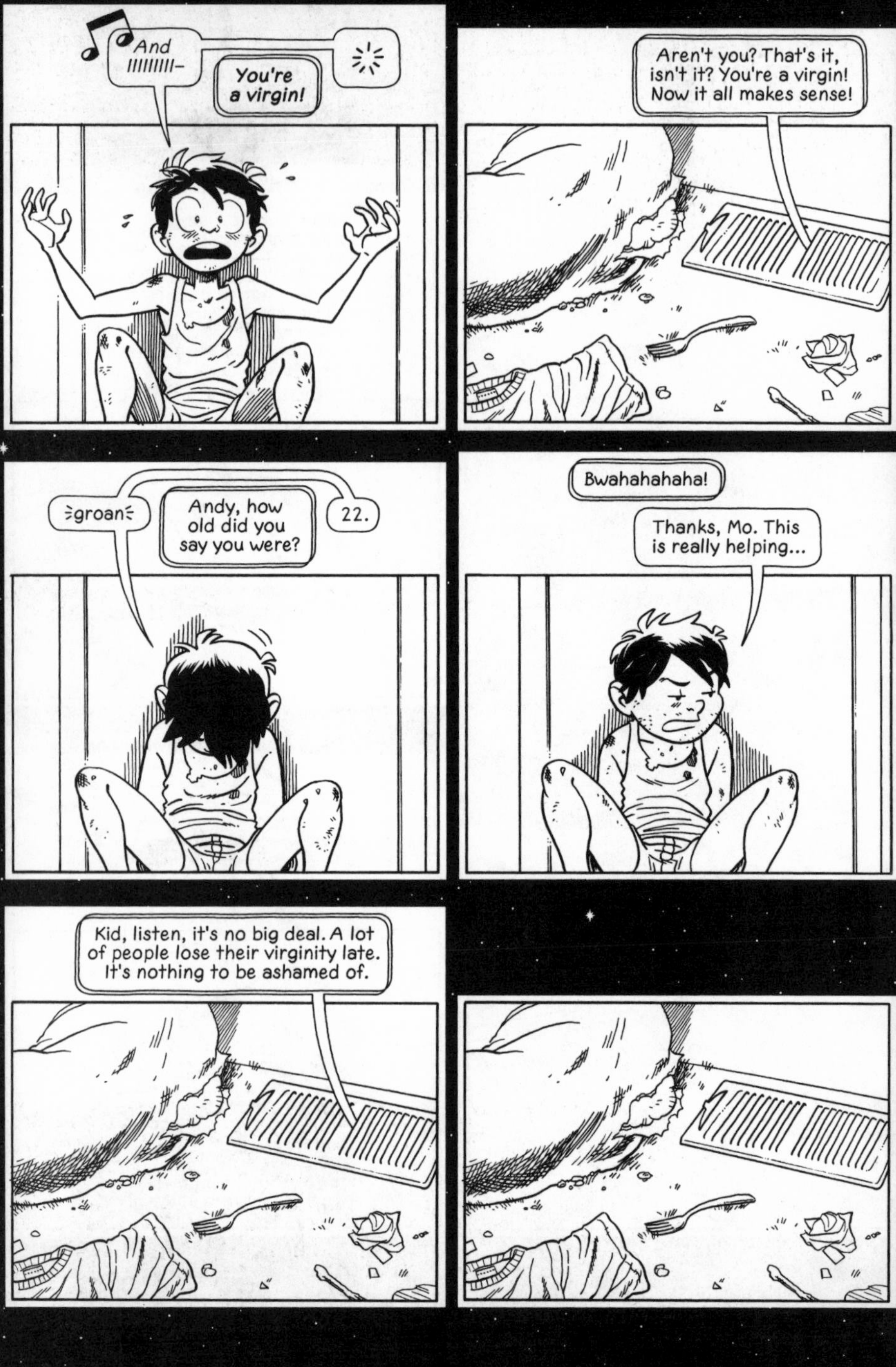
And
IIIIIIII–
You're a virgin!
Aren't you? That's it, isn't it? You're a virgin! Now it all makes sense!
groan
Andy, how old did you say you were?
22.
Bwahahahaha!
Thanks, Mo. This is really helping...
Kid, listen, it's no big deal. A lot of people lose their virginity late. It's nothing to be ashamed of.

Bwahahahaha!!

Mo, I don't want to die a virgin. I don't want to die a virgin...

Well, you won't have to worry about that, kid. Heh heh...

Mo, for the last time, I am not humping anything in the refrigerator!

I'm not talking about that. You're gonna have a woman in there soon.

...

What? What're you talking about?

Are you really this dumb? Haven't you ever been to a zoo? They always try to get both sexes in an exhibit.

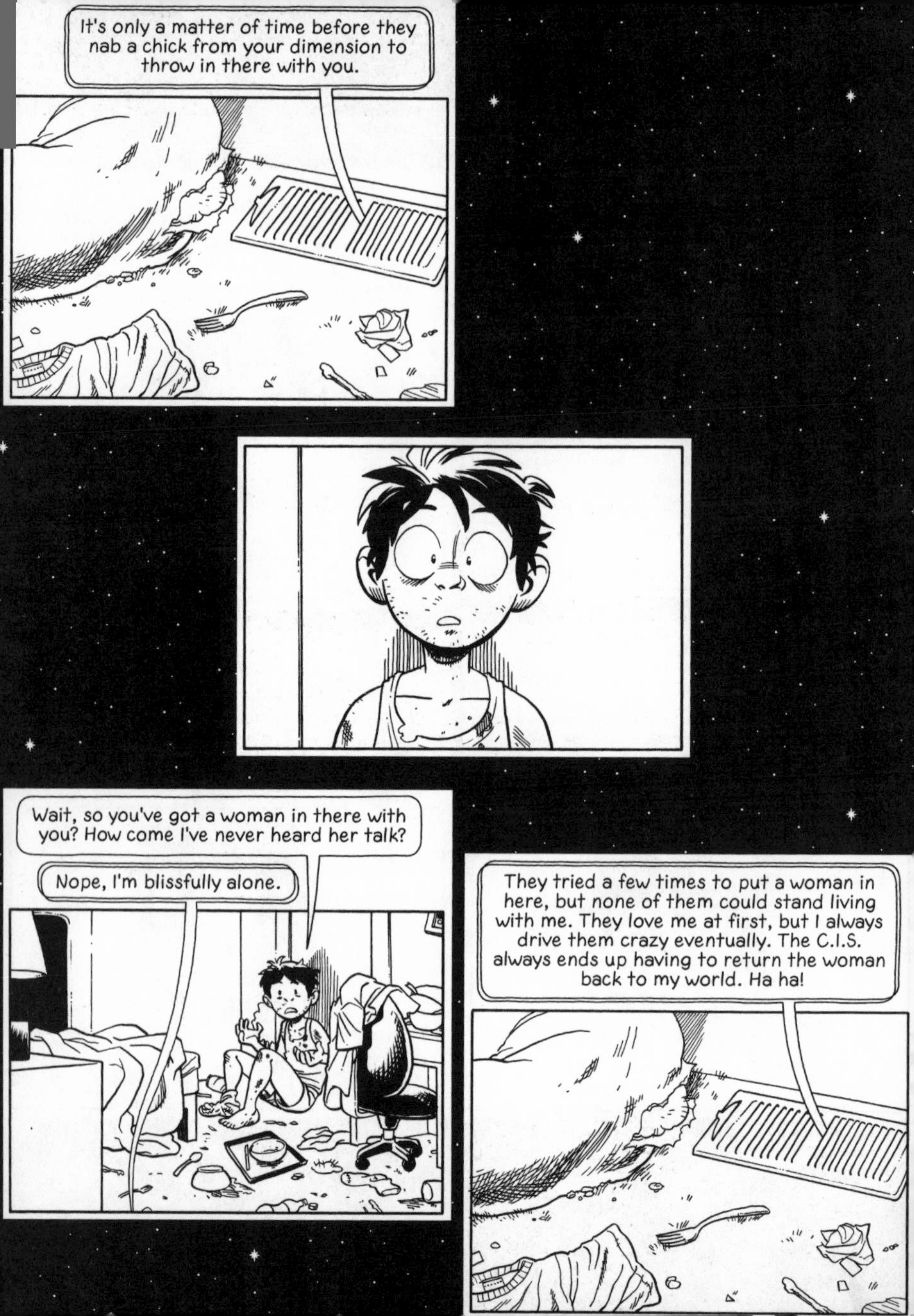
It's only a matter of time before they nab a chick from your dimension to throw in there with you.
Wait, so you've got a woman in there with you? How come I've never heard her talk?
Nope, I'm blissfully alone.
They tried a few times to put a woman in here, but none of them could stand living with me. They love me at first, but I always drive them crazy eventually. The C.I.S. always ends up having to return the woman back to my world. Ha ha!

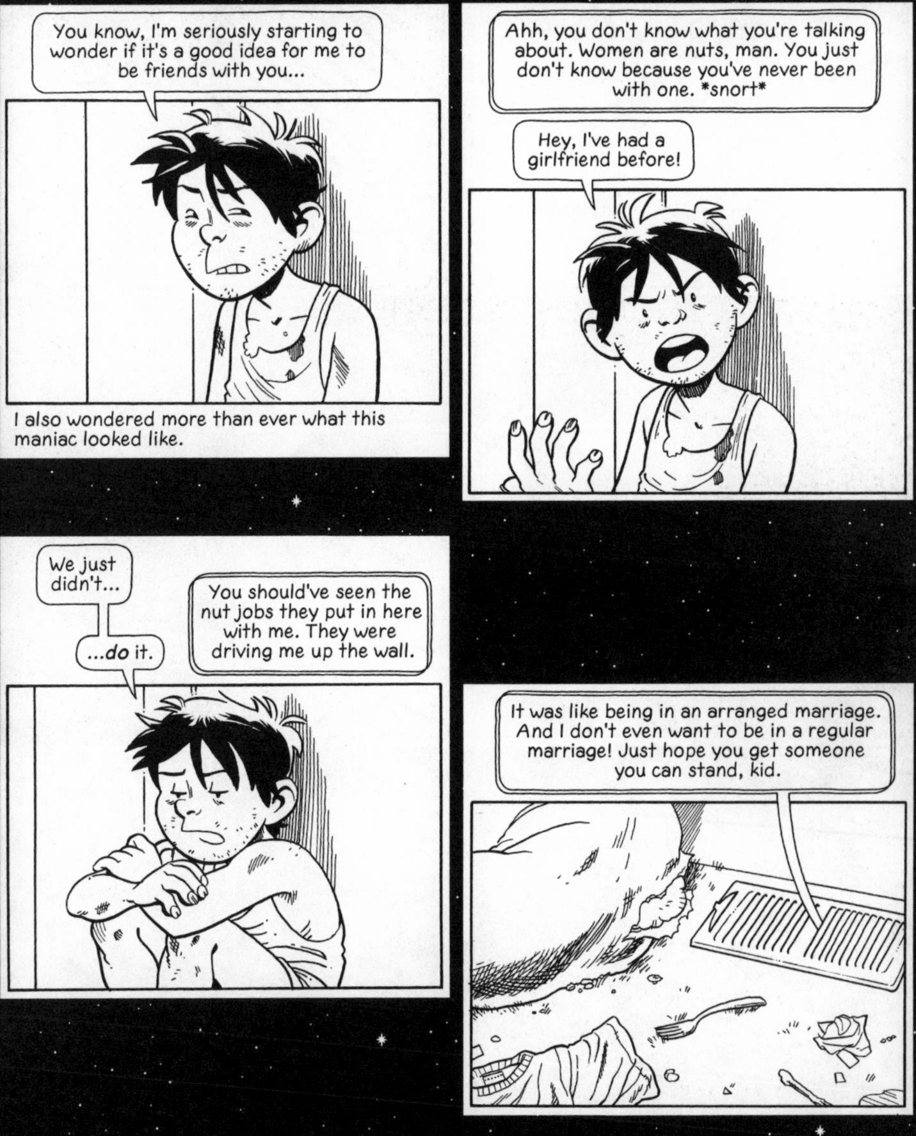
You know, I'm seriously starting to wonder if it's a good idea for me to be friends with you...
I also wondered more than ever what this maniac looked like.
Ahh, you don't know what you're talking about. Women are nuts, man. You just don't know because you've never been with one. *snort*
Hey, I've had a girlfriend before!
We just didn't...
...*do* it.
You should've seen the nut jobs they put in here with me. They were driving me up the wall.
It was like being in an arranged marriage. And I don't even want to be in a regular marriage! Just hope you get someone you can stand, kid.

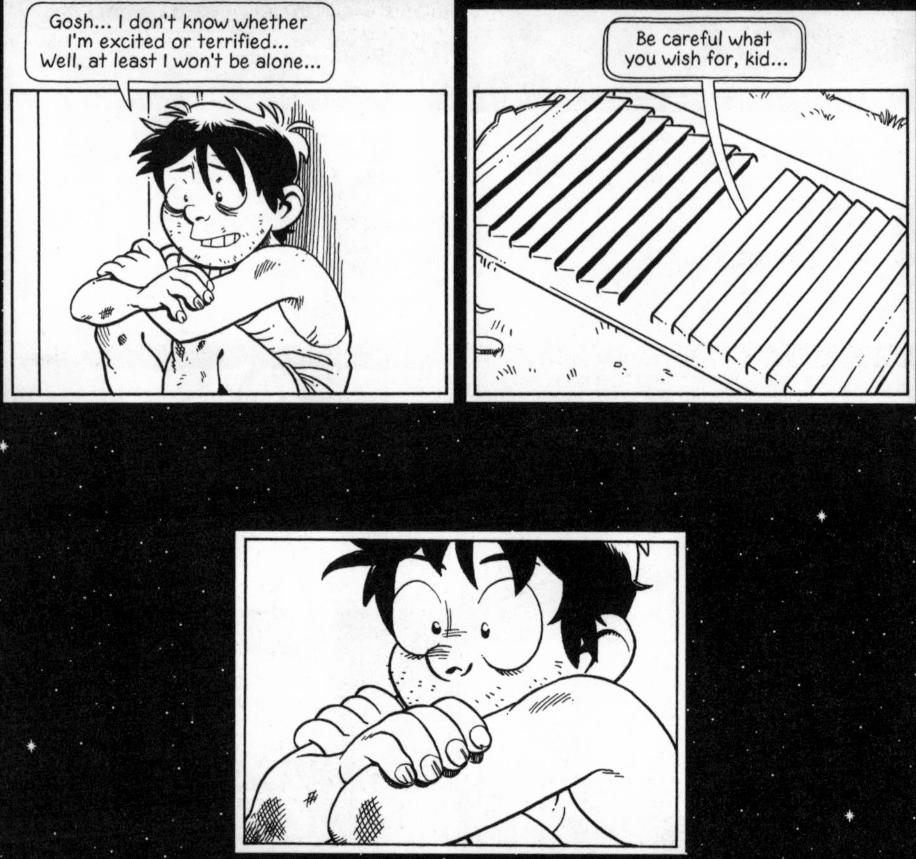
Gosh... I don't know whether I'm excited or terrified... Well, at least I won't be alone...
Be careful what you wish for, kid...

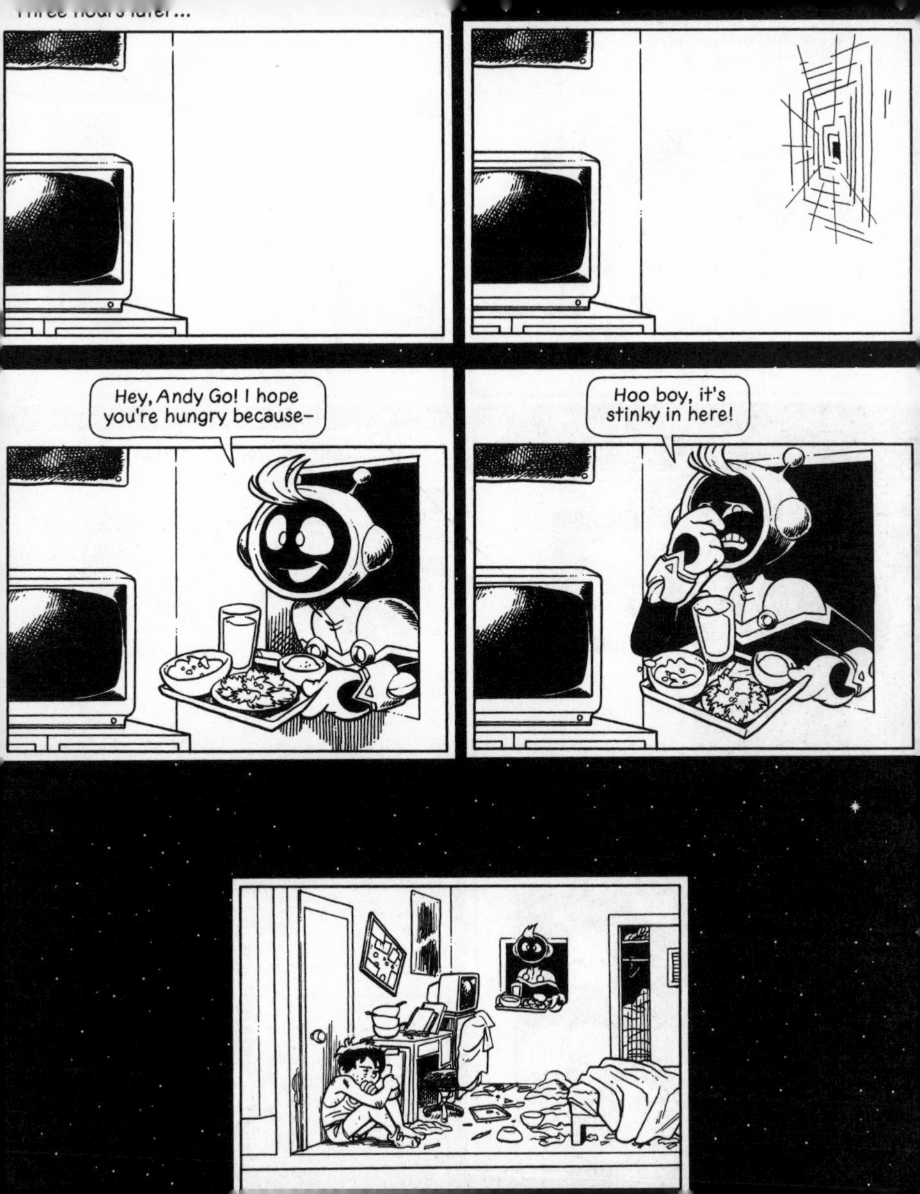
Hey, Andy Go! I hope you're hungry because-
Hoo boy, it's stinky in here!

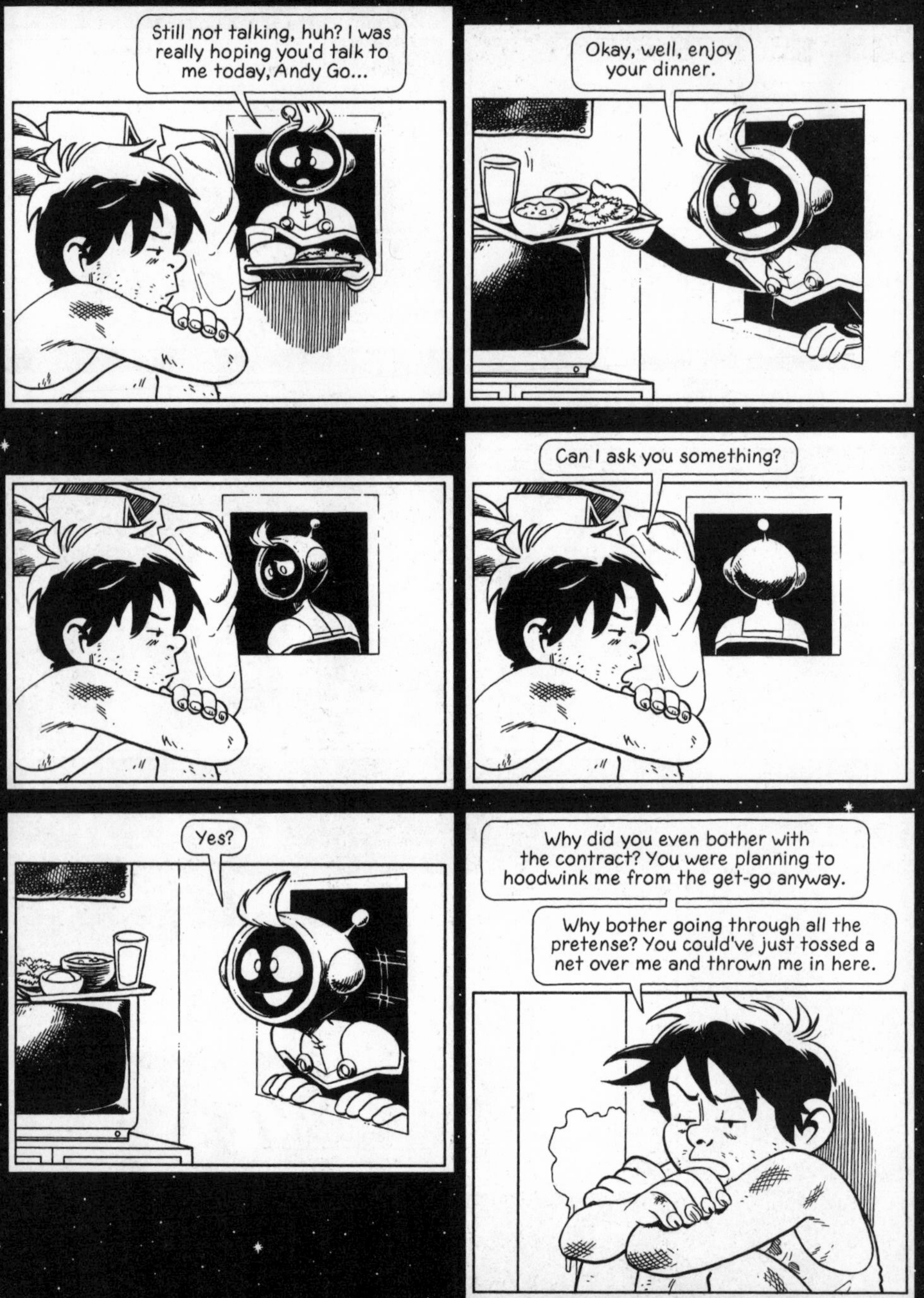

Still not talking, huh? I was really hoping you'd talk to me today, Andy Go...
Okay, well, enjoy your dinner.
Can I ask you something?
Yes?
Why did you even bother with the contract? You were planning to hoodwink me from the get-go anyway.
Why bother going through all the pretense? You could've just tossed a net over me and thrown me in here.

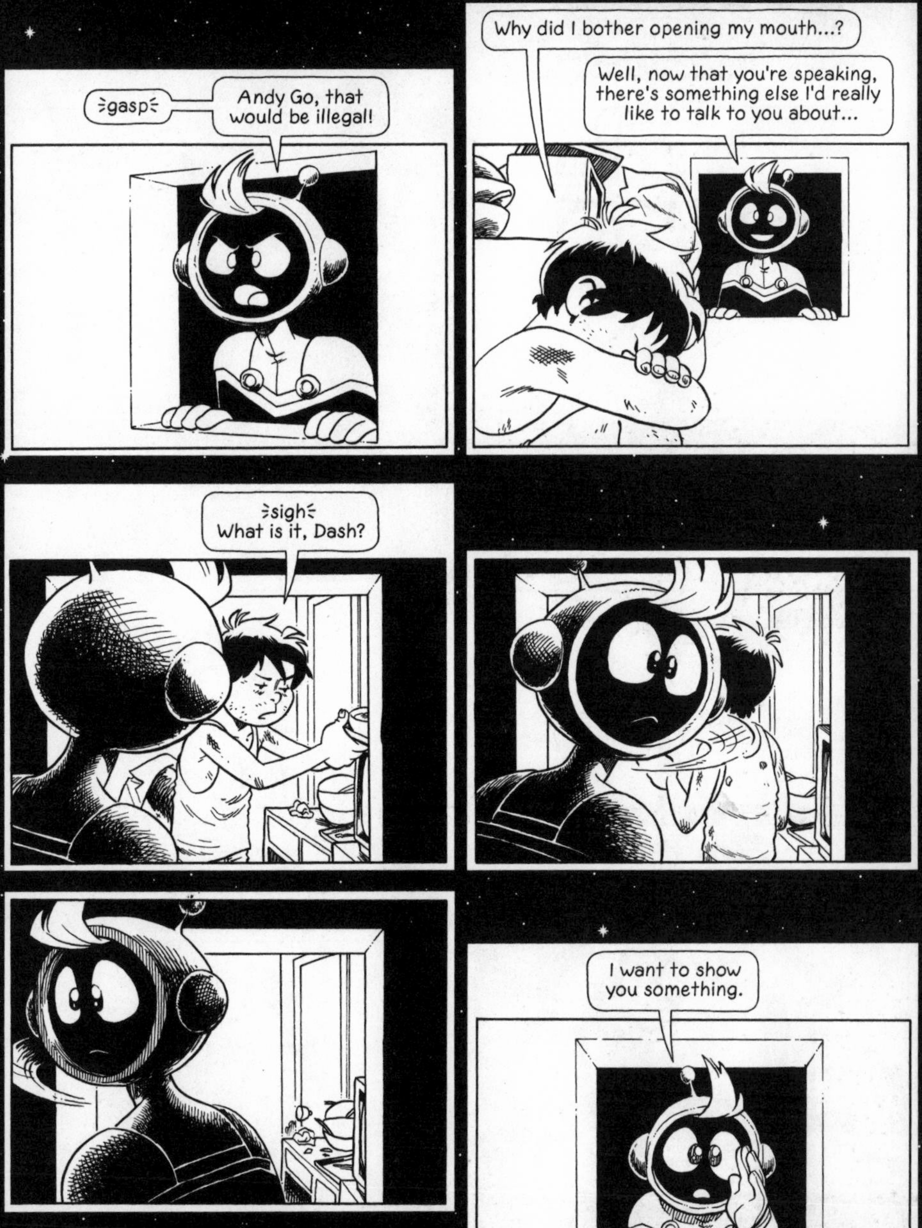

≷gasp≶
Andy Go, that would be illegal!
Why did I bother opening my mouth...?
Well, now that you're speaking, there's something else I'd really like to talk to you about...
≷sigh≶ What is it, Dash?
I want to show you something.

What? Speak up!
Shh!
Come here, I want to show you something!

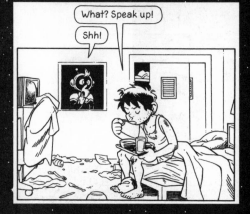

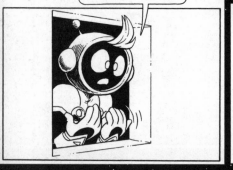

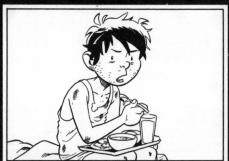

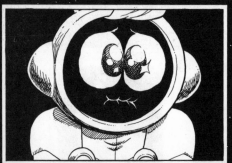

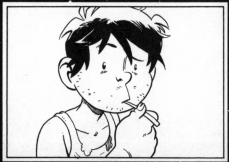

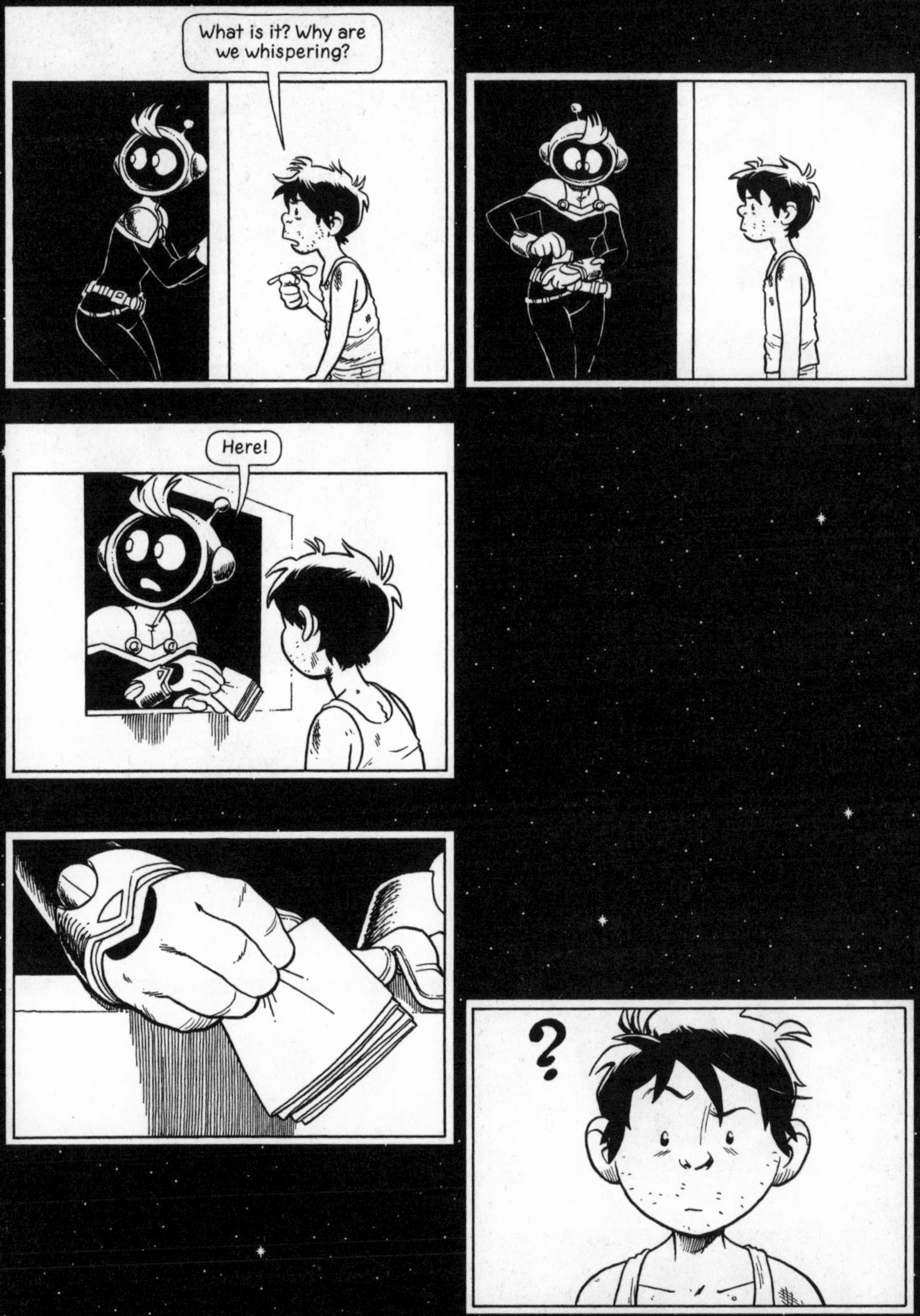
What is it? Why are we whispering?
Here!
?

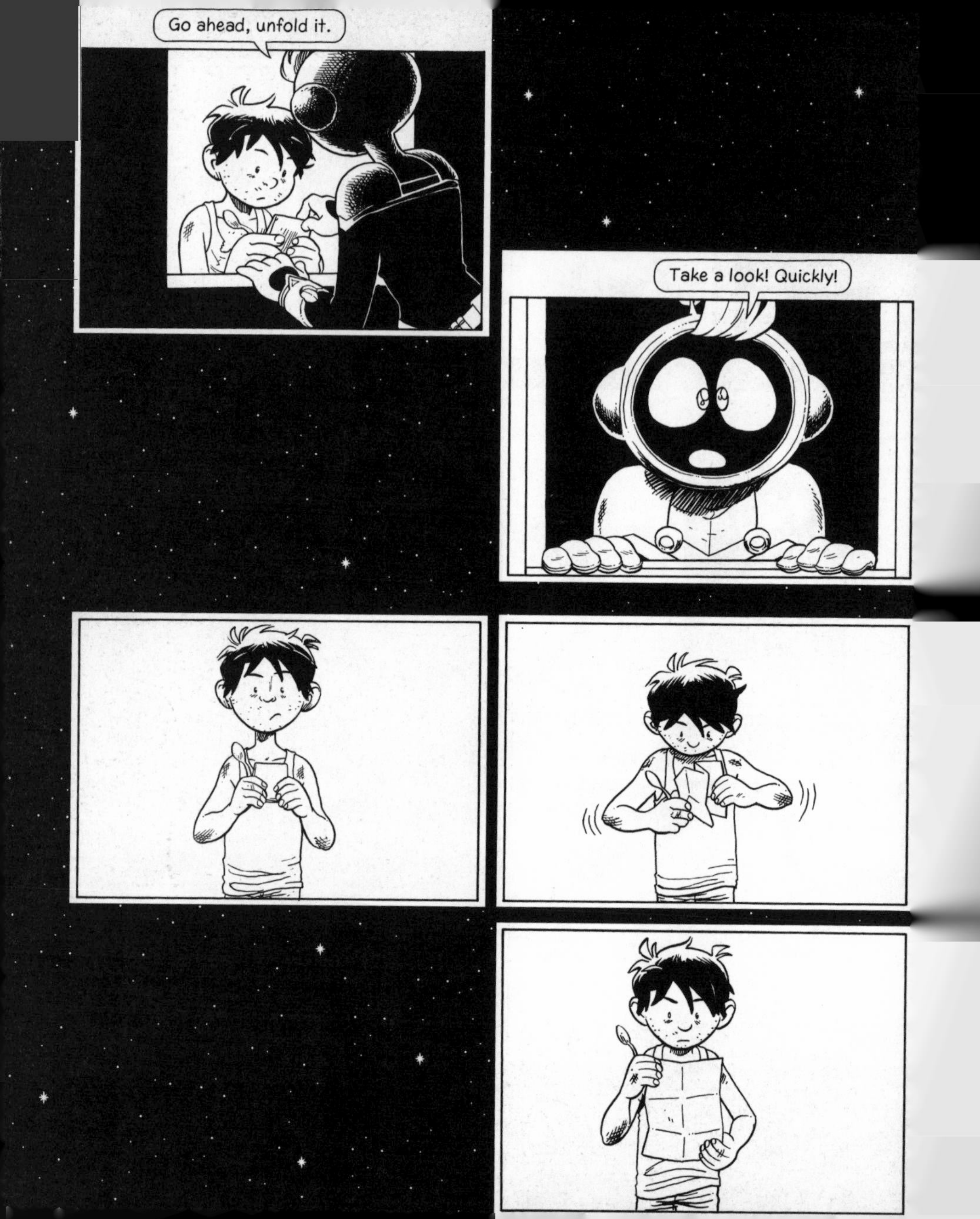
Go ahead, unfold it.
Take a look! Quickly!

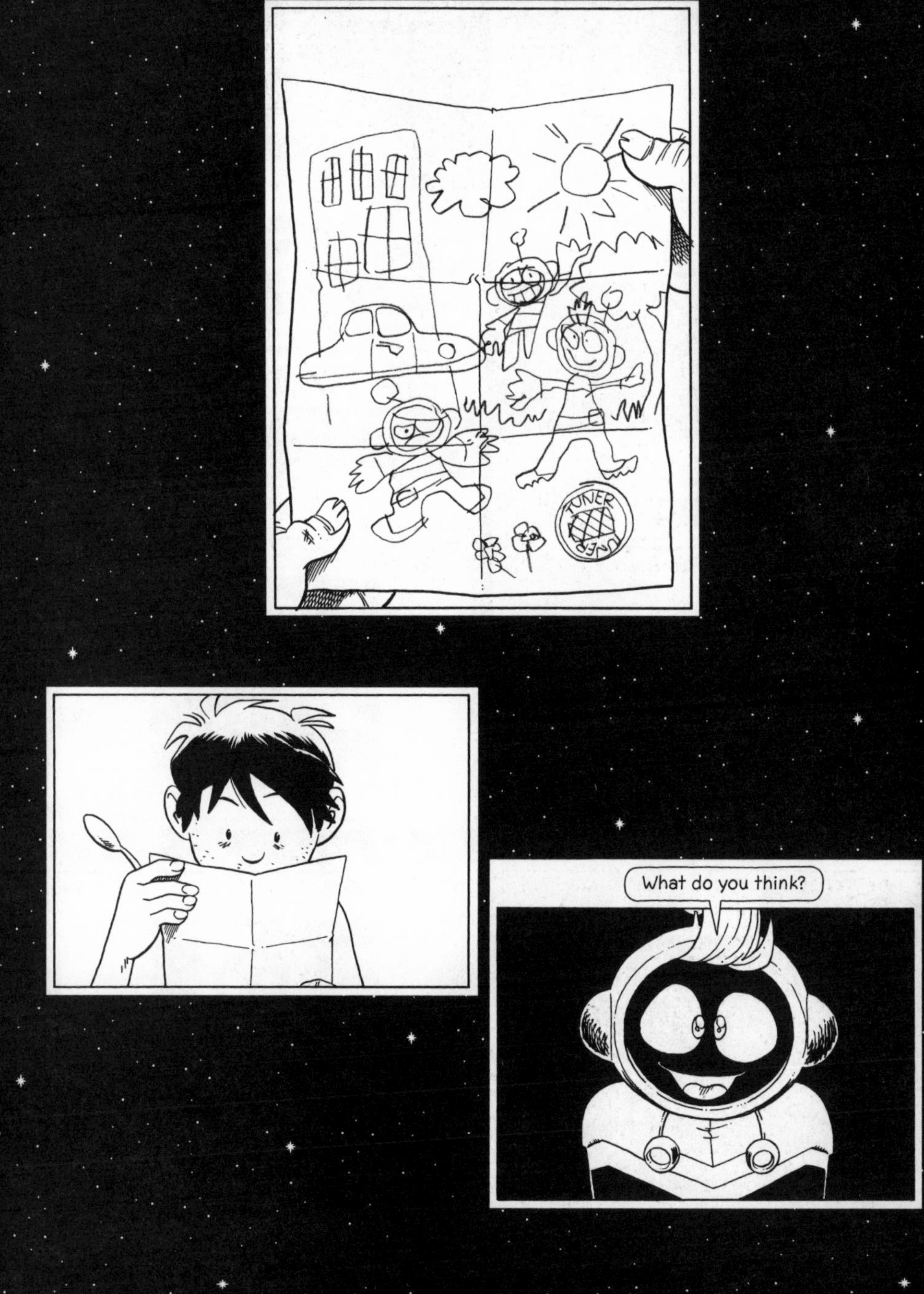
TUNER
What do you think?

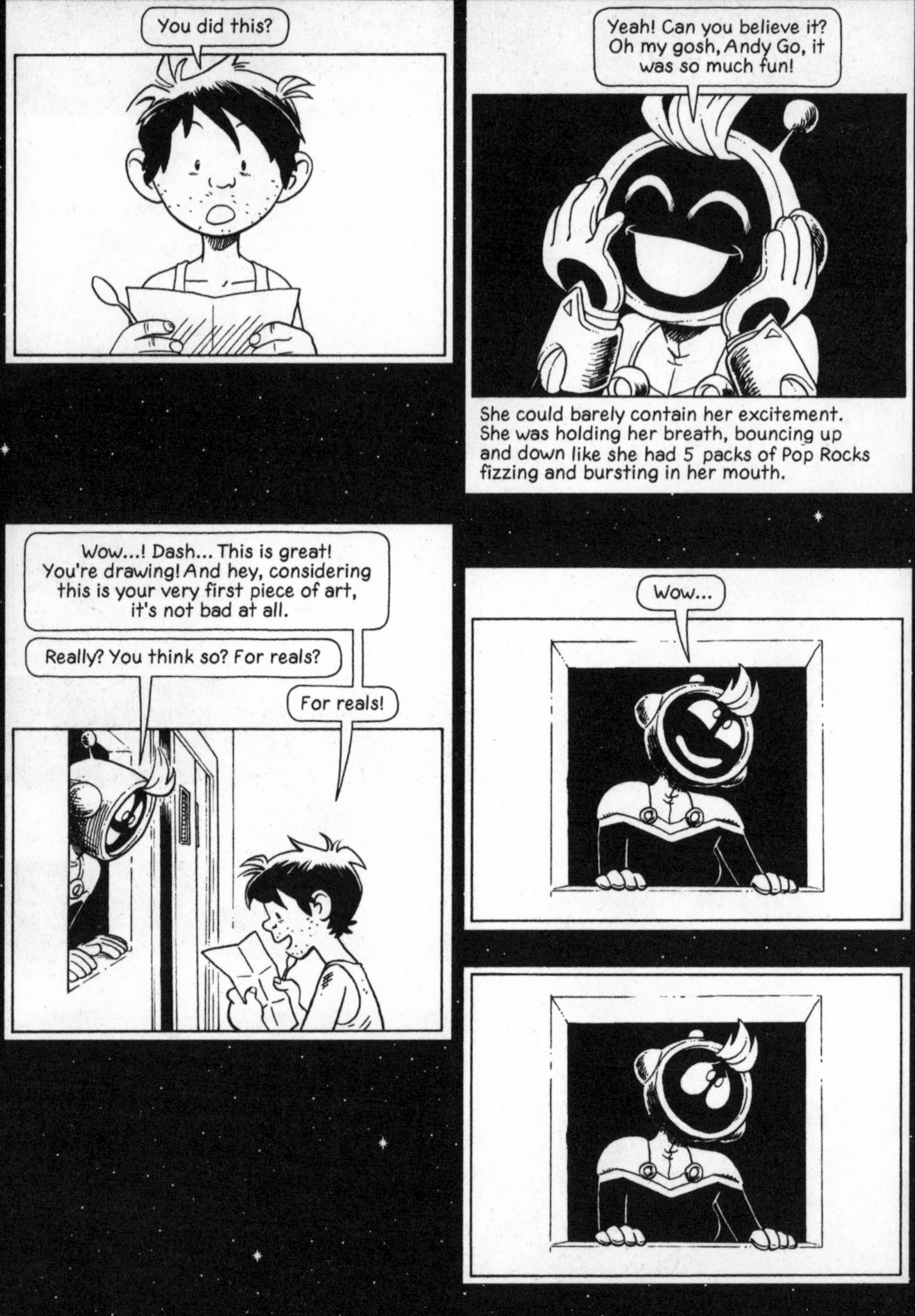
You did this?
Yeah! Can you believe it? Oh my gosh, Andy Go, it was so much fun!
She could barely contain her excitement. She was holding her breath, bouncing up and down like she had 5 packs of Pop Rocks fizzing and bursting in her mouth.
Wow...! Dash... This is great! You're drawing! And hey, considering this is your very first piece of art, it's not bad at all.
Really? You think so? For reals?
For reals!
Wow...

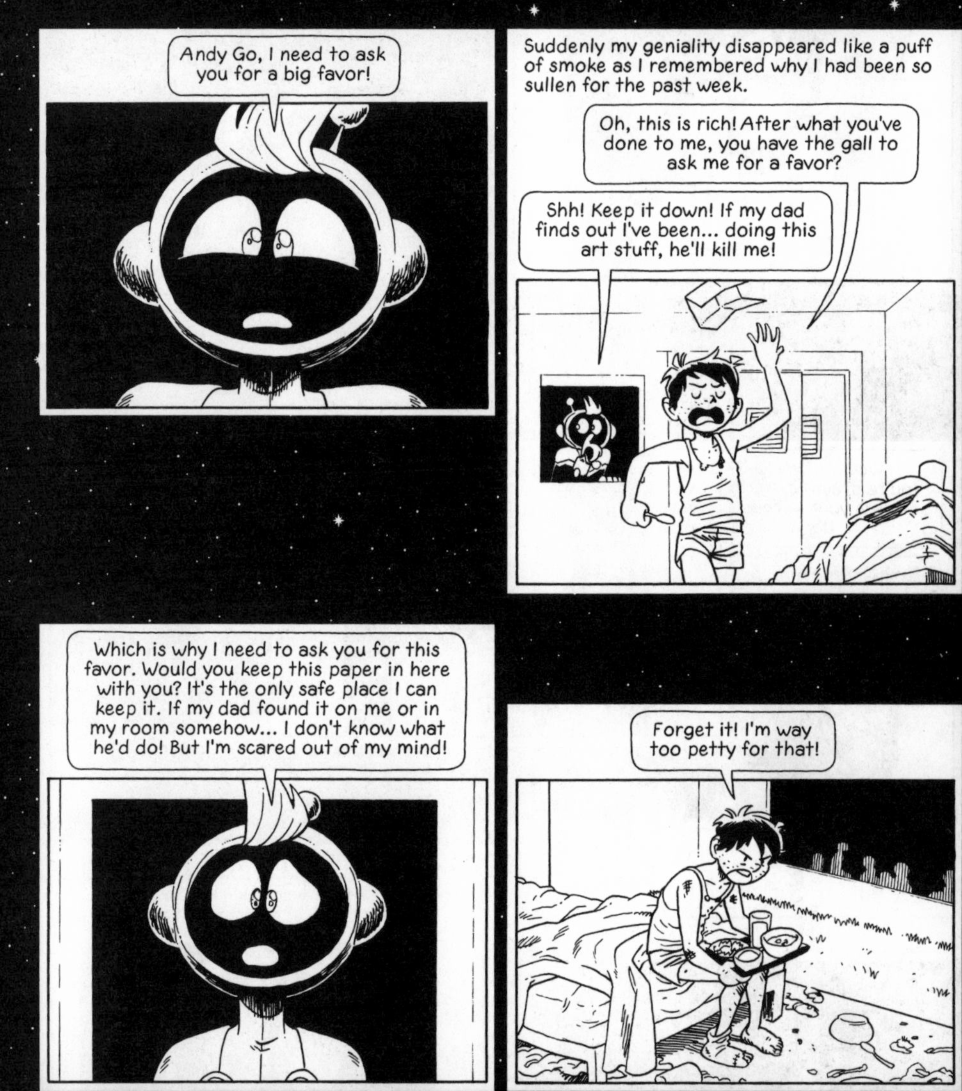
Andy Go, I need to ask you for a big favor!
Suddenly my geniality disappeared like a puff of smoke as I remembered why I had been so sullen for the past week.
Oh, this is rich! After what you've done to me, you have the gall to ask me for a favor?
Shh! Keep it down! If my dad finds out I've been... doing this art stuff, he'll kill me!
Which is why I need to ask you for this favor. Would you keep this paper in here with you? It's the only safe place I can keep it. If my dad found it on me or in my room somehow... I don't know what he'd do! But I'm scared out of my mind!
Forget it! I'm way too petty for that!

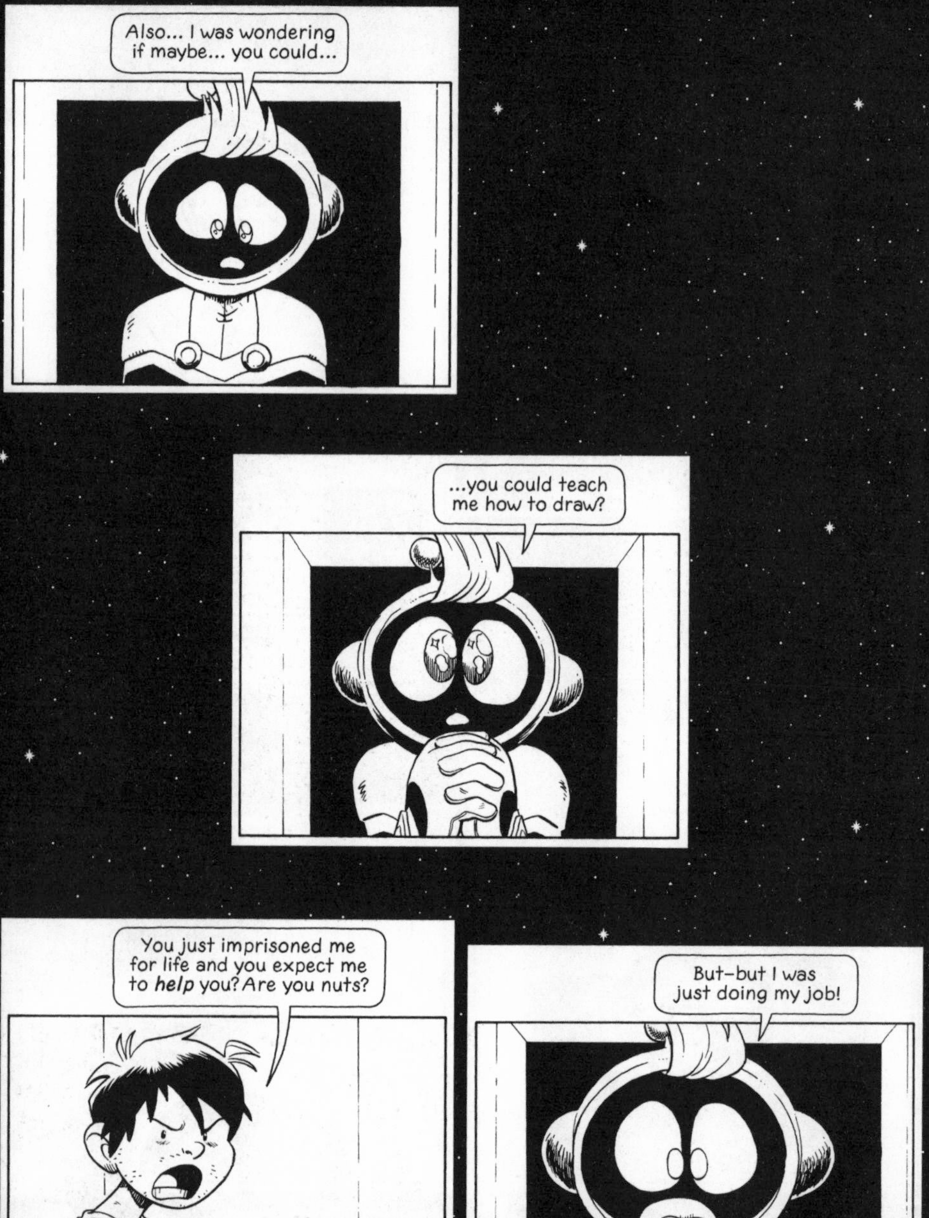
Also... I was wondering if maybe... you could...
...you could teach me how to draw?
You just imprisoned me for life and you expect me to *help* you? Are you nuts?
But–but I was just doing my job!

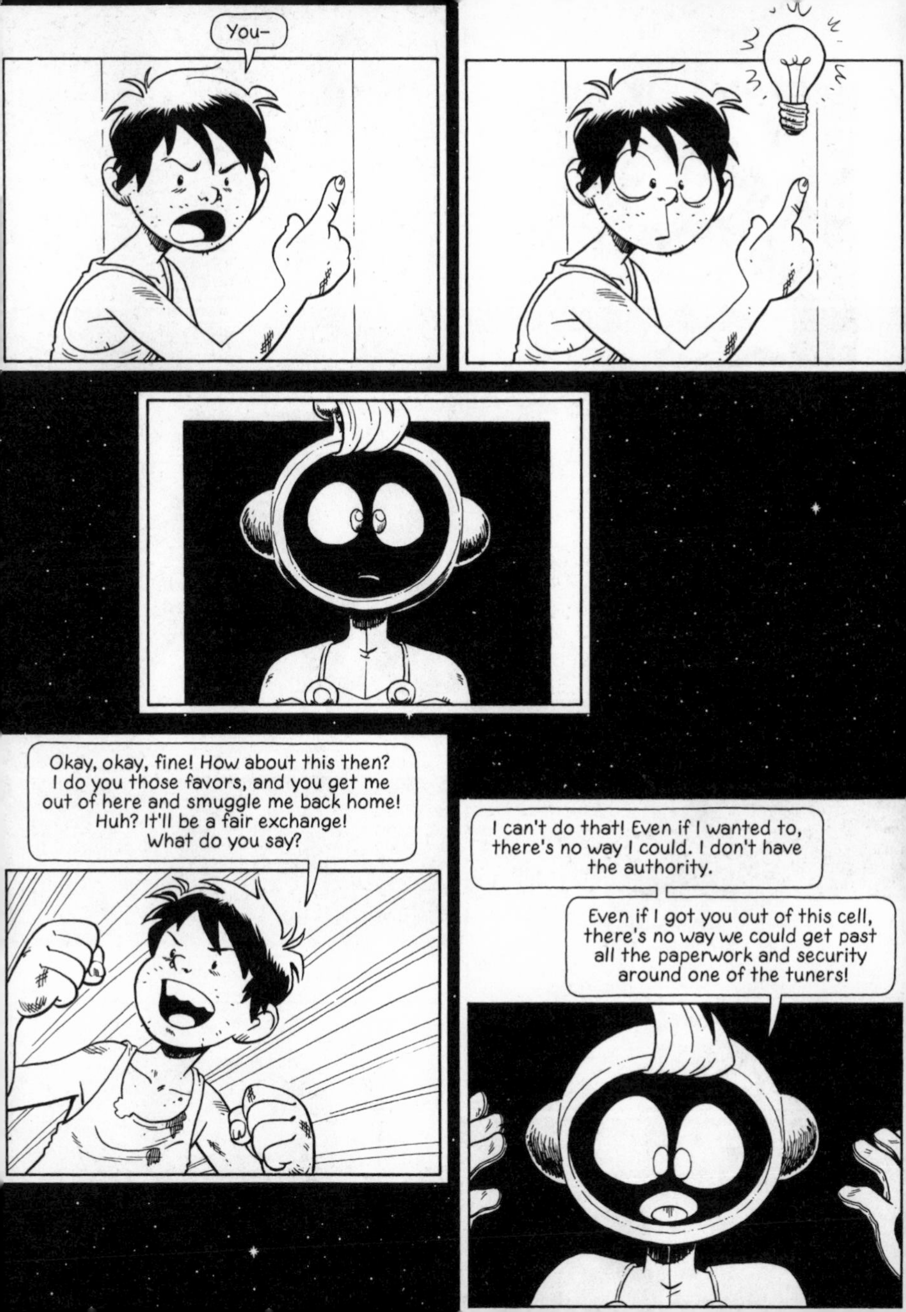
You-
Okay, okay, fine! How about this then? I do you those favors, and you get me out of here and smuggle me back home! Huh? It'll be a fair exchange! What do you say?
I can't do that! Even if I wanted to, there's no way I could. I don't have the authority.
Even if I got you out of this cell, there's no way we could get past all the paperwork and security around one of the tuners!

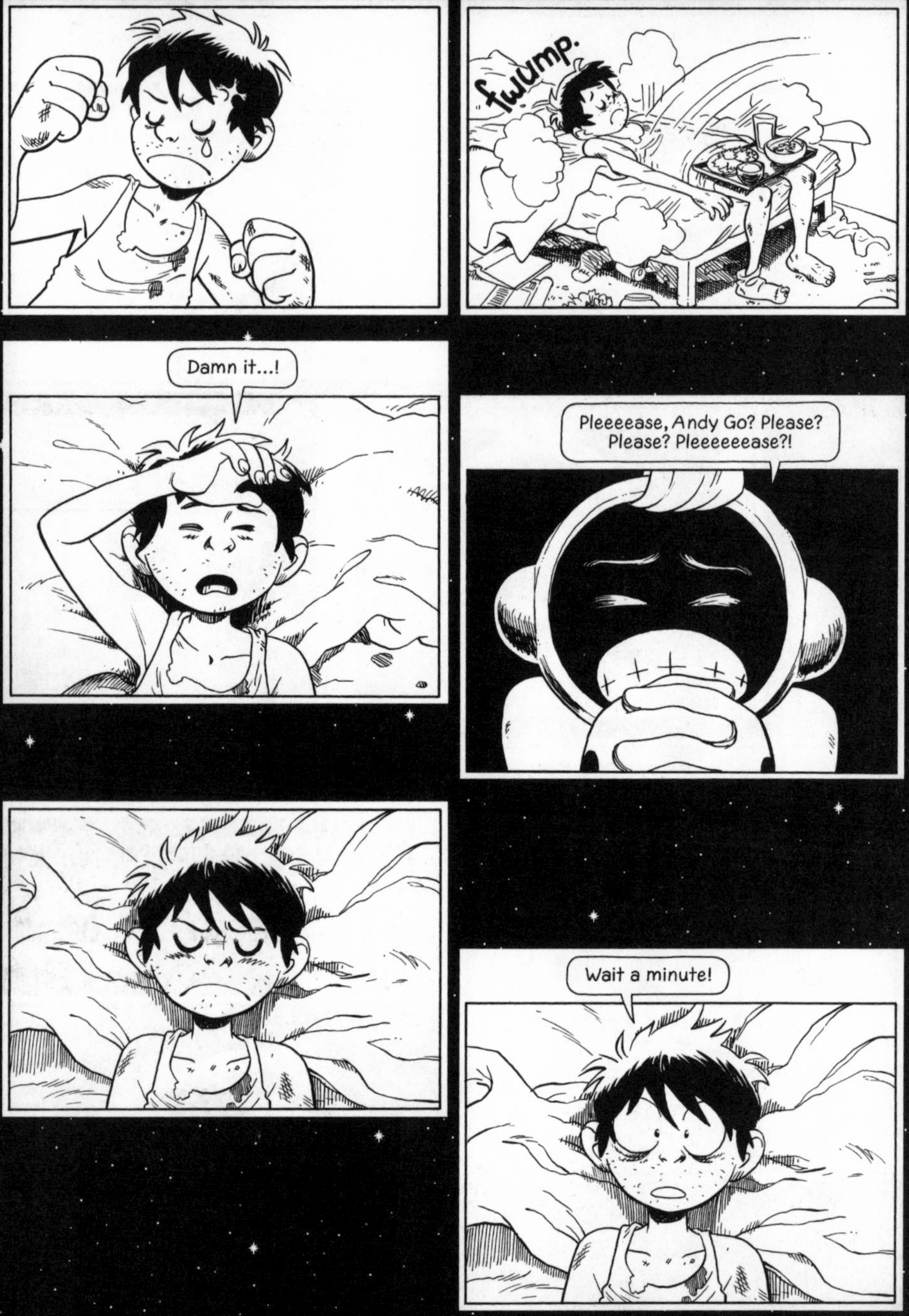
fwump.
Damn it...!
Pleeeease, Andy Go? Please? Please? Pleeeeeease?!
Wait a minute!

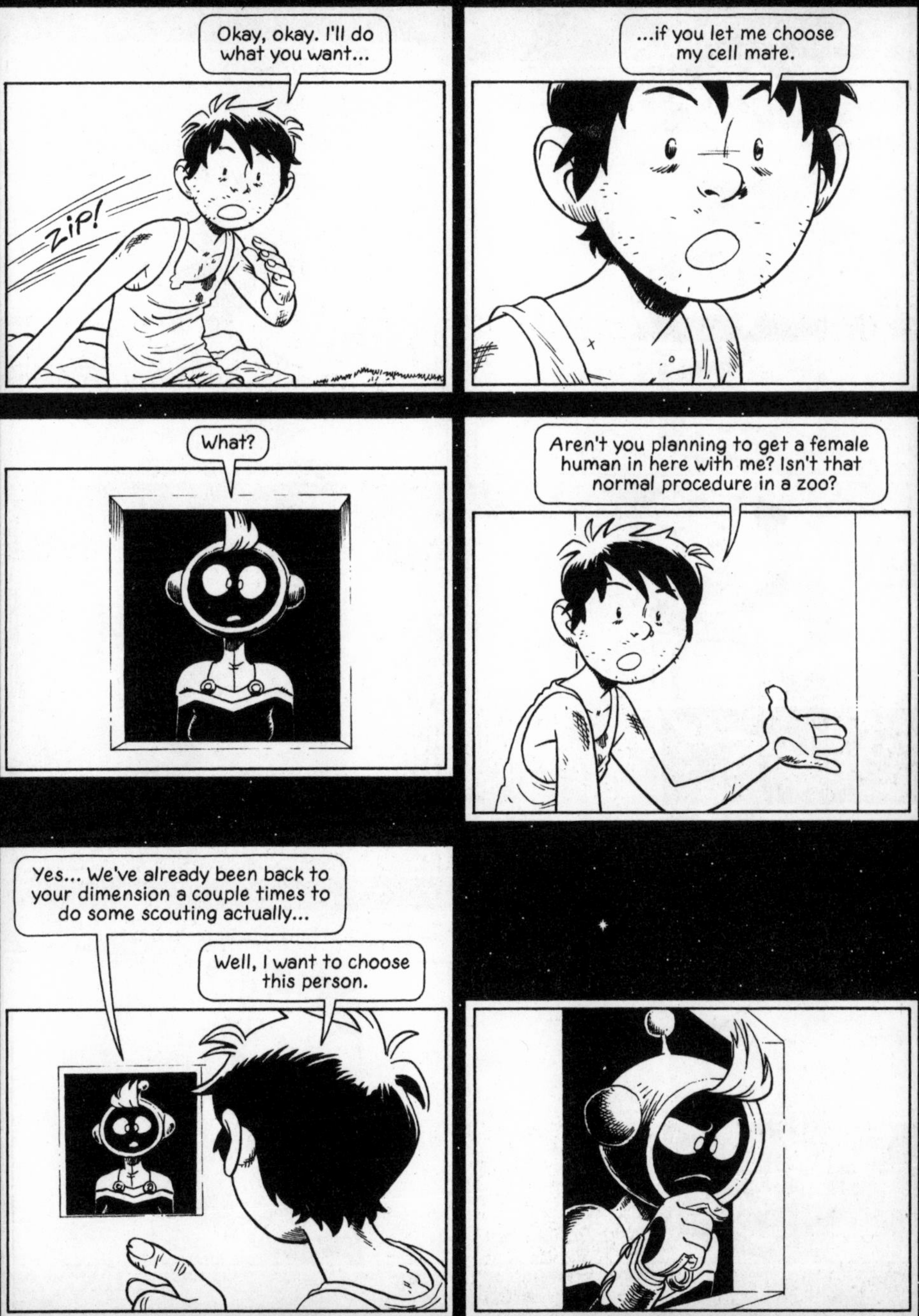
Okay, okay. I'll do what you want...
ZIP!
...if you let me choose my cell mate.
What?
Aren't you planning to get a female human in here with me? Isn't that normal procedure in a zoo?
Yes... We've already been back to your dimension a couple times to do some scouting actually...
Well, I want to choose this person.

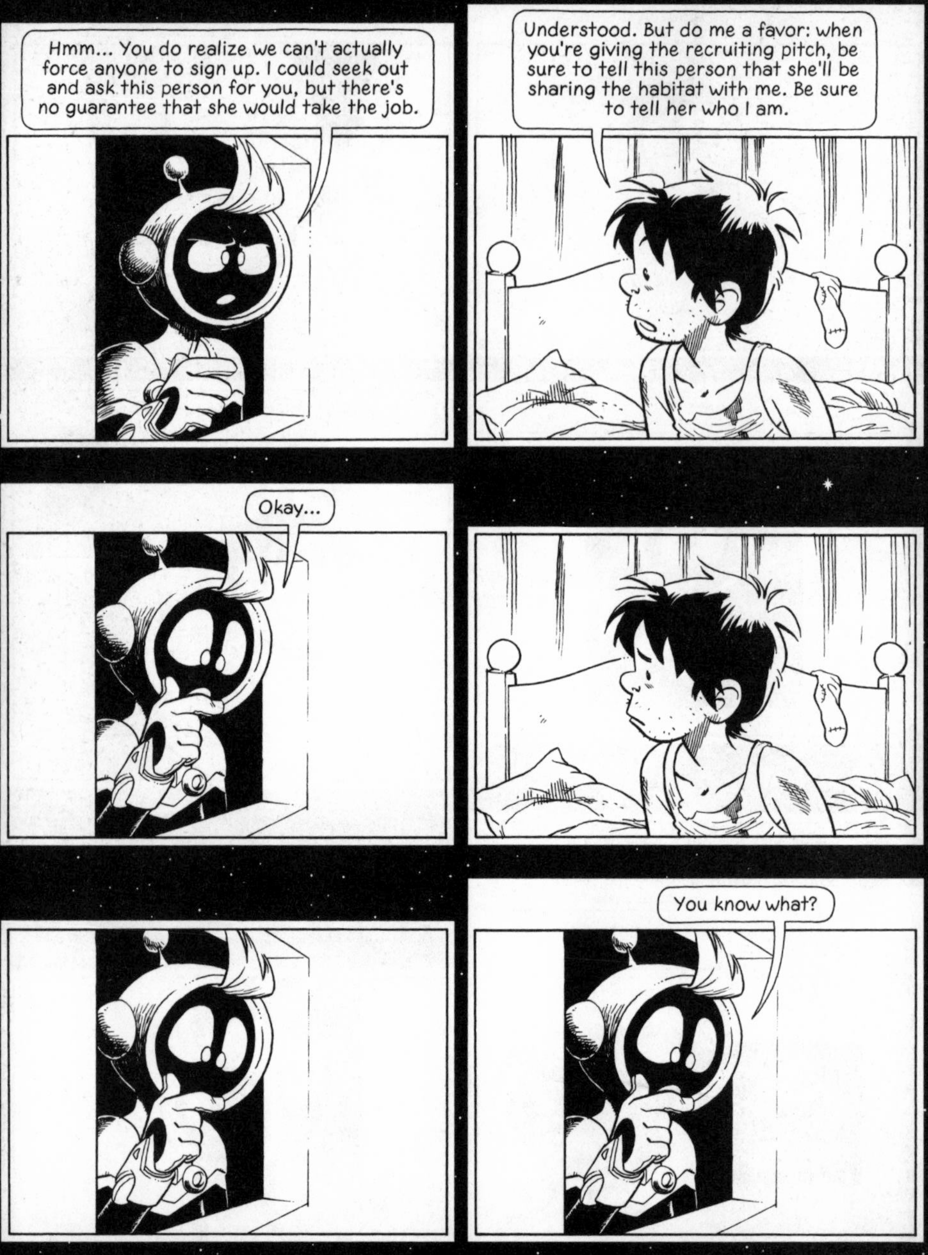

Hmm... You do realize we can't actually force anyone to sign up. I could seek out and ask this person for you, but there's no guarantee that she would take the job.
Understood. But do me a favor: when you're giving the recruiting pitch, be sure to tell this person that she'll be sharing the habitat with me. Be sure to tell her who I am.
Okay...
You know what?

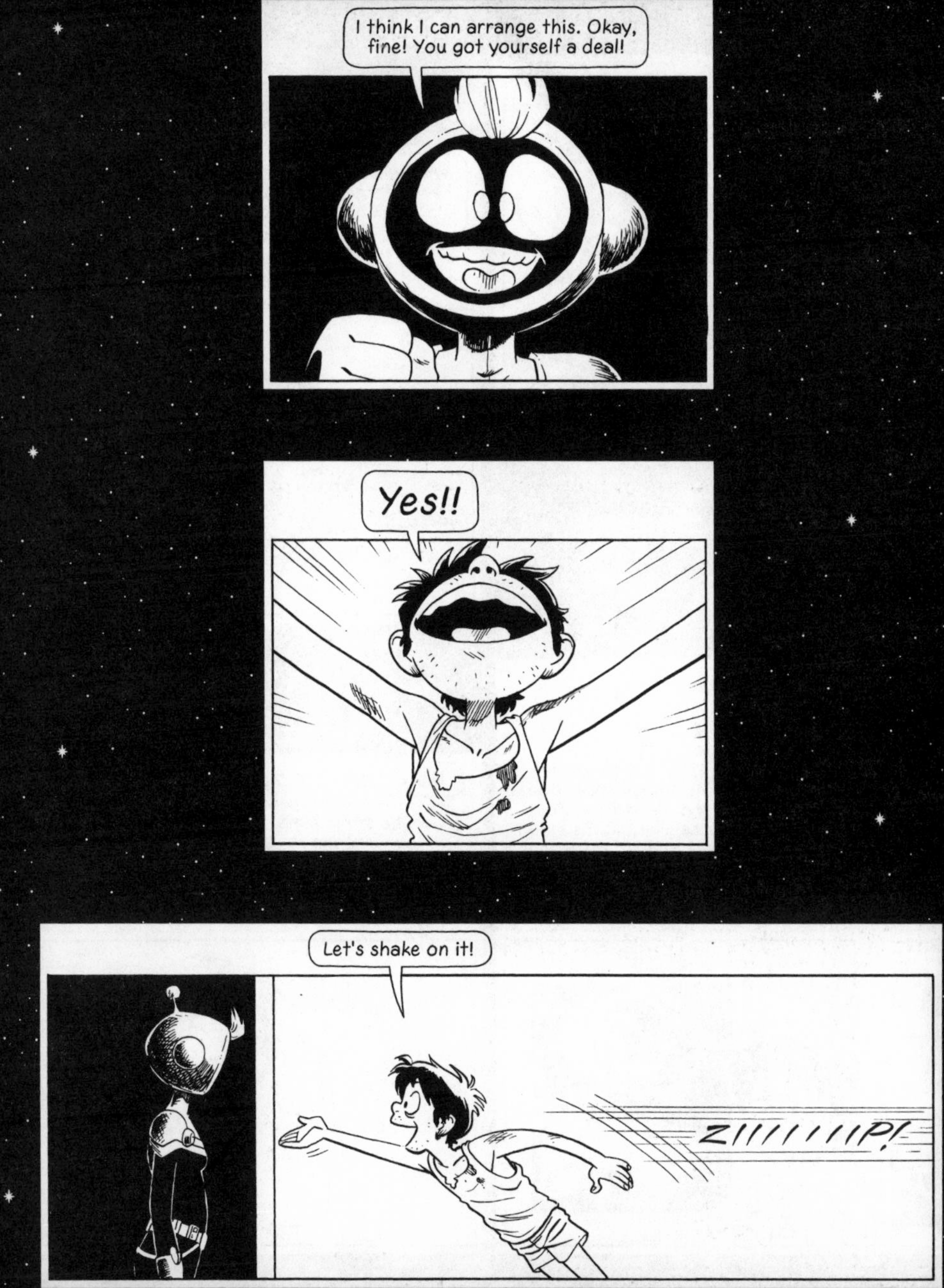

I think I can arrange this. Okay, fine! You got yourself a deal!
Yes!!
Let's shake on it!
ZIIIIIIIP!

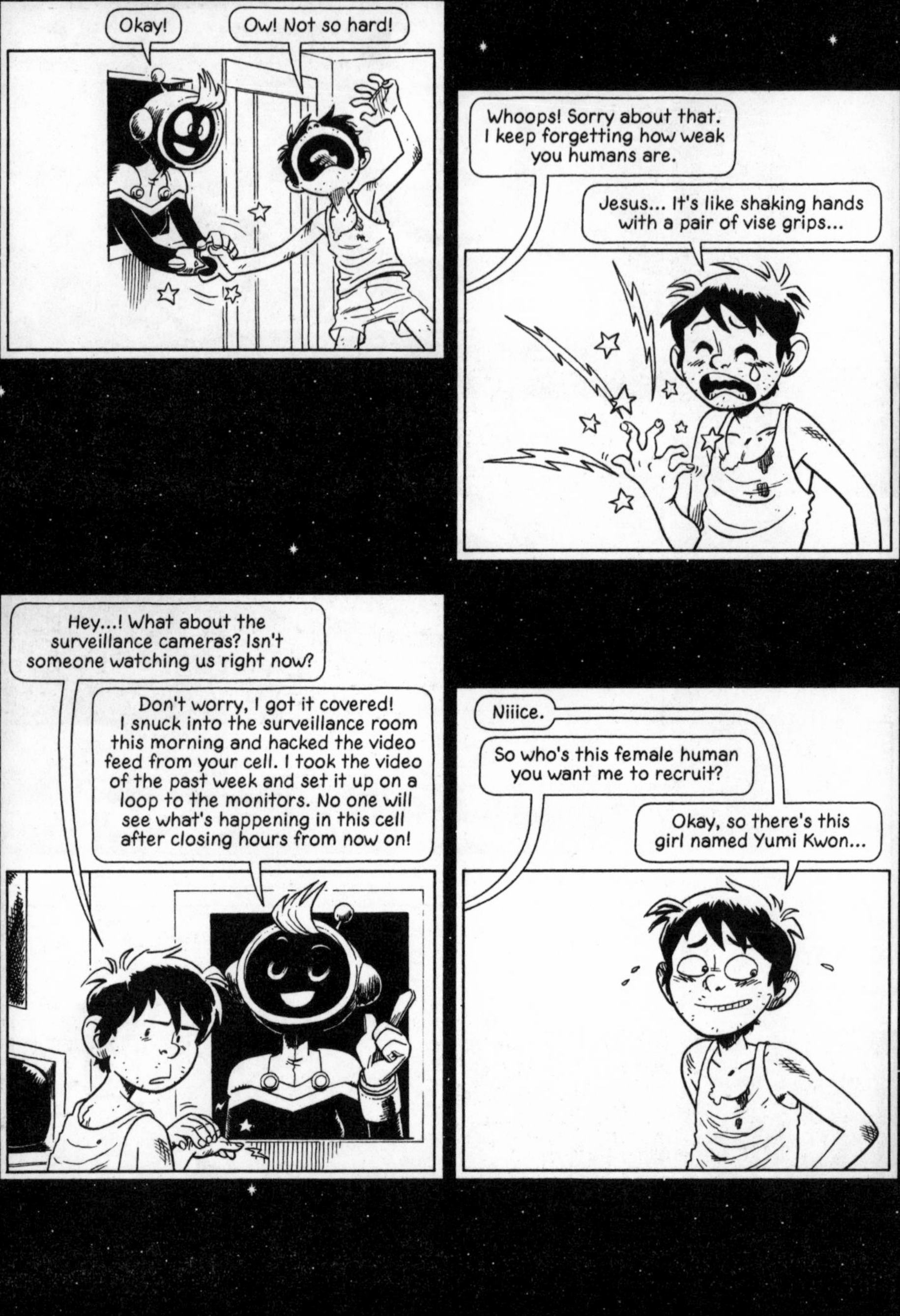
Okay!
Ow! Not so hard!
Whoops! Sorry about that. I keep forgetting how weak you humans are.
Jesus... It's like shaking hands with a pair of vise grips...
Hey...! What about the surveillance cameras? Isn't someone watching us right now?
Don't worry, I got it covered! I snuck into the surveillance room this morning and hacked the video feed from your cell. I took the video of the past week and set it up on a loop to the monitors. No one will see what's happening in this cell after closing hours from now on!
Niiice.
So who's this female human you want me to recruit?
Okay, so there's this girl named Yumi Kwon...

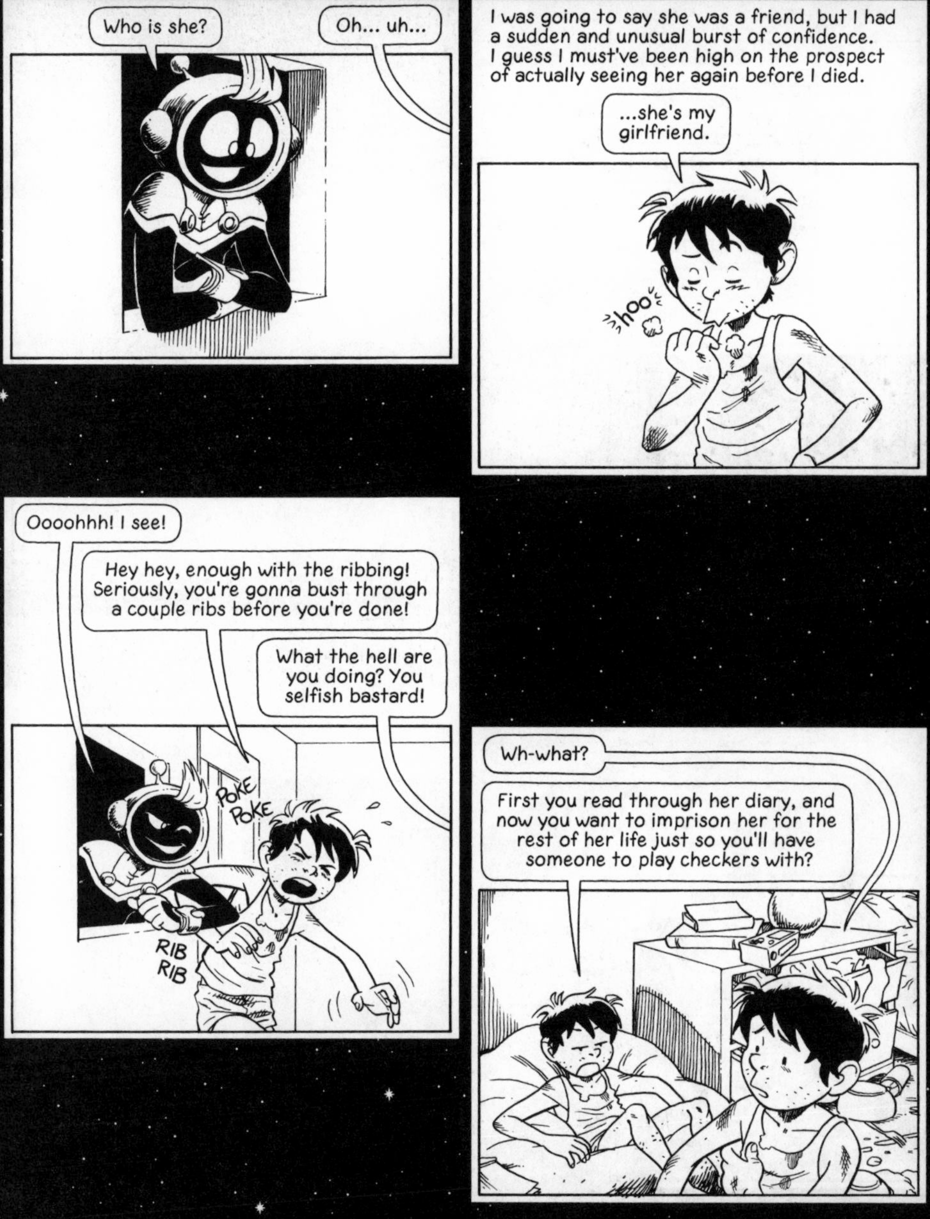
Who is she?
Oh... uh...
I was going to say she was a friend, but I had a sudden and unusual burst of confidence. I guess I must've been high on the prospect of actually seeing her again before I died.
...she's my girlfriend.
hoo
Oooohhh! I see!
Hey hey, enough with the ribbing! Seriously, you're gonna bust through a couple ribs before you're done!
What the hell are you doing? You selfish bastard!
POKE POKE
RIB RIB
Wh-what?
First you read through her diary, and now you want to imprison her for the rest of her life just so you'll have someone to play checkers with?

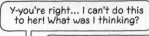

Y-you're right... I can't do this to her! What was I thinking?

Andy Go? Who are you talking to?

But... I want to see her again so badly! I need to tell her what she means to me... Oh, the humanity!

Then I remembered something else Mo had told me.

Wait!

If you bring someone here and we end up fighting constantly, the C.I.S. will send her back, right?

Dash seemed surprised at my in-depth knowledge of their procedures, but didn't say anything.

Yes...

That's it! This way I'll get to see Yumi one last time, but she won't be trapped here forever like me!

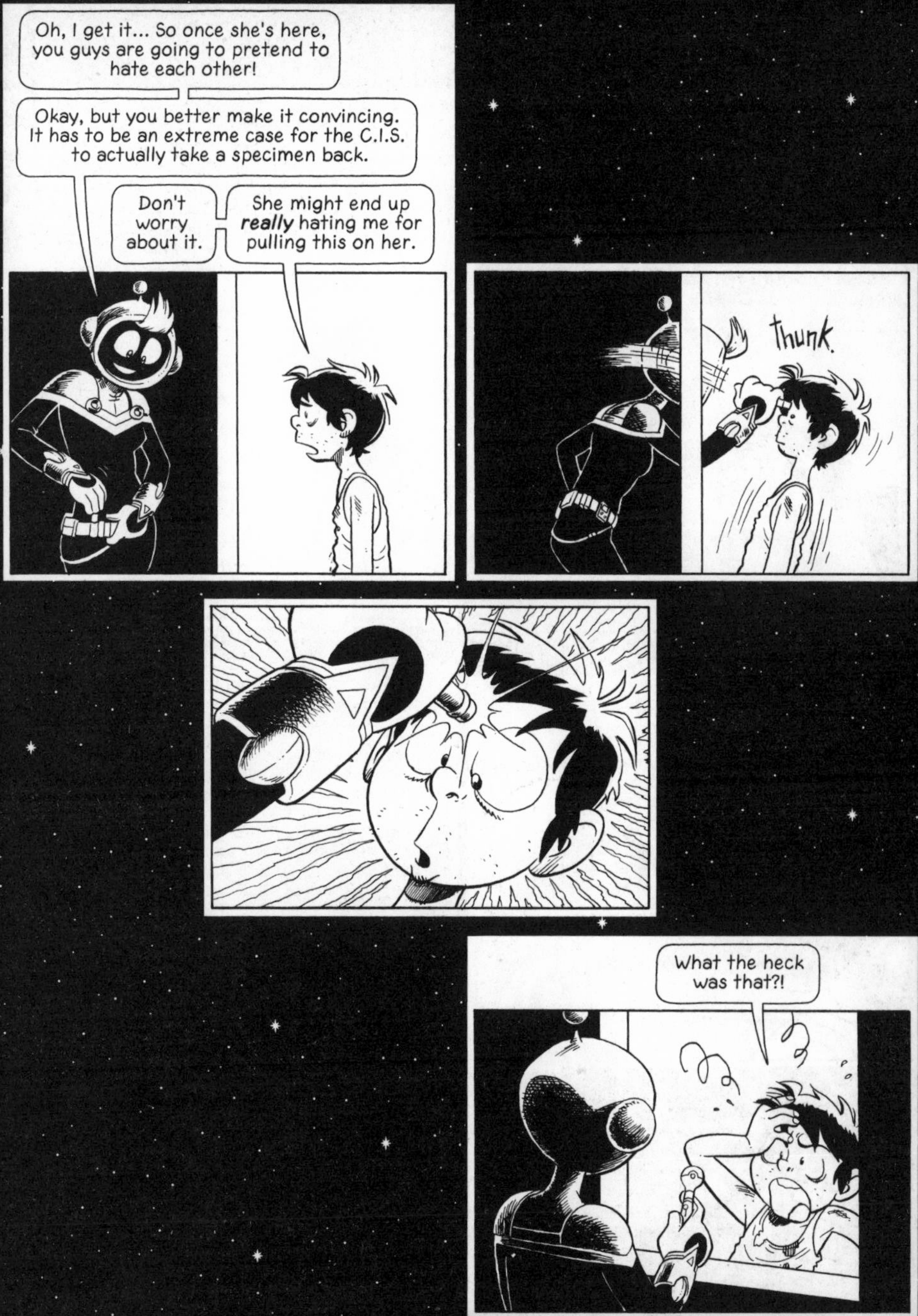
Oh, I get it... So once she's here, you guys are going to pretend to hate each other!
Okay, but you better make it convincing. It has to be an extreme case for the C.I.S. to actually take a specimen back.
Don't worry about it.
She might end up *really* hating me for pulling this on her.
thunk.
What the heck was that?!

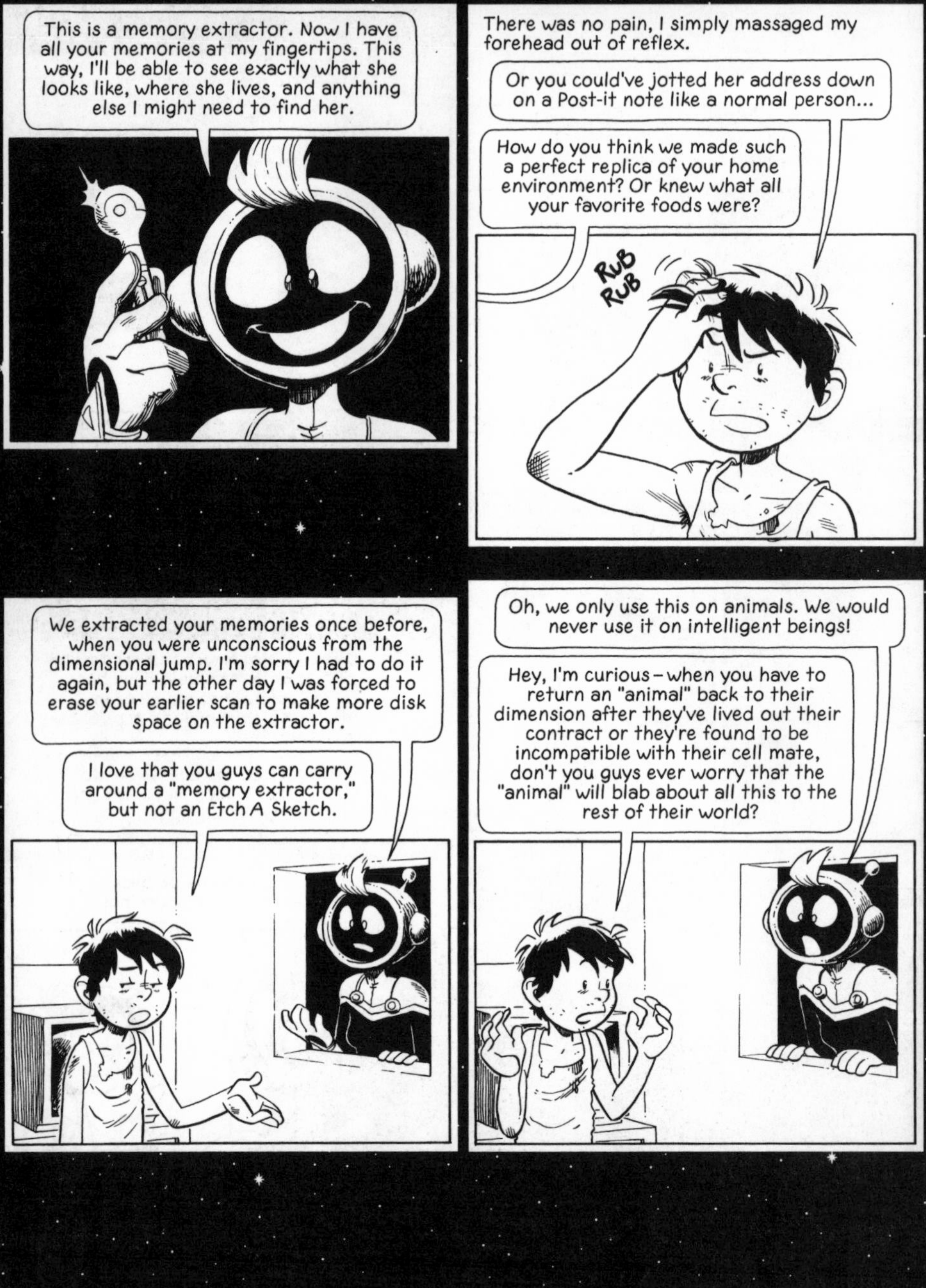
This is a memory extractor. Now I have all your memories at my fingertips. This way, I'll be able to see exactly what she looks like, where she lives, and anything else I might need to find her.
There was no pain, I simply massaged my forehead out of reflex.
Or you could've jotted her address down on a Post-it note like a normal person...
How do you think we made such a perfect replica of your home environment? Or knew what all your favorite foods were?
RUB RUB
We extracted your memories once before, when you were unconscious from the dimensional jump. I'm sorry I had to do it again, but the other day I was forced to erase your earlier scan to make more disk space on the extractor.
I love that you guys can carry around a "memory extractor," but not an Etch A Sketch.
Oh, we only use this on animals. We would never use it on intelligent beings!
Hey, I'm curious – when you have to return an "animal" back to their dimension after they've lived out their contract or they're found to be incompatible with their cell mate, don't you guys ever worry that the "animal" will blab about all this to the rest of their world?

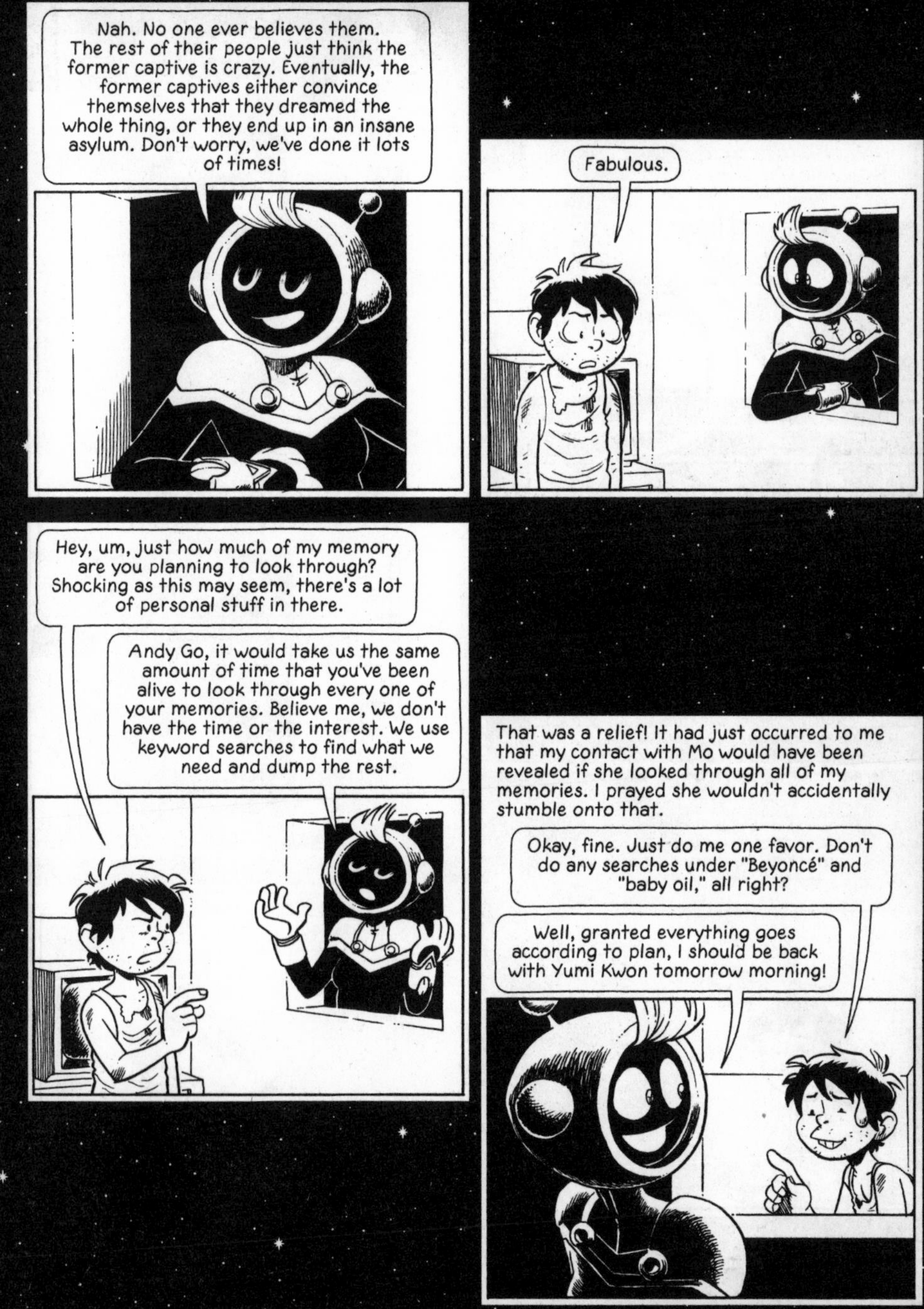
Nah. No one ever believes them. The rest of their people just think the former captive is crazy. Eventually, the former captives either convince themselves that they dreamed the whole thing, or they end up in an insane asylum. Don't worry, we've done it lots of times!
Fabulous.
Hey, um, just how much of my memory are you planning to look through? Shocking as this may seem, there's a lot of personal stuff in there.
Andy Go, it would take us the same amount of time that you've been alive to look through every one of your memories. Believe me, we don't have the time or the interest. We use keyword searches to find what we need and dump the rest.
That was a relief! It had just occurred to me that my contact with Mo would have been revealed if she looked through all of my memories. I prayed she wouldn't accidentally stumble onto that.
Okay, fine. Just do me one favor. Don't do any searches under "Beyoncé" and "baby oil," all right?
Well, granted everything goes according to plan, I should be back with Yumi Kwon tomorrow morning!

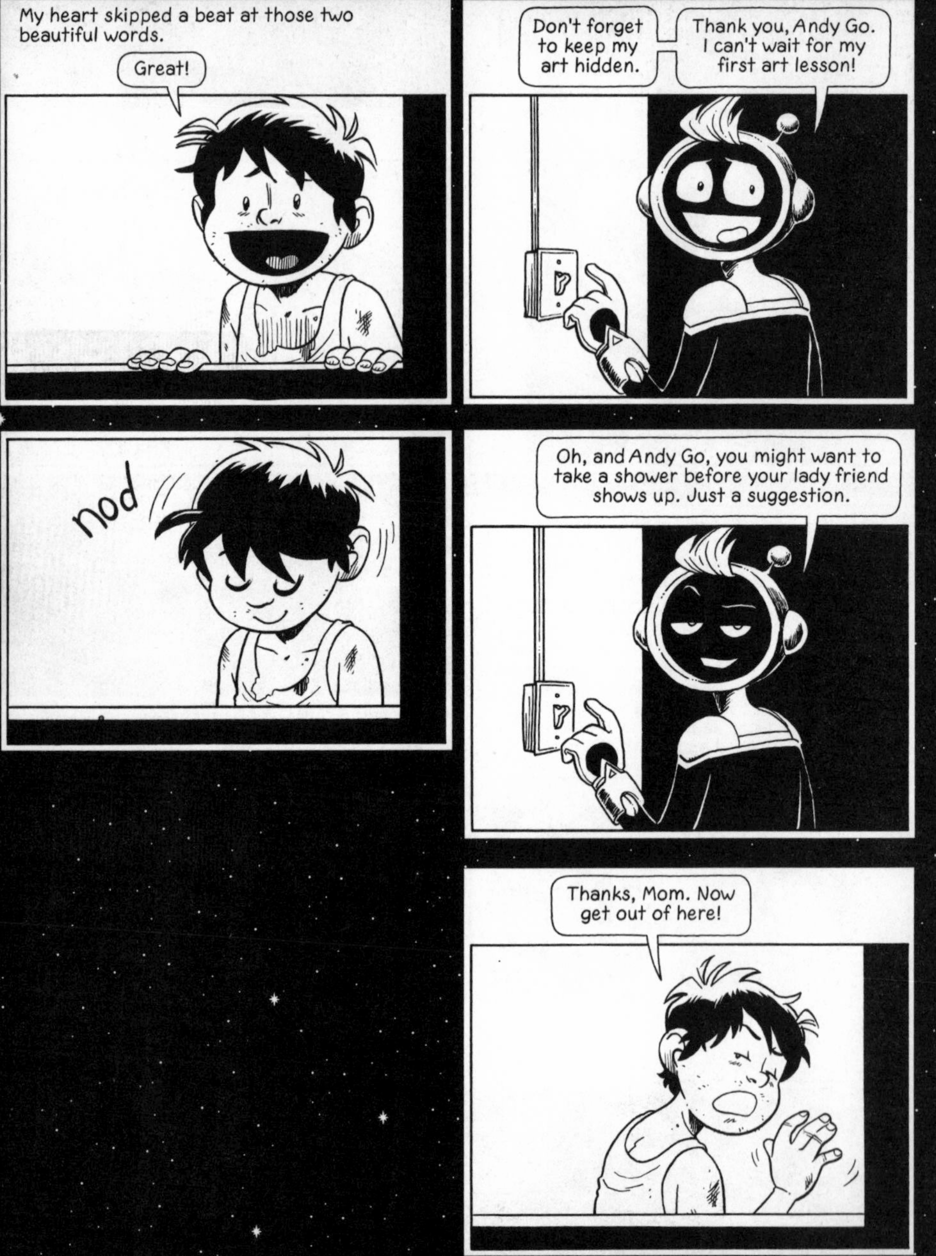
My heart skipped a beat at those two beautiful words.
Great!
Don't forget to keep my art hidden.
Thank you, Andy Go. I can't wait for my first art lesson!
nod
Oh, and Andy Go, you might want to take a shower before your lady friend shows up. Just a suggestion.
Thanks, Mom. Now get out of here!

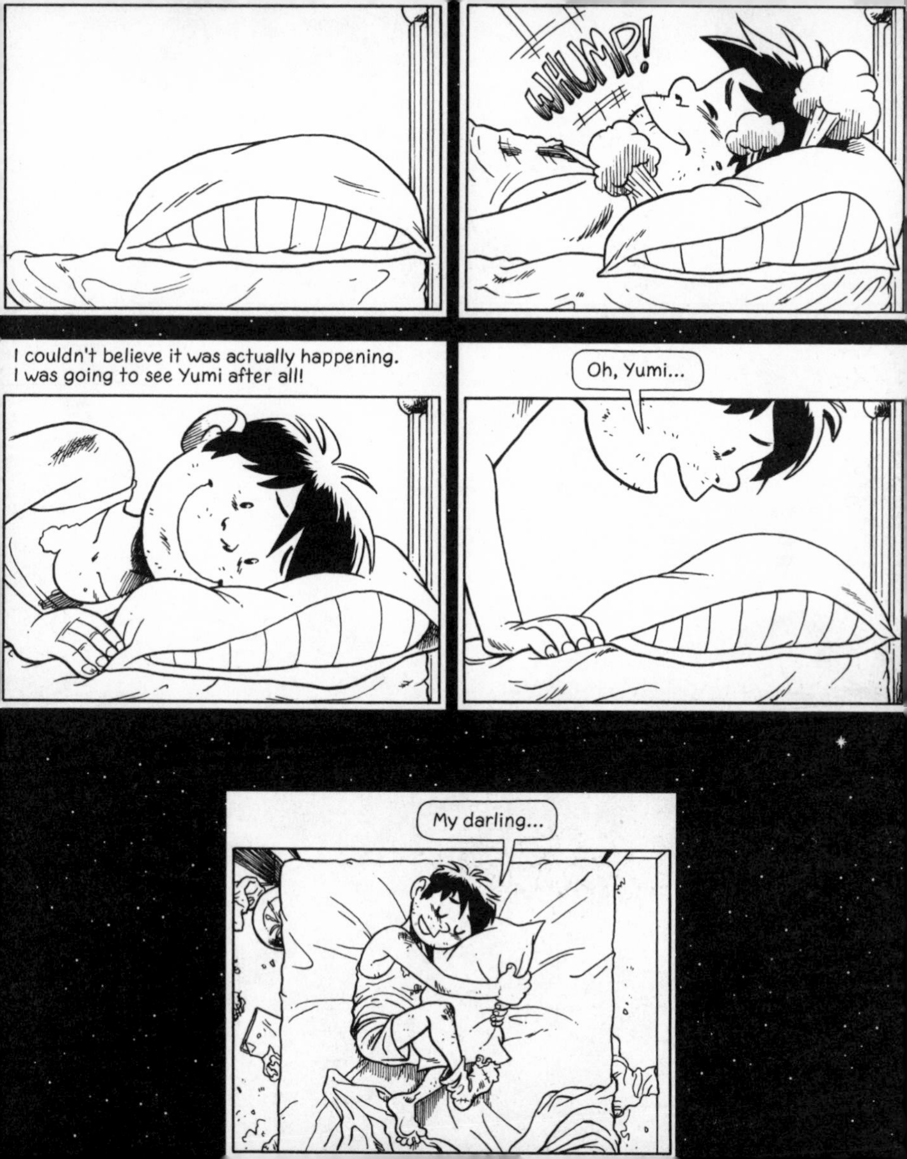
WHUMP!
I couldn't believe it was actually happening.
I was going to see Yumi after all!
Oh, Yumi...
My darling...

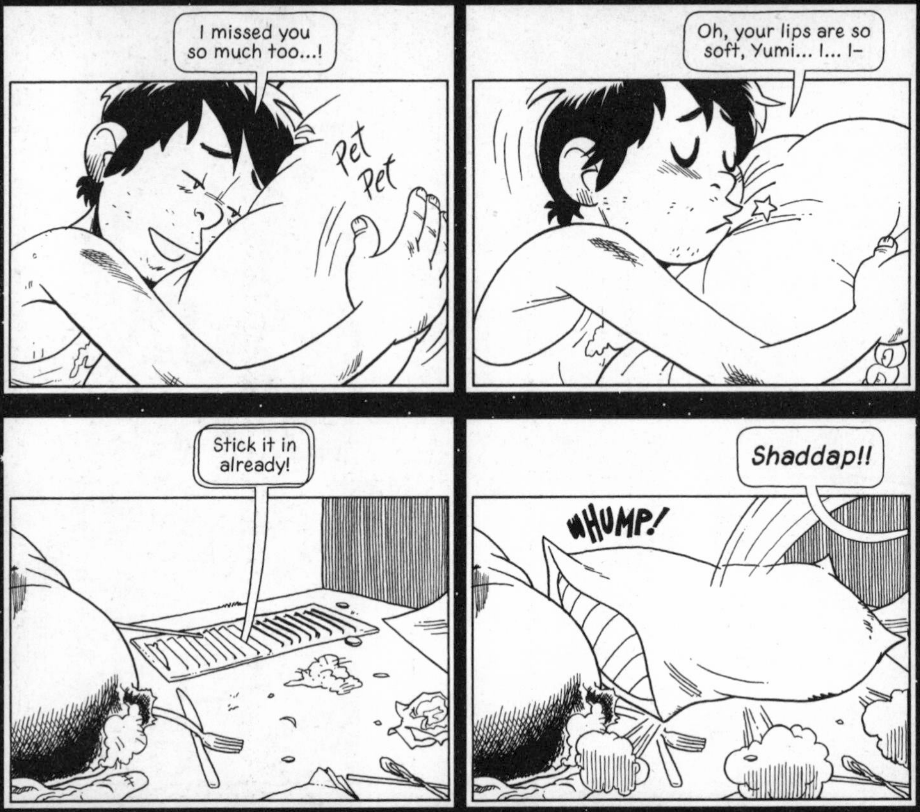
I missed you so much too...!
Pet Pet
Oh, your lips are so soft, Yumi... I... I-
Stick it in already!
Shaddap!!
WHUMP!

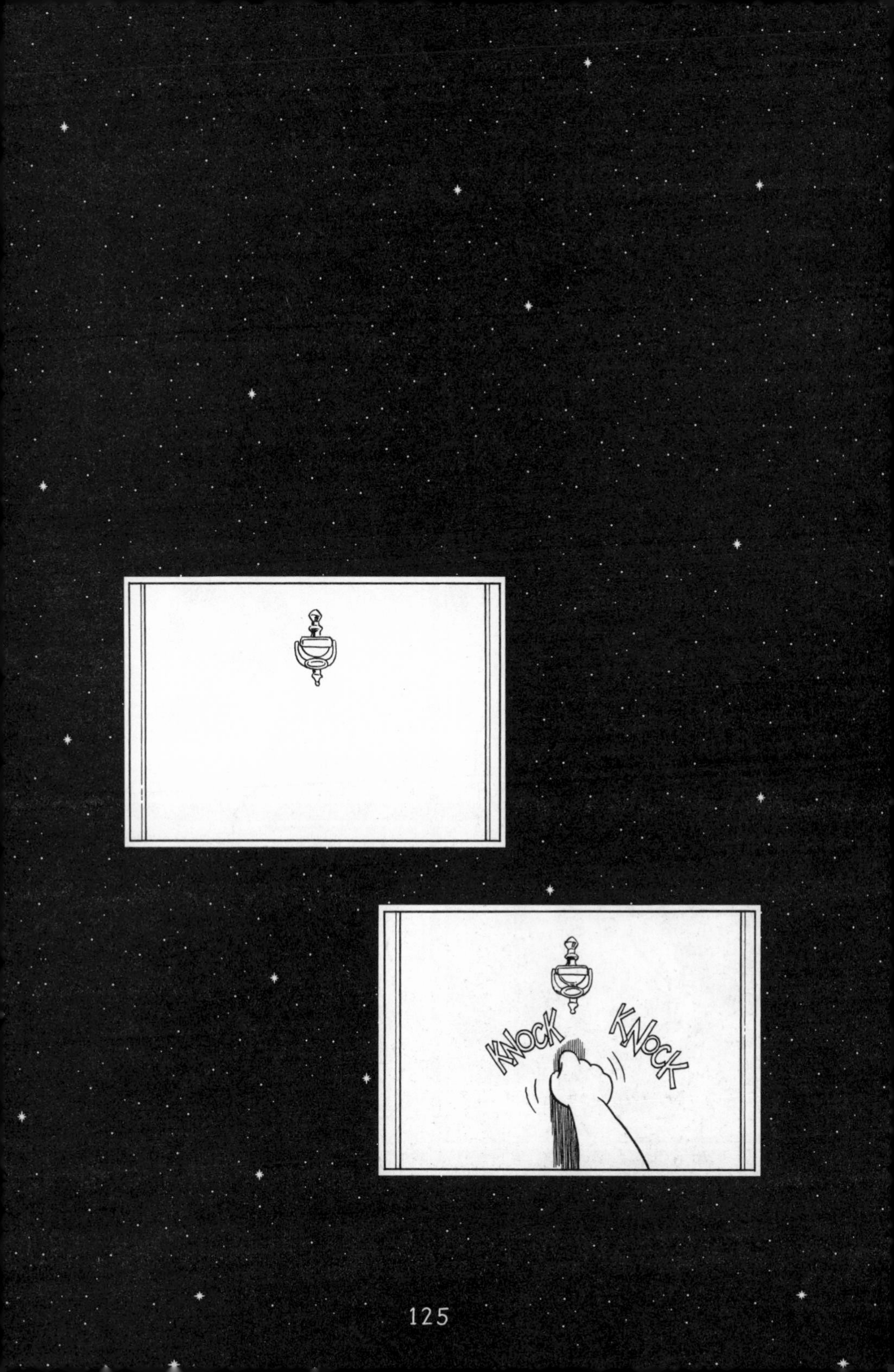
KNOCK
KNOCK

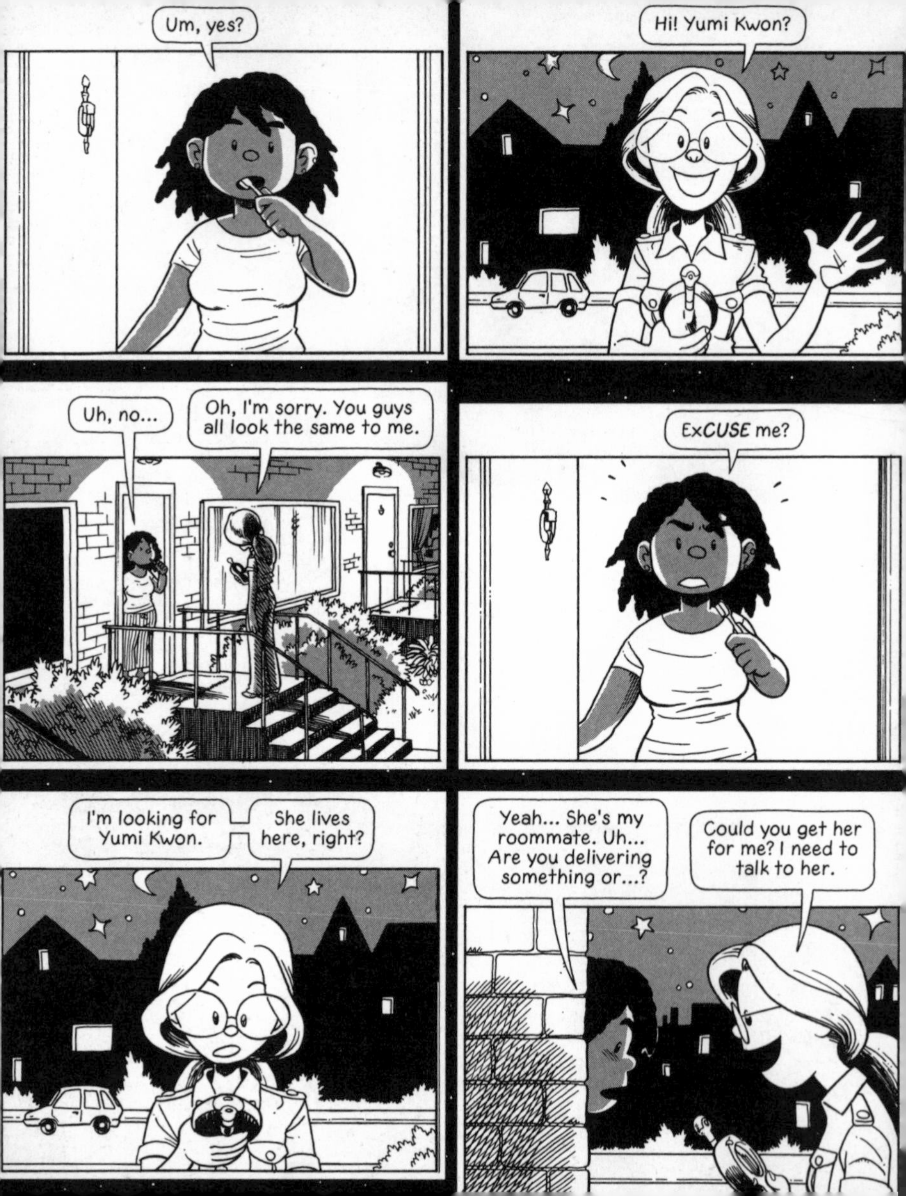
Um, yes?
Hi! Yumi Kwon?
Uh, no...
Oh, I'm sorry. You guys all look the same to me.
ExCUSE me?
I'm looking for Yumi Kwon.
She lives here, right?
Yeah... She's my roommate. Uh... Are you delivering something or...?
Could you get her for me? I need to talk to her.

Sorry, she just left for a trip to Europe. She won't be back for a month.
What's this about?

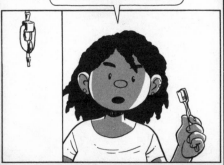

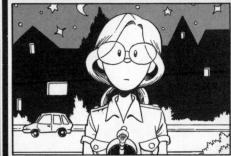

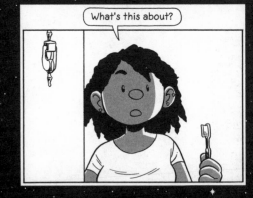

CHAPTER 16

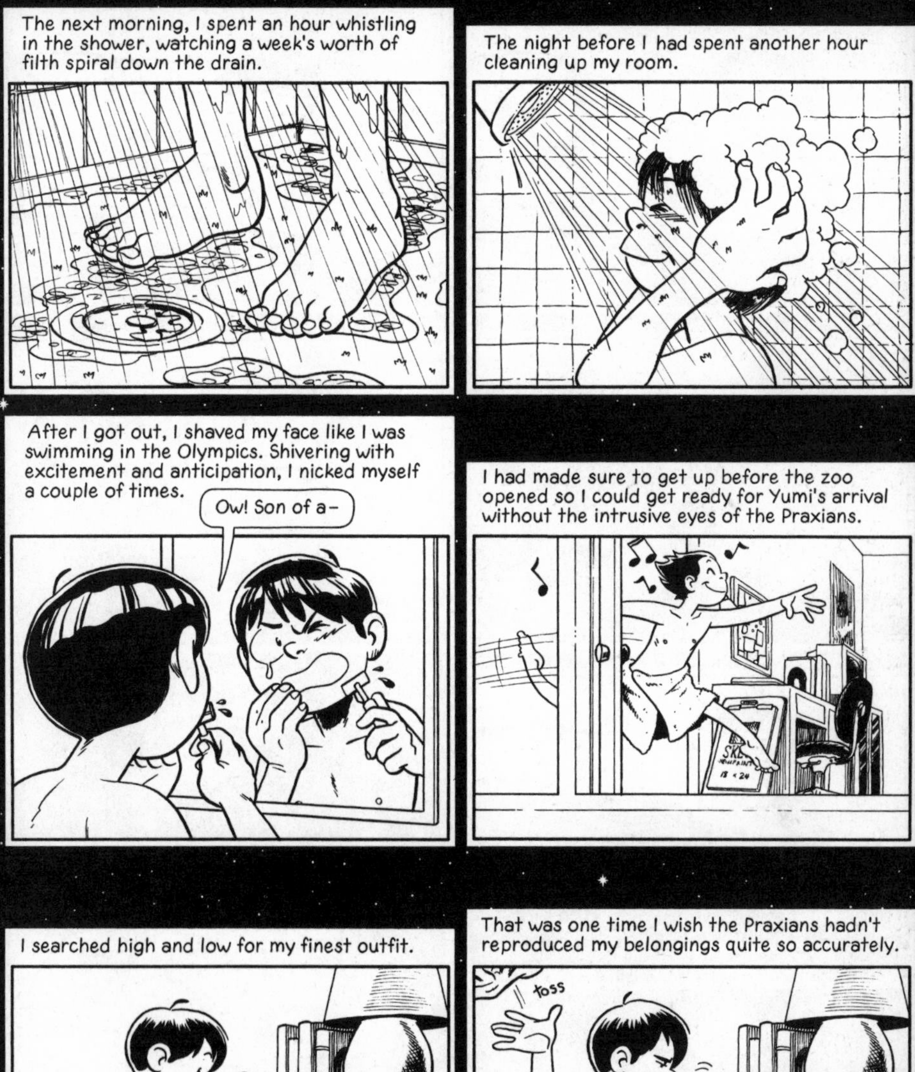
The next morning, I spent an hour whistling in the shower, watching a week's worth of filth spiral down the drain.
The night before I had spent another hour cleaning up my room.
After I got out, I shaved my face like I was swimming in the Olympics. Shivering with excitement and anticipation, I nicked myself a couple of times.
Ow! Son of a-
I had made sure to get up before the zoo opened so I could get ready for Yumi's arrival without the intrusive eyes of the Praxians.
I searched high and low for my finest outfit.
That was one time I wish the Praxians hadn't reproduced my belongings quite so accurately.
toss

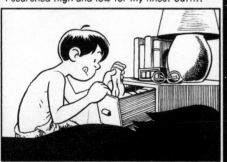

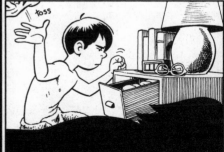

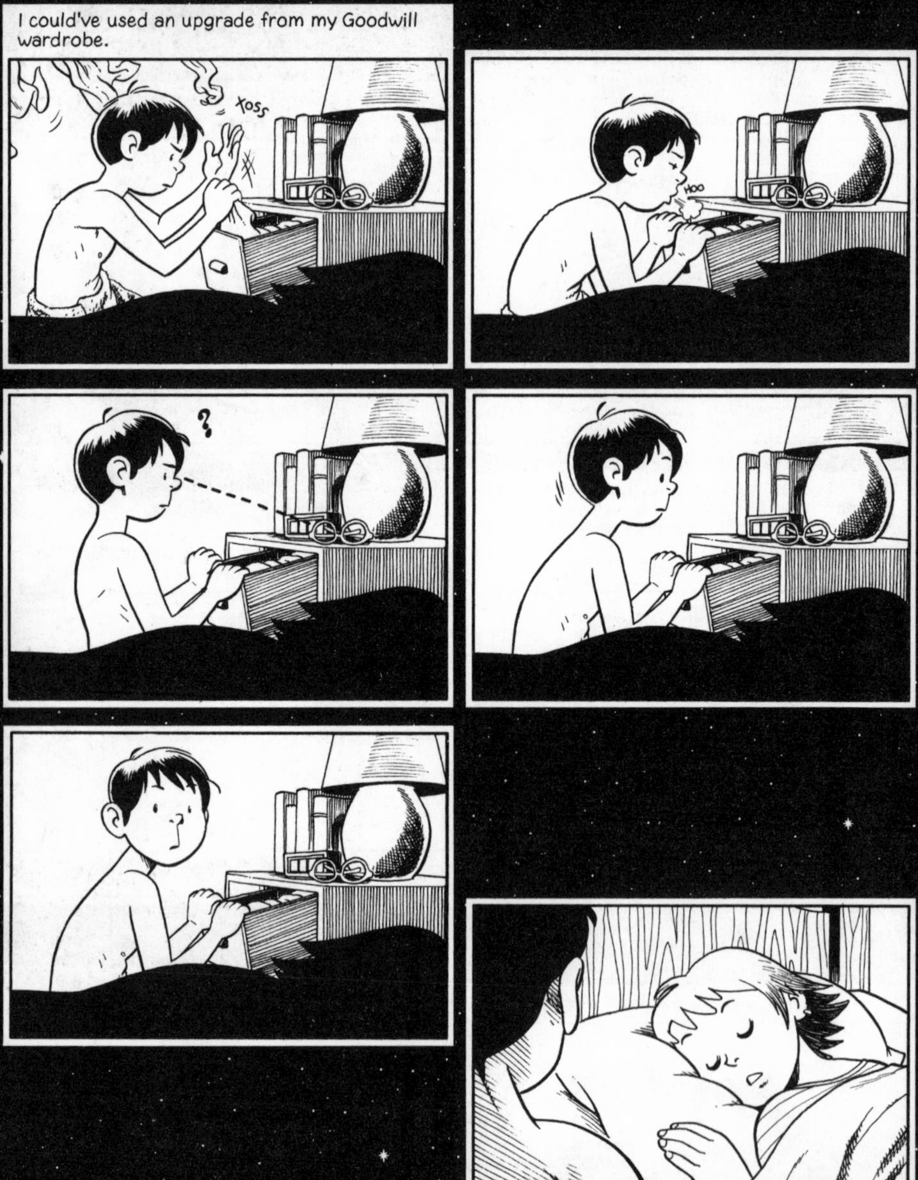
I could've used an upgrade from my Goodwill wardrobe.
TOSS
HOO
?

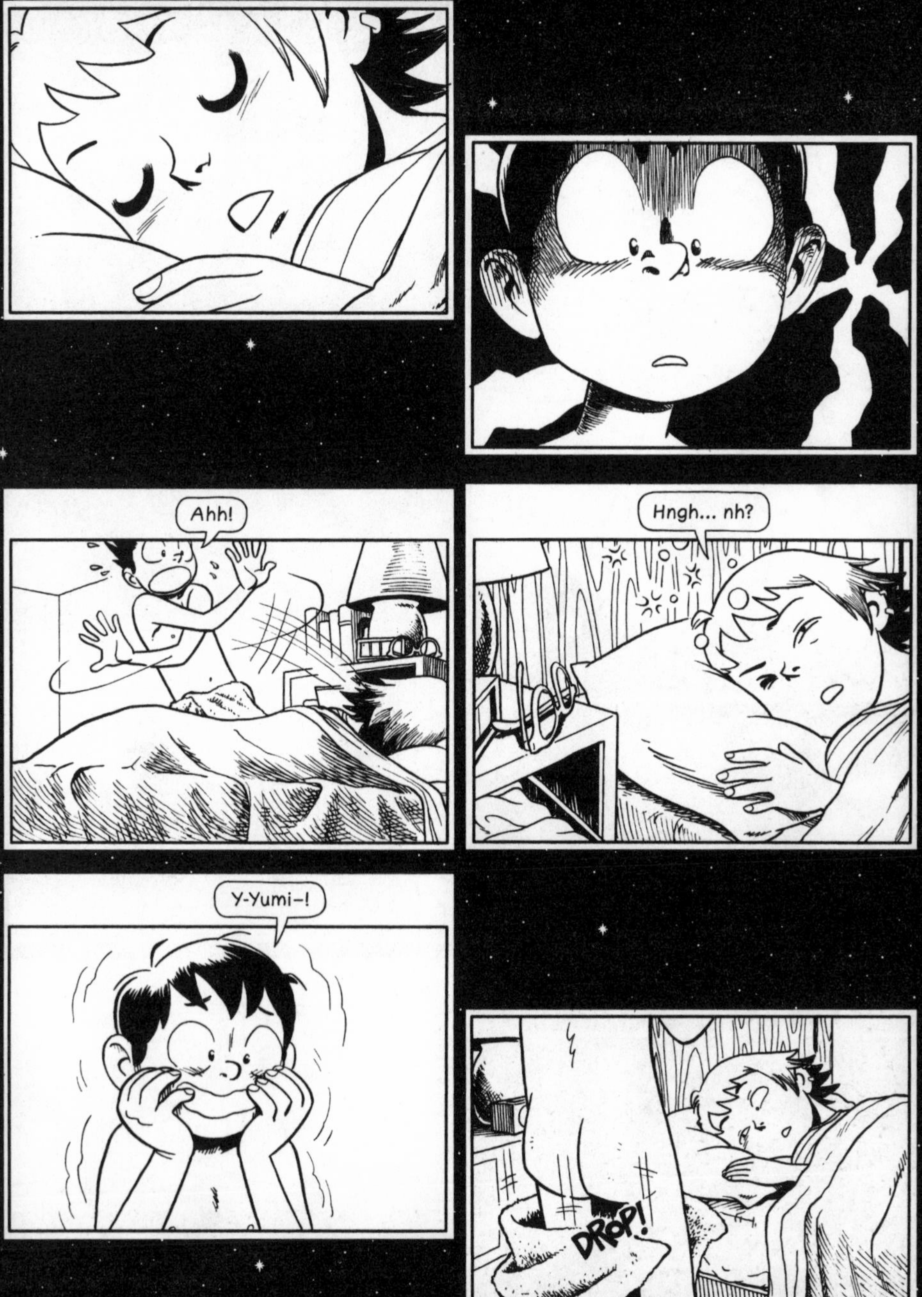
Ahh!
Hngh... nh?
Y-Yumi-!
DROP!

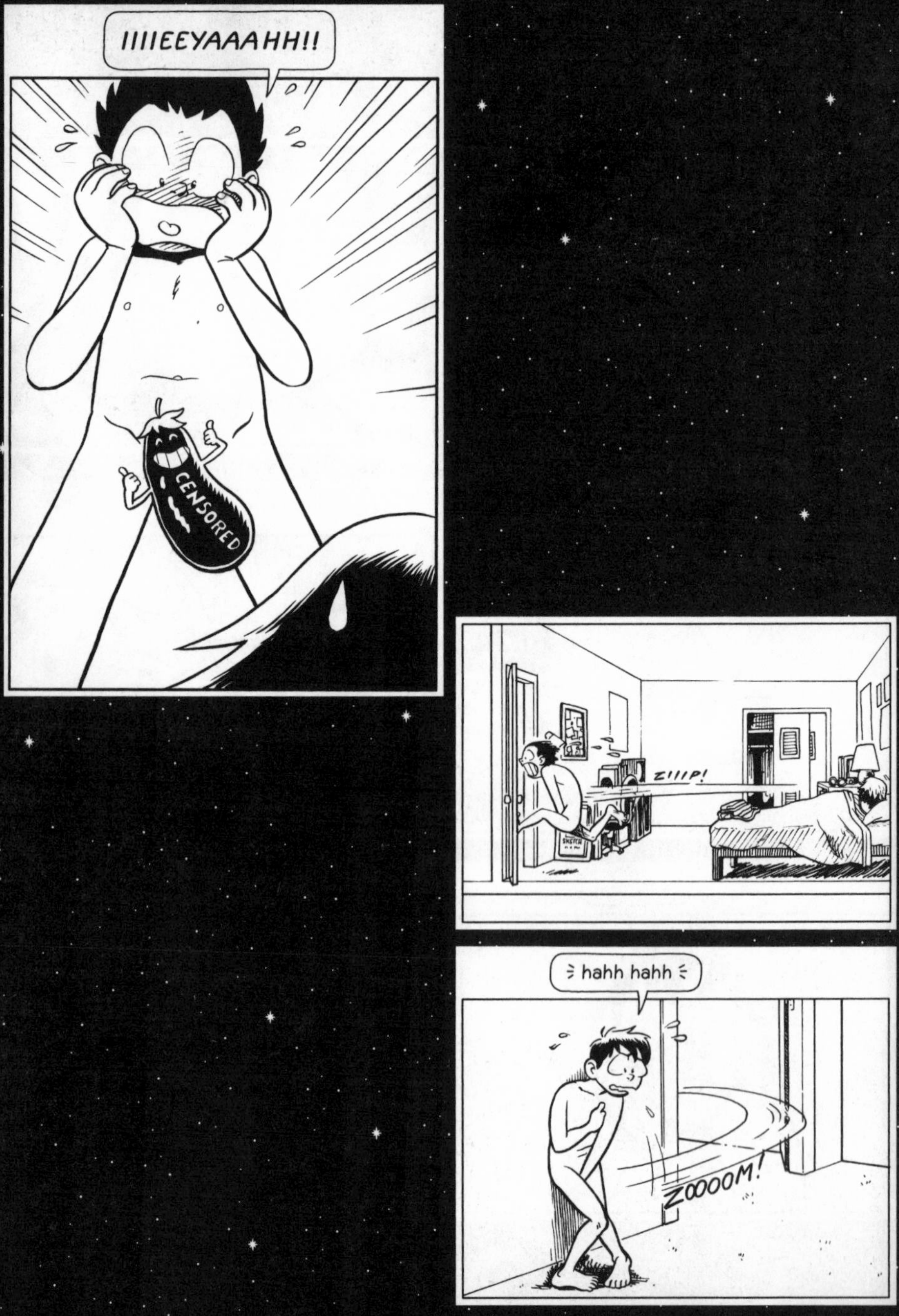
IIIIEEYAAAHH!!
CENSORED
ZIIIP!
hahh hahh
ZOOOOM!

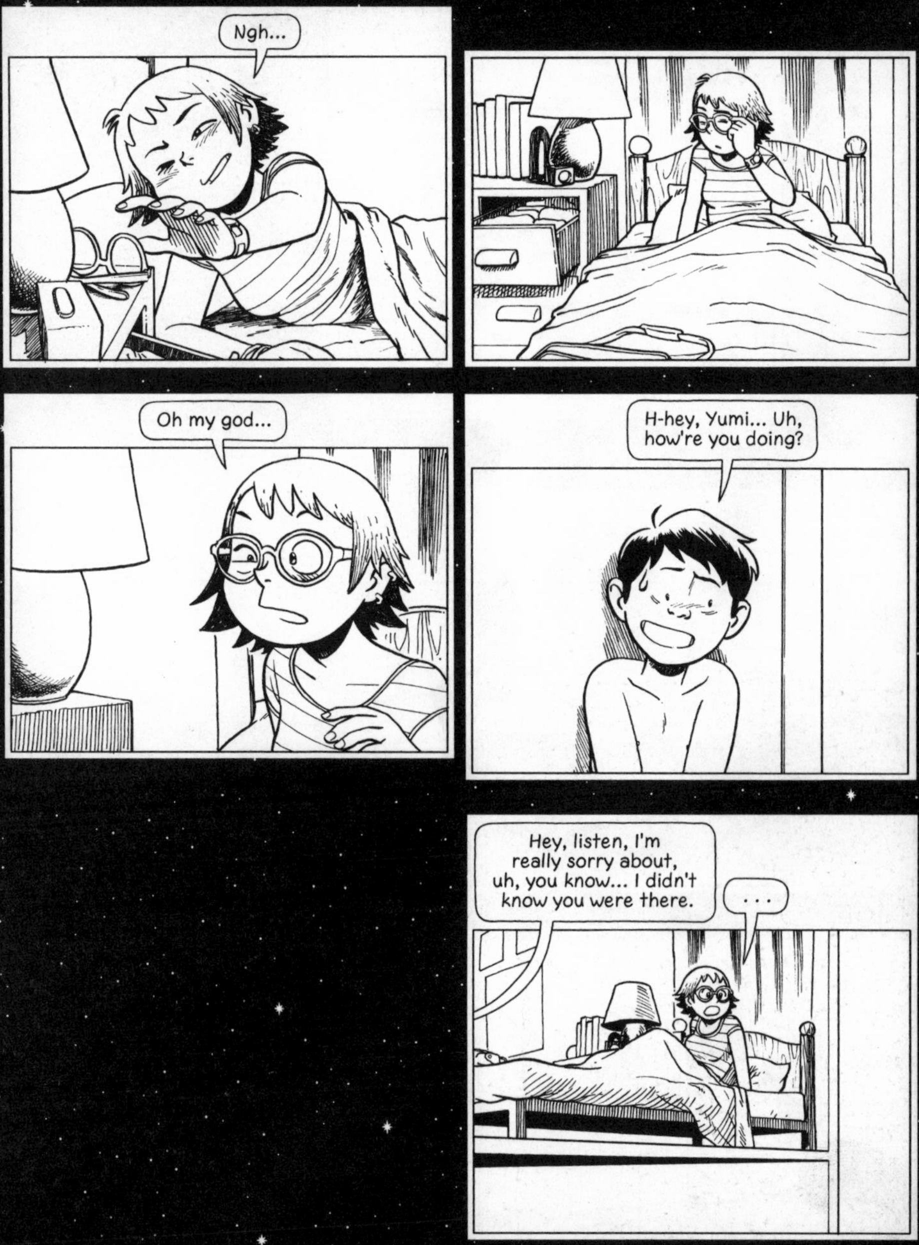
Ngh...
Oh my god...
H-hey, Yumi... Uh, how're you doing?
Hey, listen, I'm really sorry about, uh, you know... I didn't know you were there.
. . .

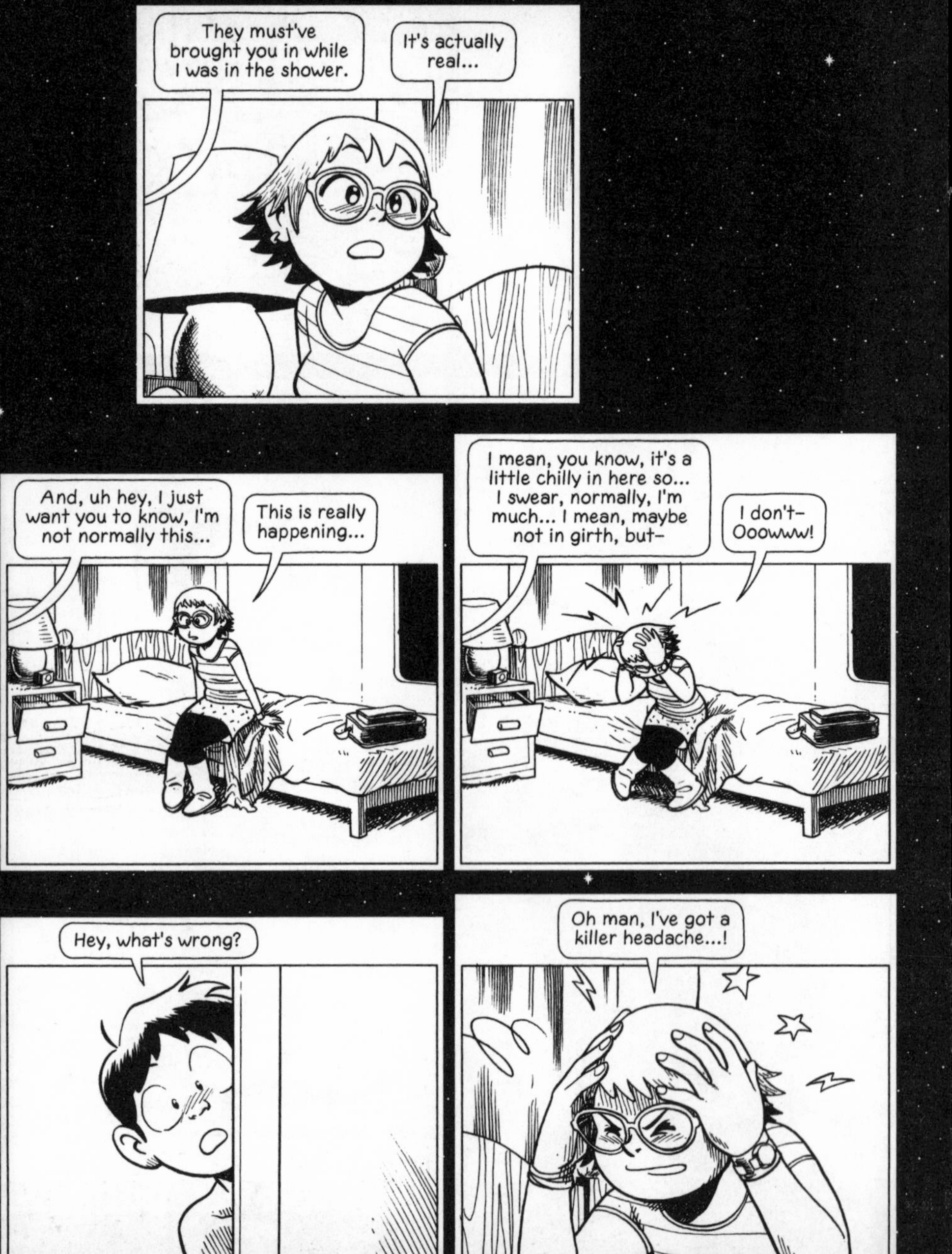
They must've brought you in while I was in the shower.
It's actually real...
And, uh hey, I just want you to know, I'm not normally this...
This is really happening...
I mean, you know, it's a little chilly in here so... I swear, normally, I'm much... I mean, maybe not in girth, but-
I don't- Ooowww!
Hey, what's wrong?
Oh man, I've got a killer headache...!

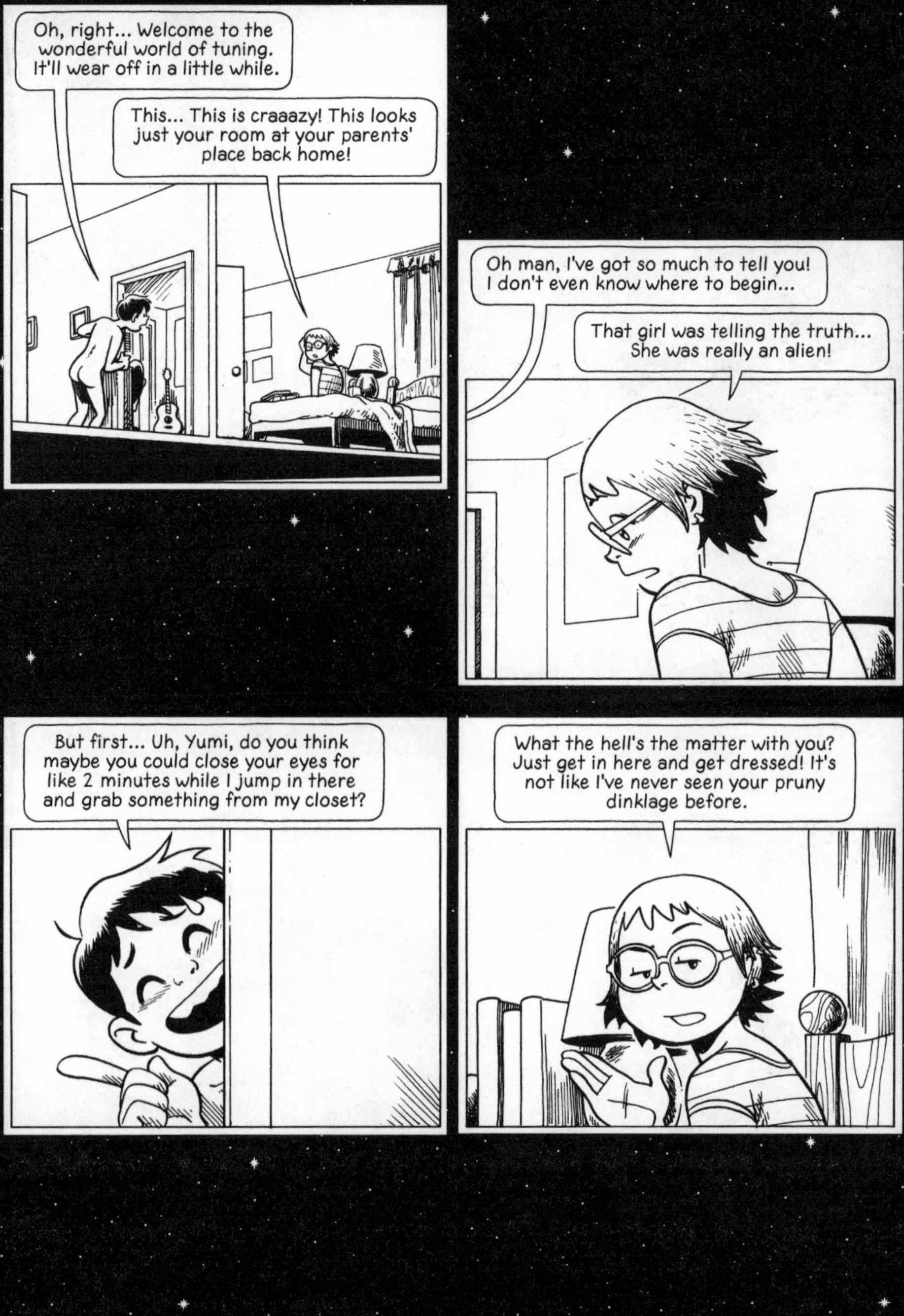
Oh, right... Welcome to the wonderful world of tuning. It'll wear off in a little while.
This... This is craaazy! This looks just your room at your parents' place back home!
Oh man, I've got so much to tell you! I don't even know where to begin...
That girl was telling the truth... She was really an alien!
But first... Uh, Yumi, do you think maybe you could close your eyes for like 2 minutes while I jump in there and grab something from my closet?
What the hell's the matter with you? Just get in here and get dressed! It's not like I've never seen your pruny dinklage before.

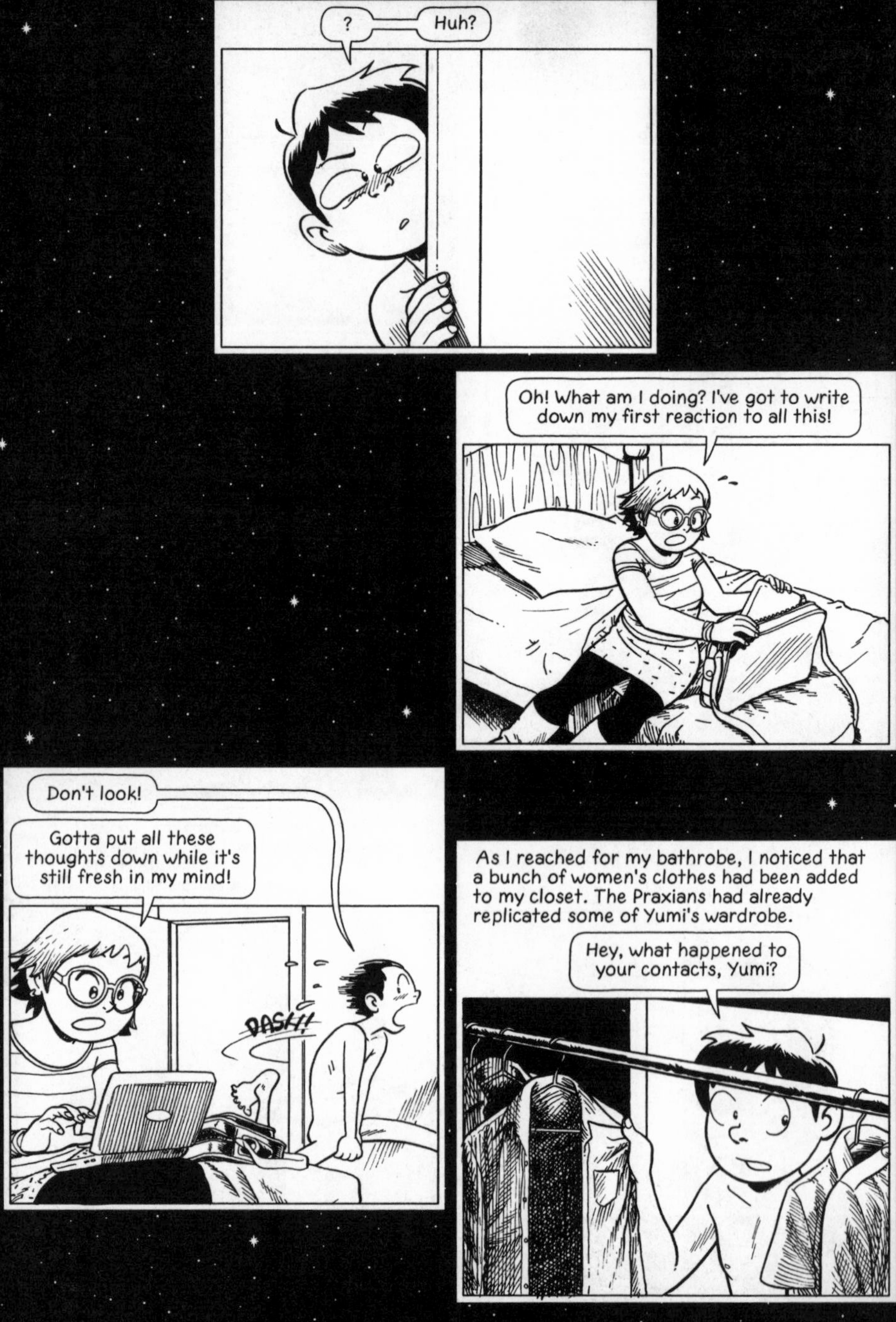
?
Huh?
Oh! What am I doing? I've got to write down my first reaction to all this!
Don't look!
Gotta put all these thoughts down while it's still fresh in my mind!
DASH!!
As I reached for my bathrobe, I noticed that a bunch of women's clothes had been added to my closet. The Praxians had already replicated some of Yumi's wardrobe.
Hey, what happened to your contacts, Yumi?

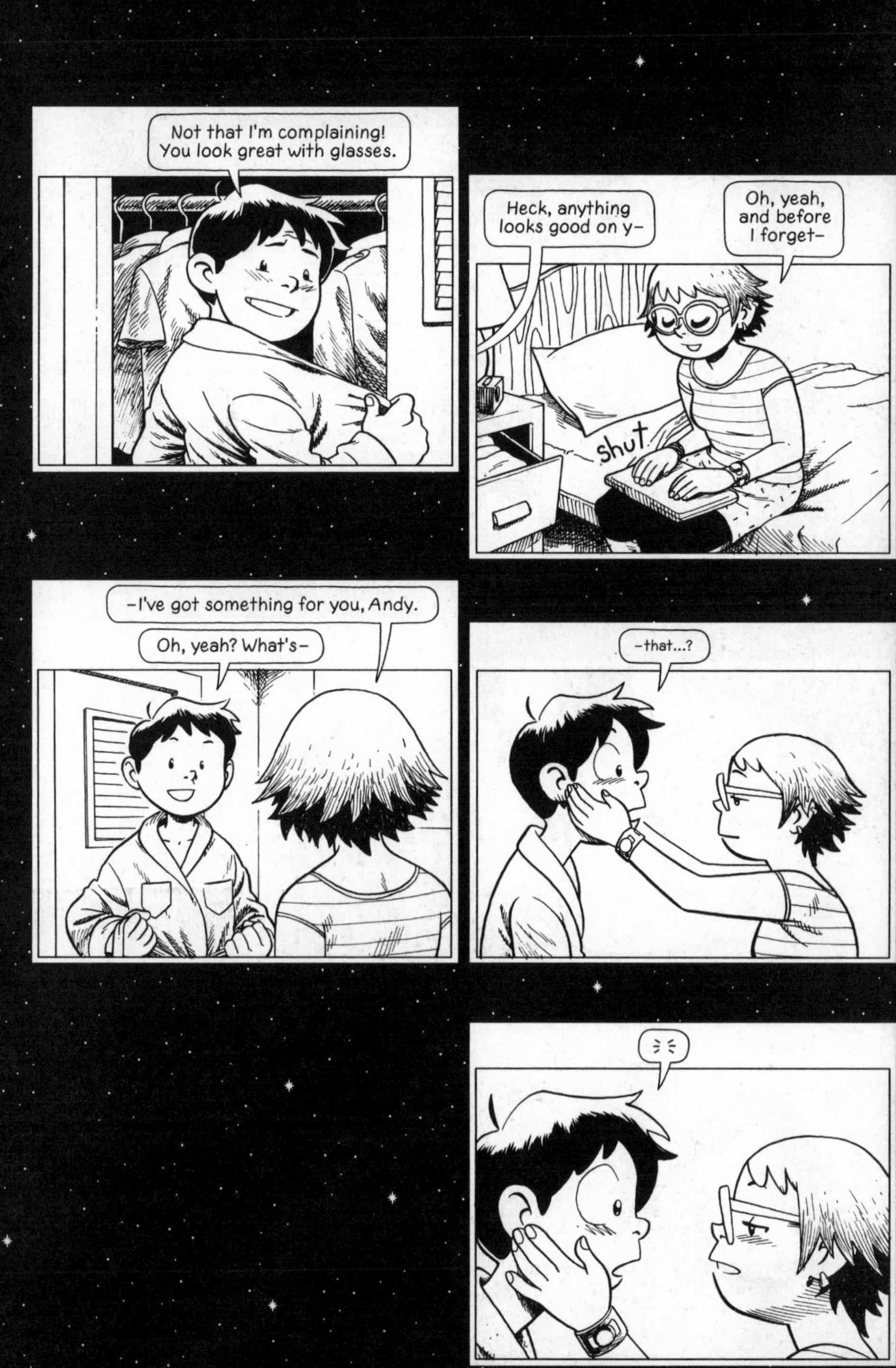
Not that I'm complaining! You look great with glasses.
Heck, anything looks good on y-
Oh, yeah, and before I forget-
shut
-I've got something for you, Andy.
Oh, yeah? What's-
-that...?

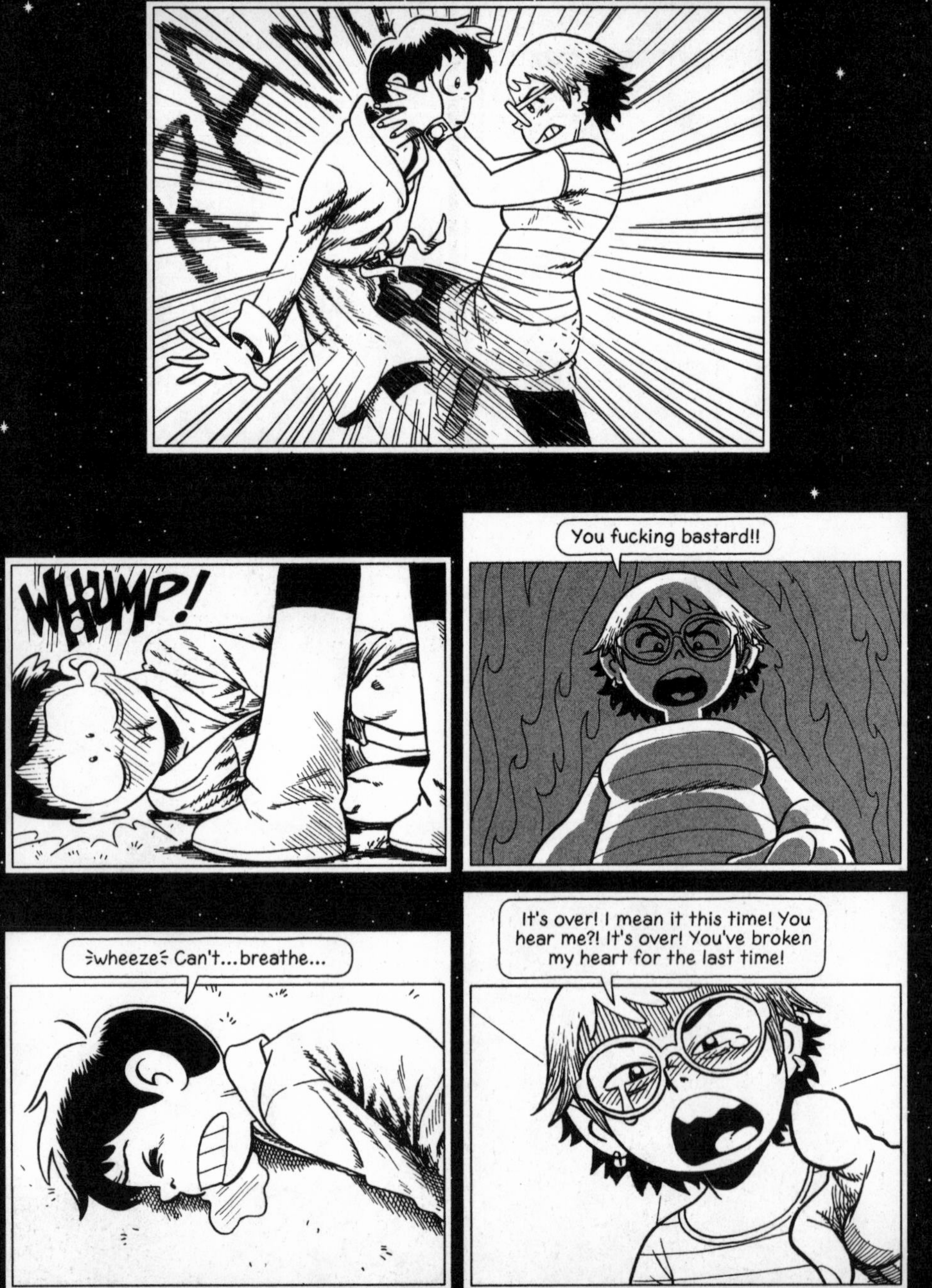
BAM!
WHUMP!
You fucking bastard!!
≶wheeze≶ Can't...breathe...
It's over! I mean it this time! You hear me?! It's over! You've broken my heart for the last time!

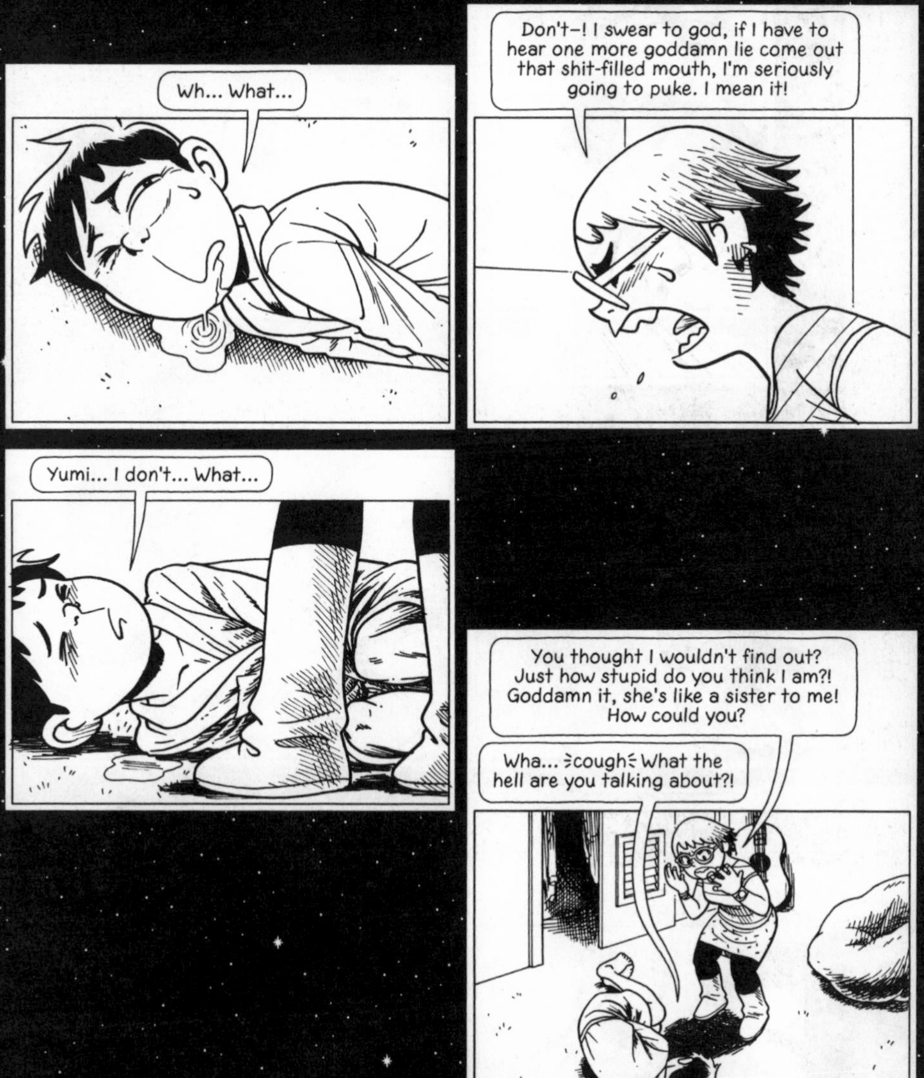
Wh... What...
Don't-! I swear to god, if I have to hear one more goddamn lie come out that shit-filled mouth, I'm seriously going to puke. I mean it!
Yumi... I don't... What...
You thought I wouldn't find out? Just how stupid do you think I am?! Goddamn it, she's like a sister to me! How could you?
Wha... ≷cough≶ What the hell are you talking about?!

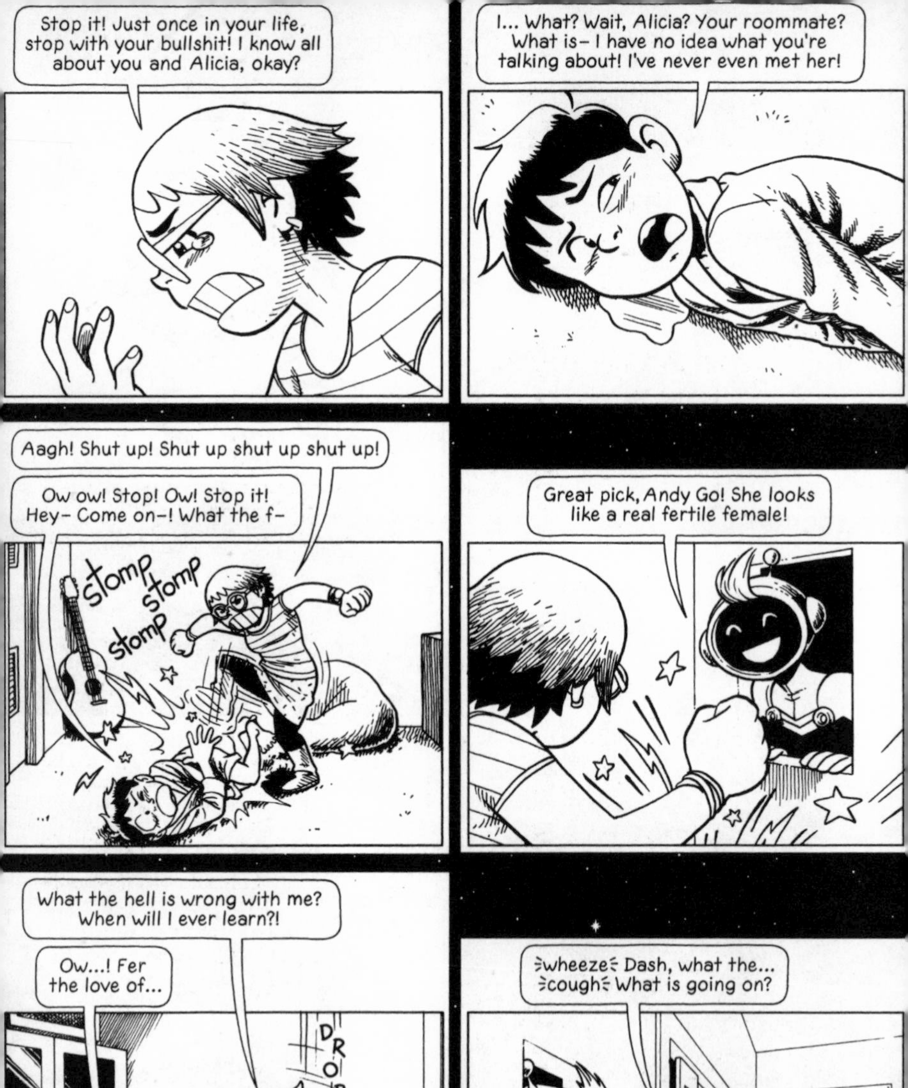
Stop it! Just once in your life, stop with your bullshit! I know all about you and Alicia, okay?
I... What? Wait, Alicia? Your roommate? What is– I have no idea what you're talking about! I've never even met her!
Aagh! Shut up! Shut up shut up shut up!
Ow ow! Stop! Ow! Stop it! Hey– Come on–! What the f–
stomp stomp stomp
Great pick, Andy Go! She looks like a real fertile female!
What the hell is wrong with me? When will I ever learn?!
Ow...! Fer the love of...
DROP
≷wheeze≶ Dash, what the... ≷cough≶ What is going on?

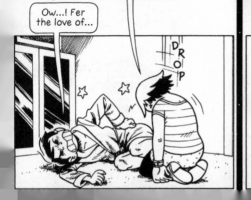

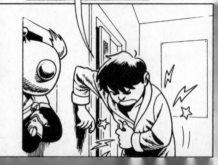

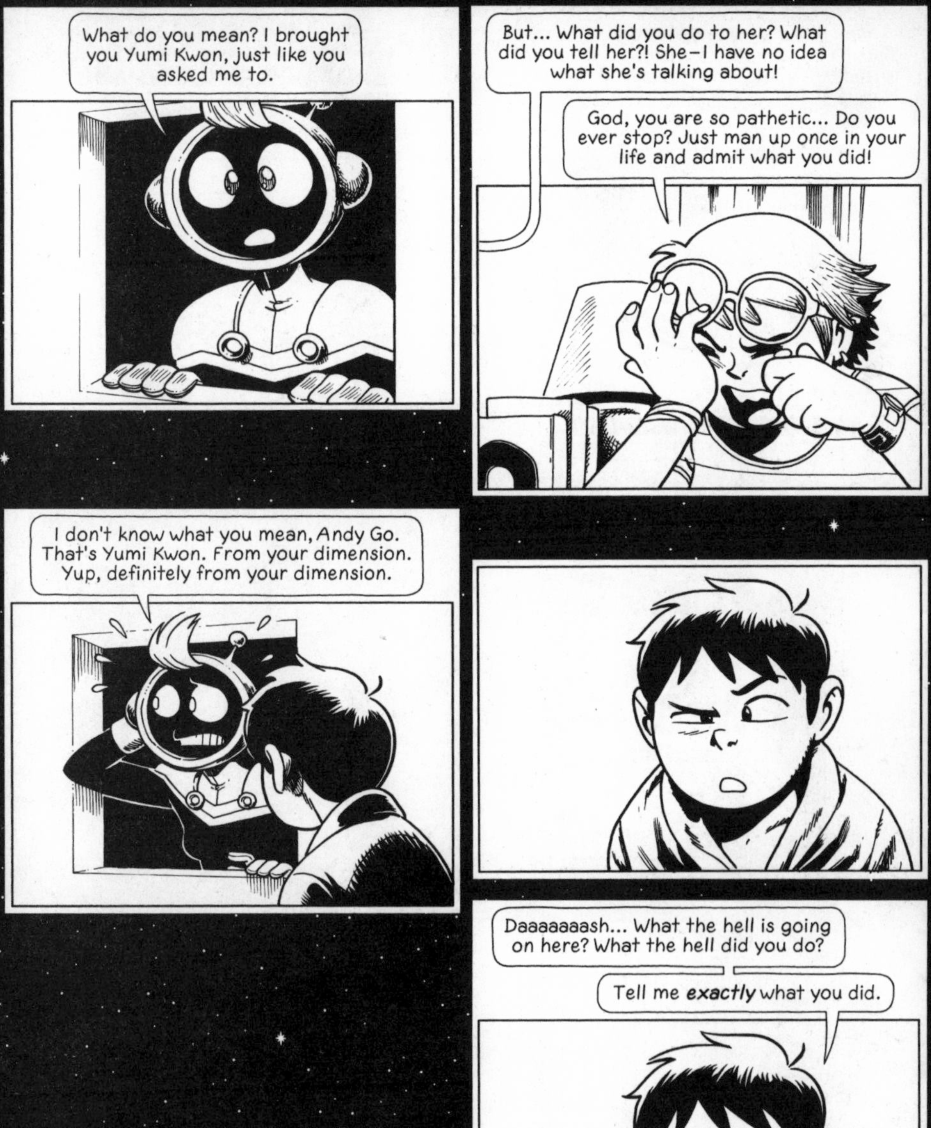
What do you mean? I brought you Yumi Kwon, just like you asked me to.
But... What did you do to her? What did you tell her?! She–I have no idea what she's talking about!
God, you are so pathetic... Do you ever stop? Just man up once in your life and admit what you did!
I don't know what you mean, Andy Go. That's Yumi Kwon. From your dimension. Yup, definitely from your dimension.
Daaaaaaash... What the hell is going on here? What the hell did you do?
Tell me *exactly* what you did.

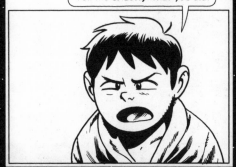

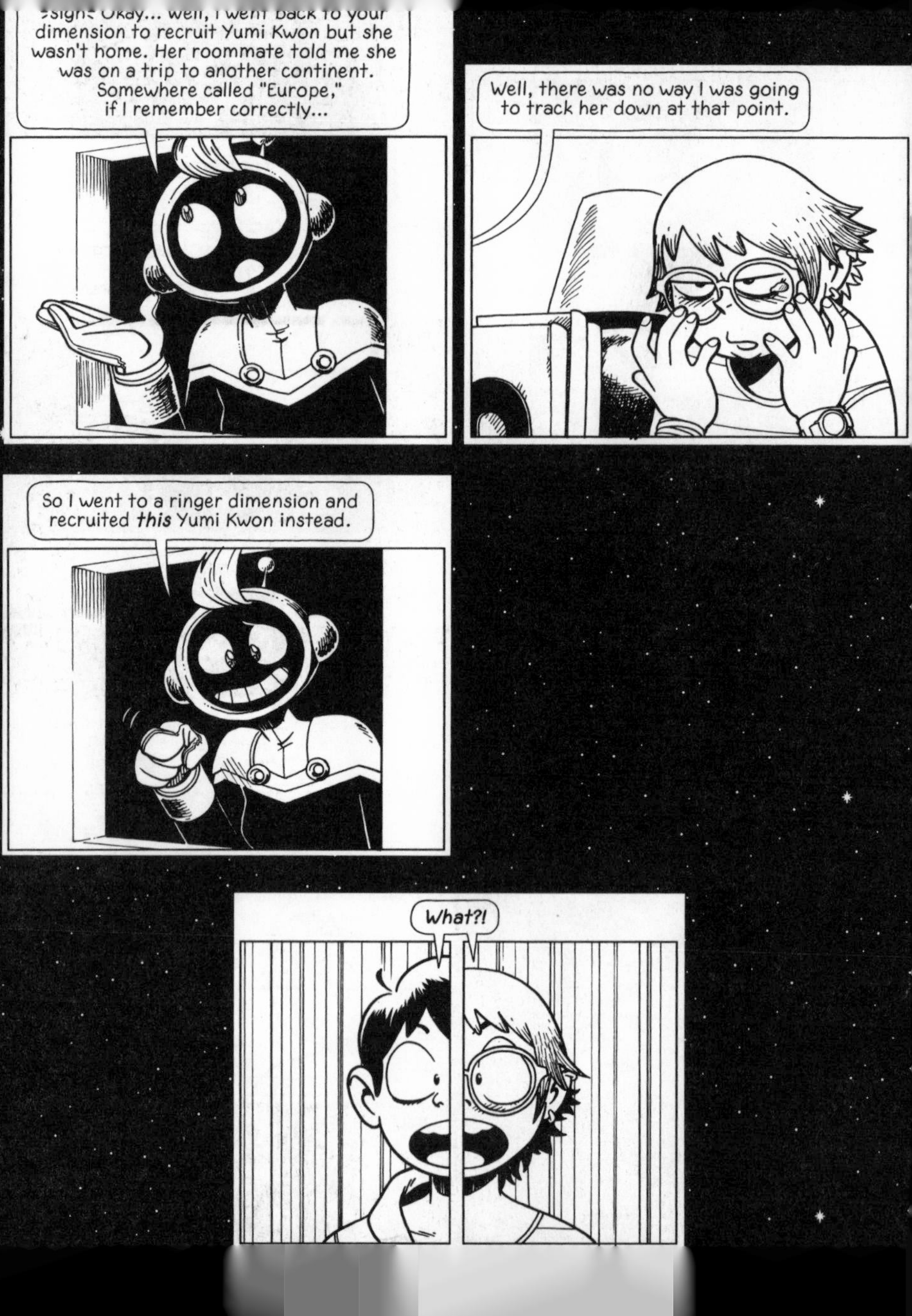
<sigh> Okay... well, I went back to your dimension to recruit Yumi Kwon but she wasn't home. Her roommate told me she was on a trip to another continent. Somewhere called "Europe," if I remember correctly...
Well, there was no way I was going to track her down at that point.
So I went to a ringer dimension and recruited *this* Yumi Kwon instead.
What?!

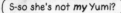

S-so she's not *my* Yumi?

Well, for all intents and purposes she should be! I told you, I recruited her from a ringer dimension.

What does that mean? Why do you keep saying "ringer dimension" like it's common knowledge?

Oh yeah, I keep forgetting I have to explain every little thing to you humans.

Look, there are an infinite number of alternate realities. Some are drastically different, like yours and mine. And some are virtually identical—we've dubbed these "ringer dimensions." You know, like a "dead ringer."

You two come from ringer dimensions. Same evolutionary pattern, same wars, same everything.

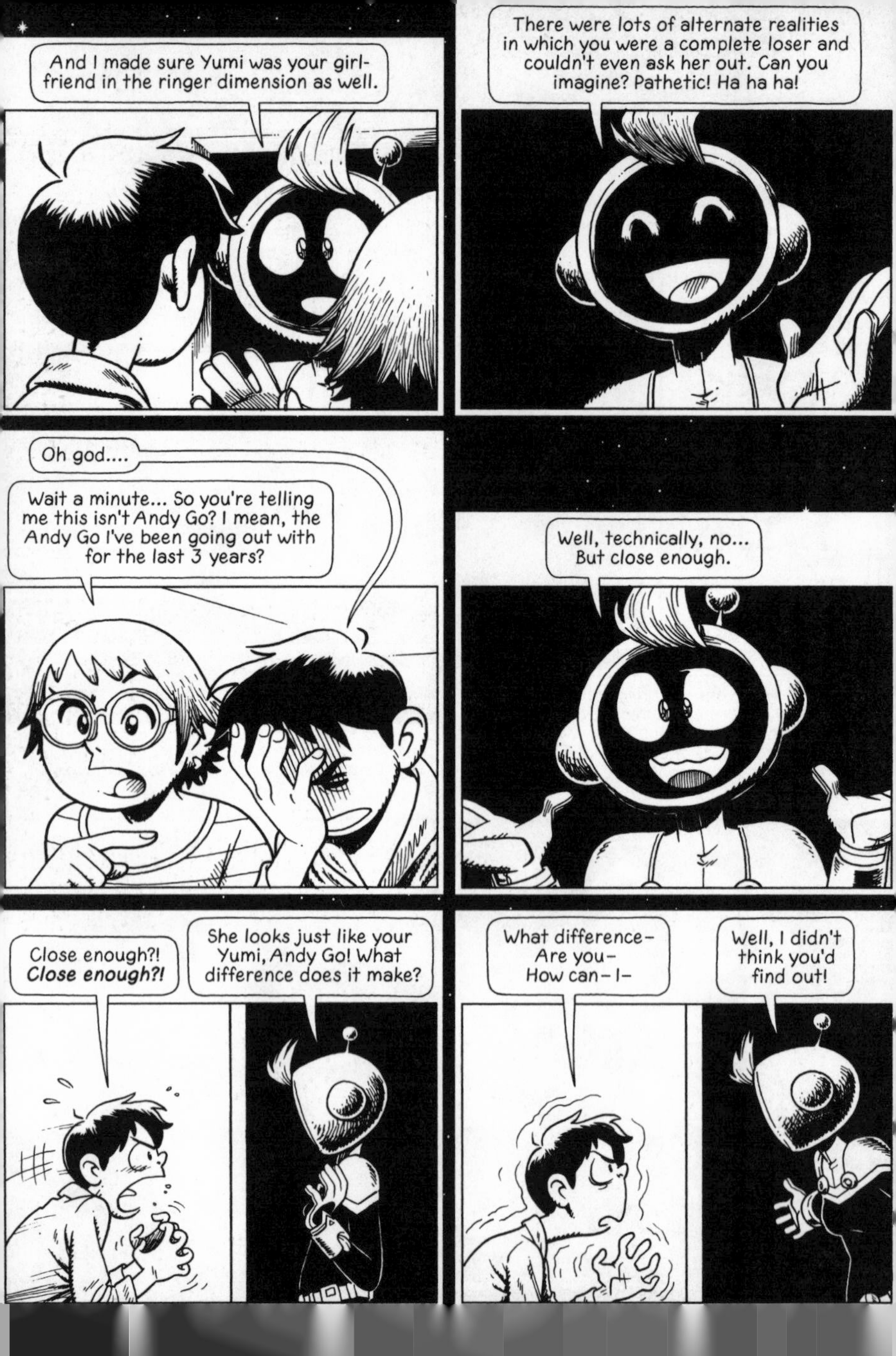
And I made sure Yumi was your girl-friend in the ringer dimension as well.
There were lots of alternate realities in which you were a complete loser and couldn't even ask her out. Can you imagine? Pathetic! Ha ha ha!
Oh god....
Wait a minute... So you're telling me this isn't Andy Go? I mean, the Andy Go I've been going out with for the last 3 years?
Well, technically, no... But close enough.
Close enough?! *Close enough?!*
She looks just like your Yumi, Andy Go! What difference does it make?
What difference- Are you- How can-I-
Well, I didn't think you'd find out!

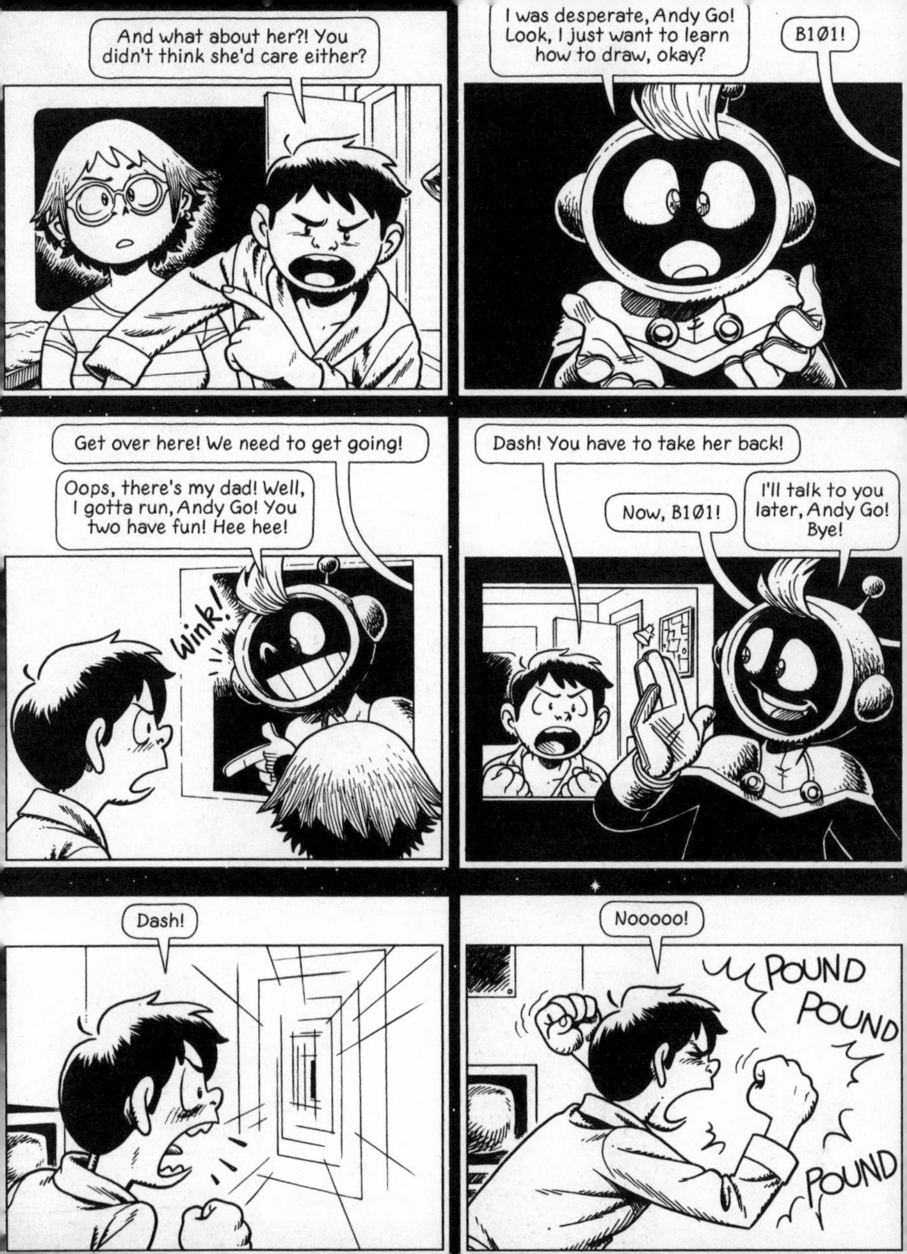
And what about her?! You didn't think she'd care either?
I was desperate, Andy Go! Look, I just want to learn how to draw, okay?
B1Ø1!
Get over here! We need to get going!
Oops, there's my dad! Well, I gotta run, Andy Go! You two have fun! Hee hee!
Wink!
Dash! You have to take her back!
Now, B1Ø1!
I'll talk to you later, Andy Go! Bye!
Dash!
Nooooo!
POUND
POUND
POUND

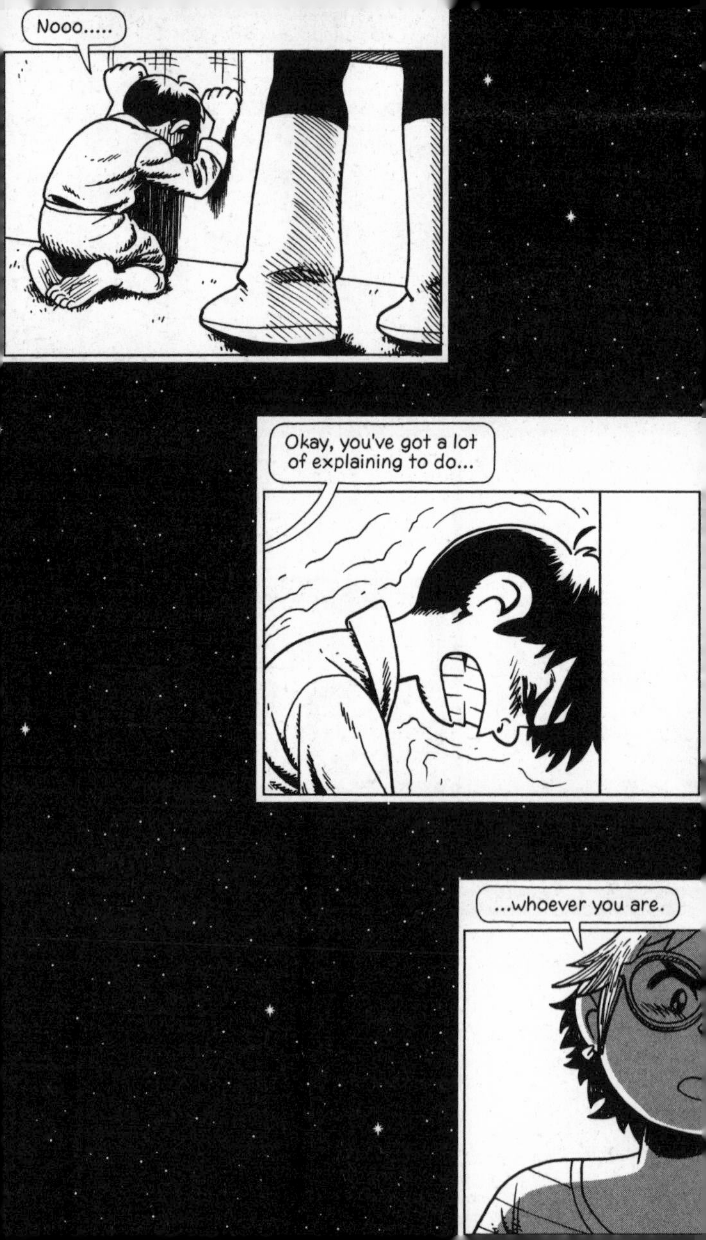
Nooo.....
Okay, you've got a lot of explaining to do...
...whoever you are.

CHAPTER 17

akkatakkatakkatakkatak

...then, as you already know, Dash brought you instead, and... here we are...

Okay, give me a sec to catch up... I don't want to miss anything...

You sure you don't want an Eggo or something?

I can't believe this... As if all this isn't unreal enough as it is...

I'm sorry to say this really is happening. You're not dreaming.

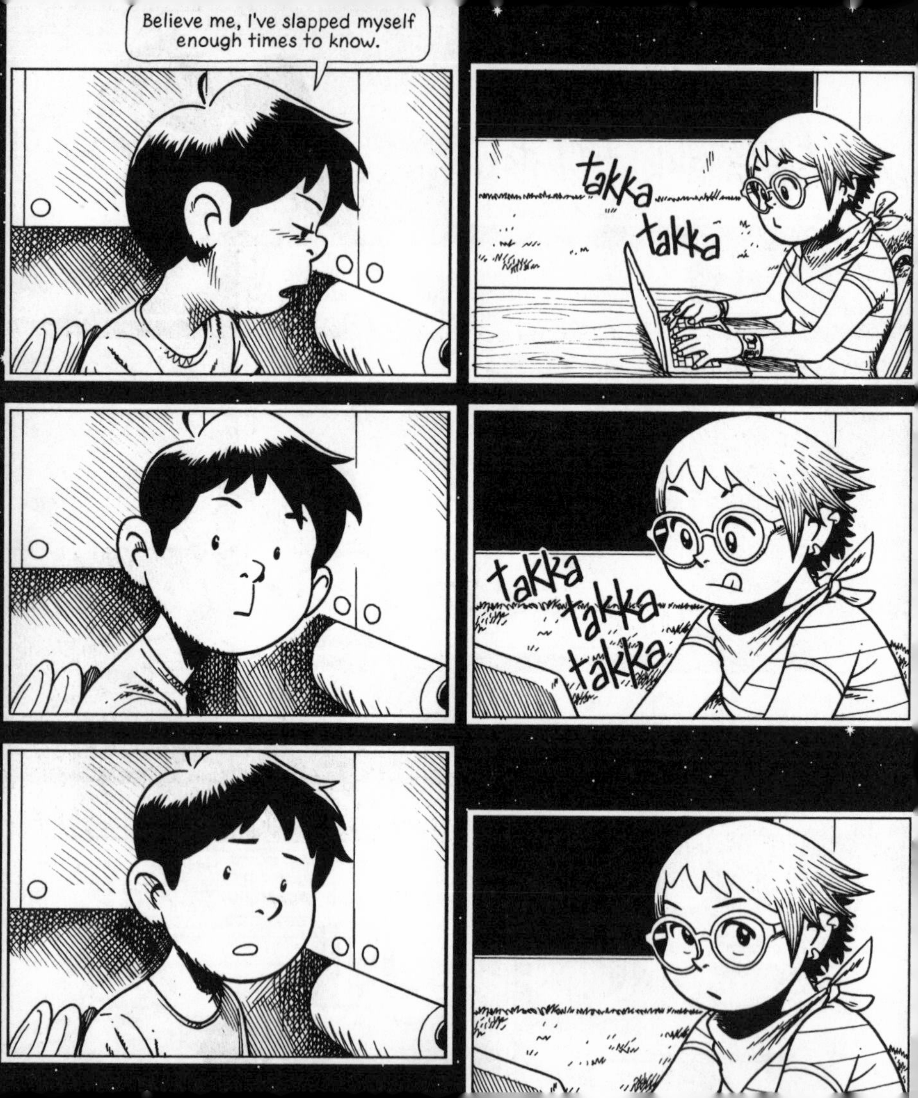

Believe me, I've slapped myself enough times to know.
takka takka
takka takka takka

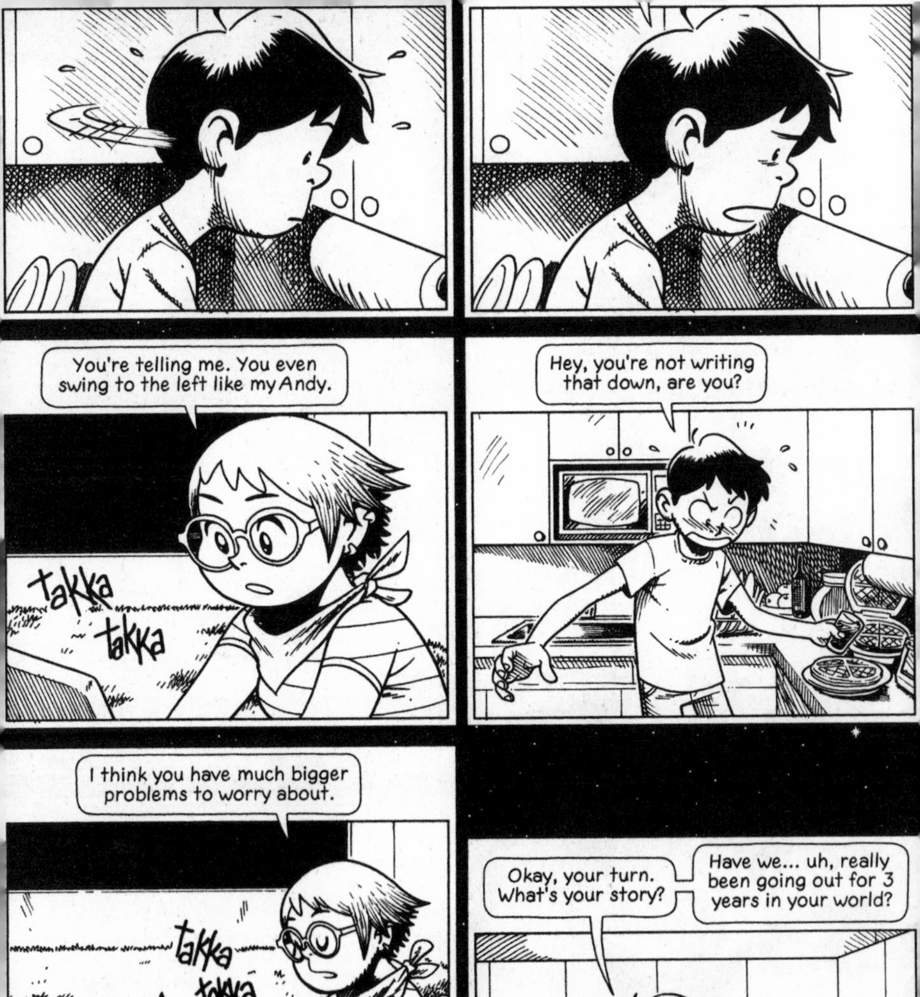
You're telling me. You even swing to the left like my Andy.
takka takka
Hey, you're not writing that down, are you?
I think you have much bigger problems to worry about.
takka takka
Okay, your turn. What's your story?
Have we... uh, really been going out for 3 years in your world?

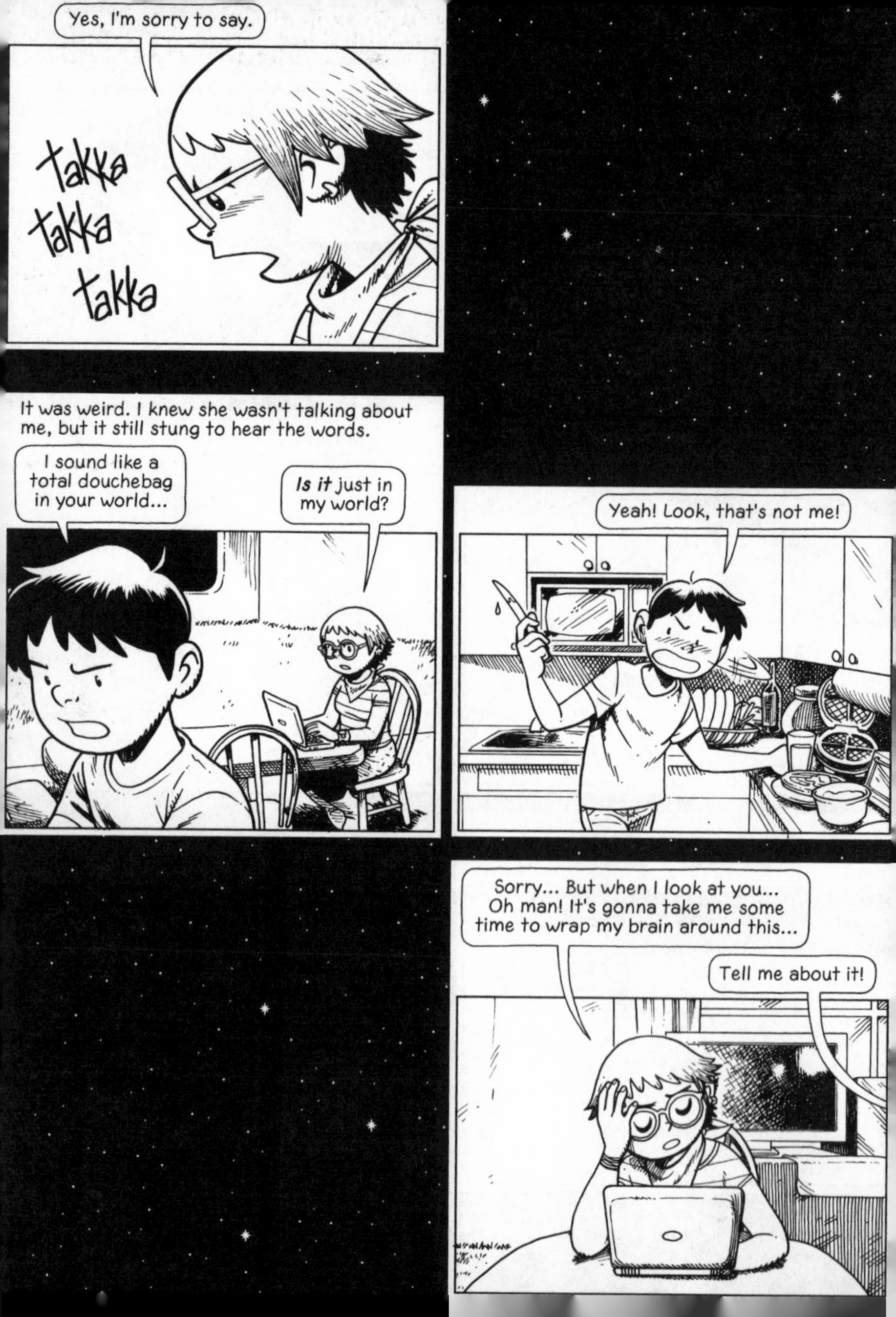

Yes, I'm sorry to say.
takka
takka
takka
It was weird. I knew she wasn't talking about me, but it still stung to hear the words.
I sound like a total douchebag in your world...
Is it just in my world?
Yeah! Look, that's not me!
Sorry... But when I look at you... Oh man! It's gonna take me some time to wrap my brain around this...
Tell me about it!

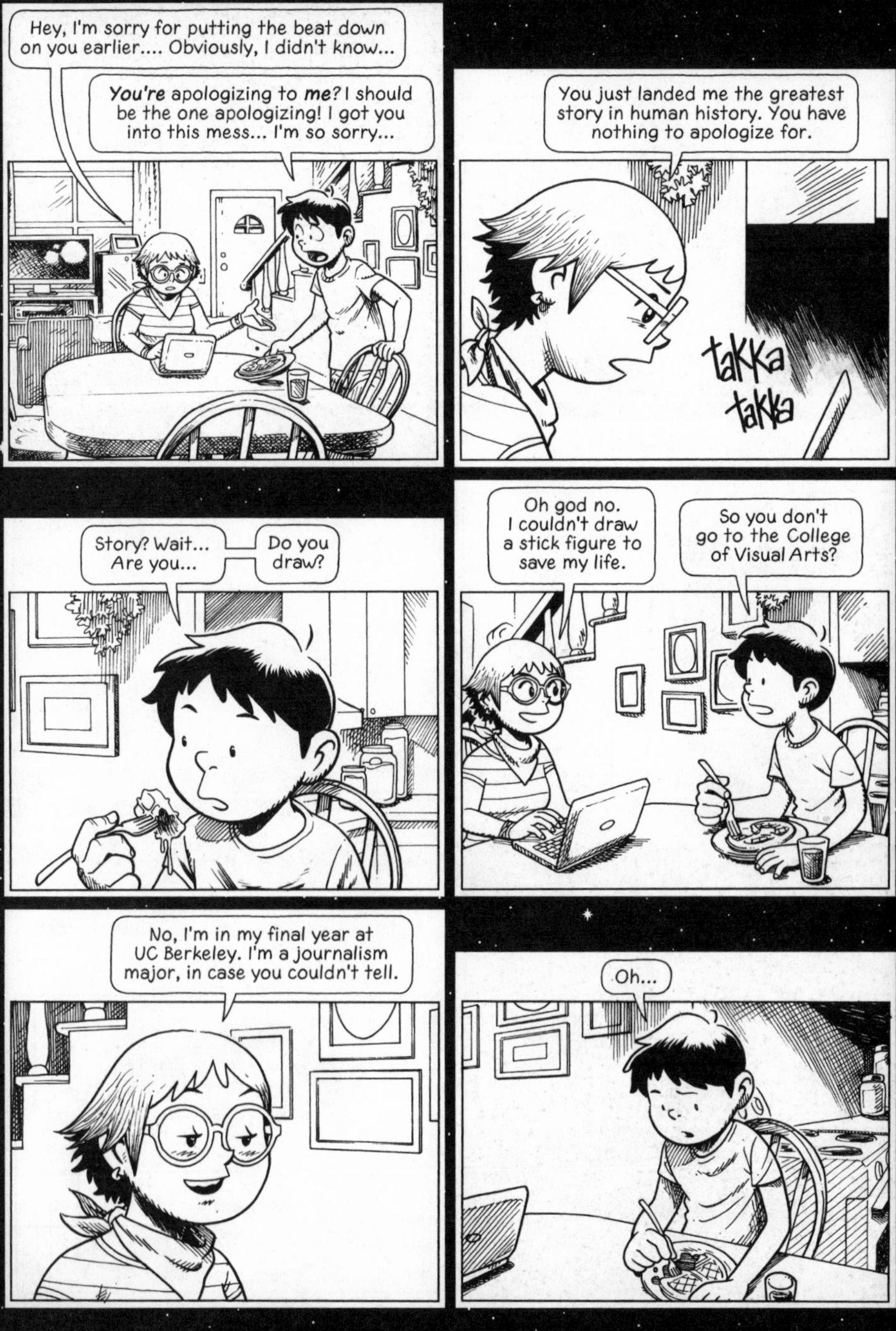
Hey, I'm sorry for putting the beat down on you earlier.... Obviously, I didn't know...
You're apologizing to *me*? I should be the one apologizing! I got you into this mess... I'm so sorry...
You just landed me the greatest story in human history. You have nothing to apologize for.
takka takka
Story? Wait... Are you...
Do you draw?
So you don't go to the College of Visual Arts?
Oh god no. I couldn't draw a stick figure to save my life.
No, I'm in my final year at UC Berkeley. I'm a journalism major, in case you couldn't tell.
Oh...

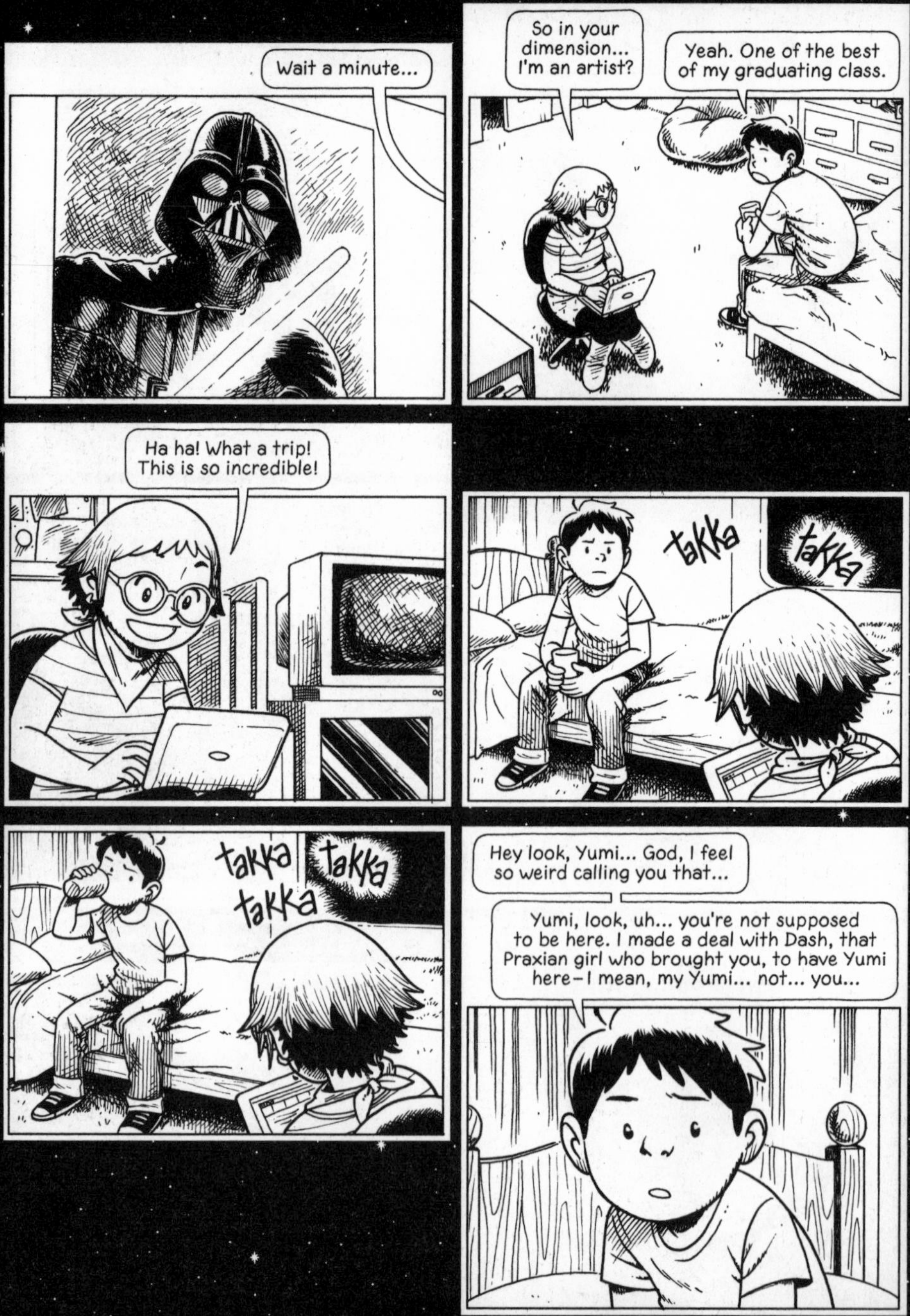
Wait a minute...
So in your dimension... I'm an artist?
Yeah. One of the best of my graduating class.
Ha ha! What a trip! This is so incredible!
takka
takka
takka
takka
takka
Hey look, Yumi... God, I feel so weird calling you that...
Yumi, look, uh... you're not supposed to be here. I made a deal with Dash, that Praxian girl who brought you, to have Yumi here—I mean, my Yumi... not... you...

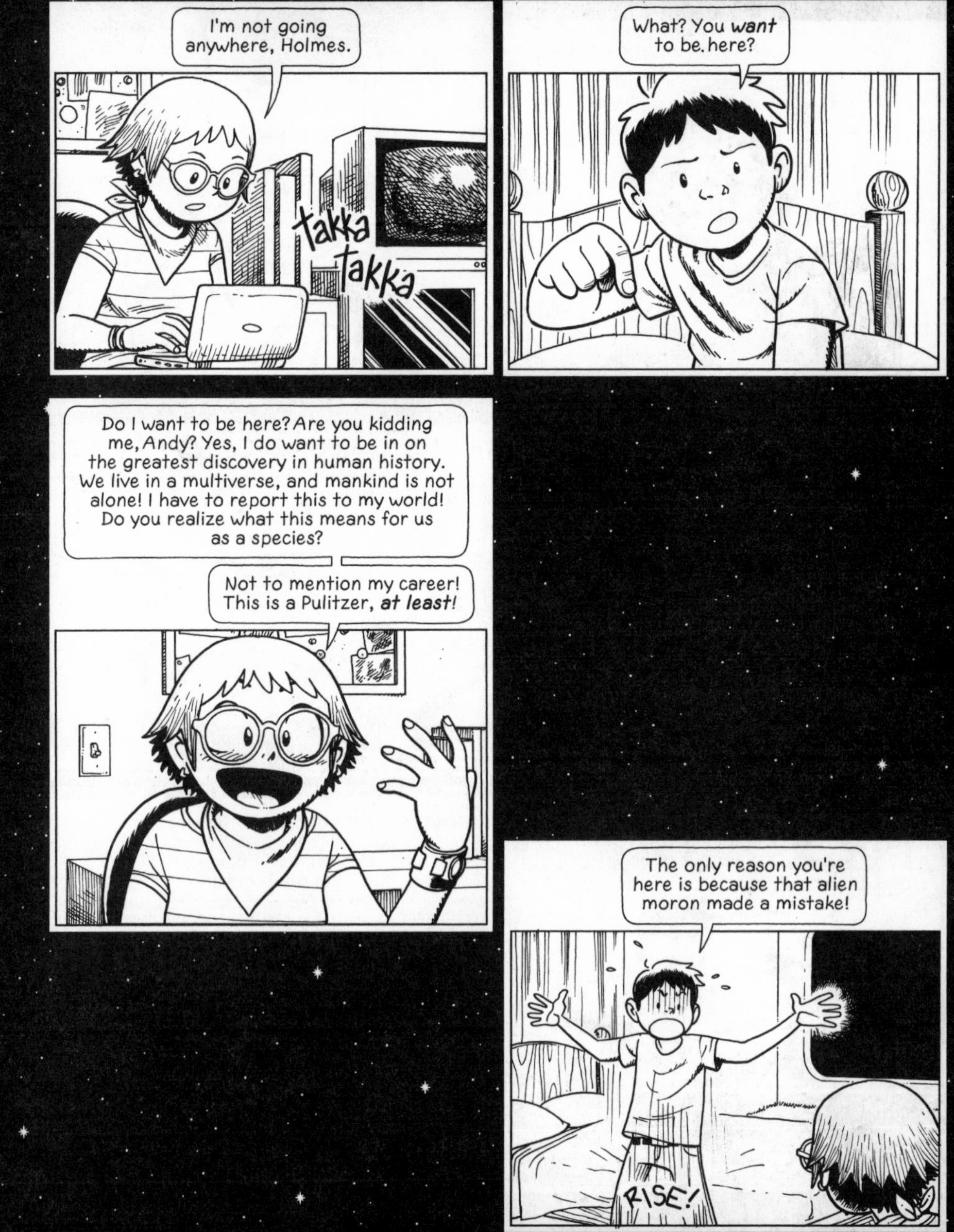

I'm not going anywhere, Holmes.
takka takka
What? You *want* to be. here?
Do I want to be here? Are you kidding me, Andy? Yes, I do want to be in on the greatest discovery in human history. We live in a multiverse, and mankind is not alone! I have to report this to my world! Do you realize what this means for us as a species?
Not to mention my career! This is a Pulitzer, ***at least***!
The only reason you're here is because that alien moron made a mistake!
RISE!

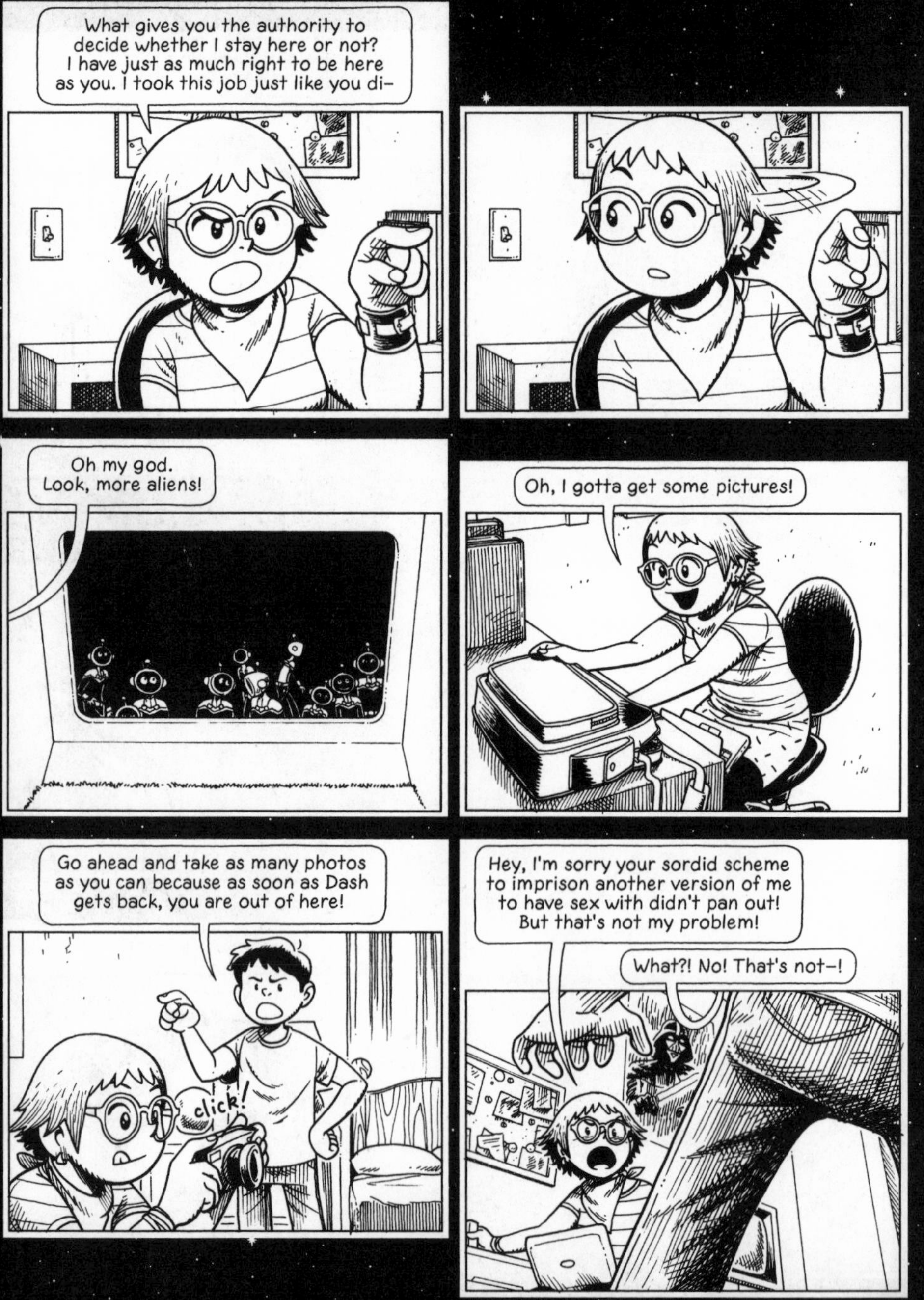
What gives you the authority to decide whether I stay here or not? I have just as much right to be here as you. I took this job just like you di–
Oh my god. Look, more aliens!
Oh, I gotta get some pictures!
Go ahead and take as many photos as you can because as soon as Dash gets back, you are out of here!
click!
Hey, I'm sorry your sordid scheme to imprison another version of me to have sex with didn't pan out! But that's not my problem!
What?! No! That's not–!

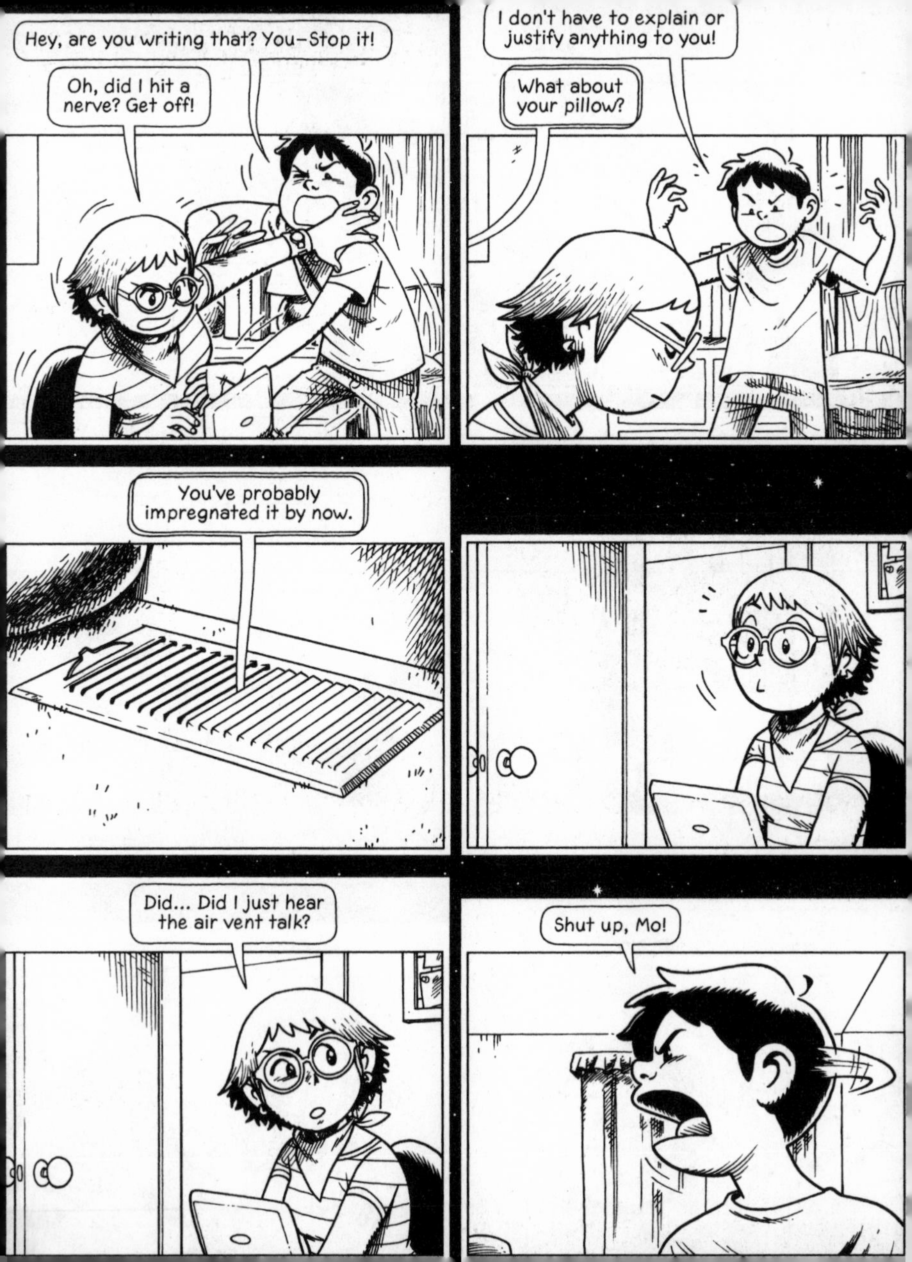
Hey, are you writing that? You–Stop it!
Oh, did I hit a nerve? Get off!
I don't have to explain or justify anything to you!
What about your pillow?
You've probably impregnated it by now.
Did... Did I just hear the air vent talk?
Shut up, Mo!

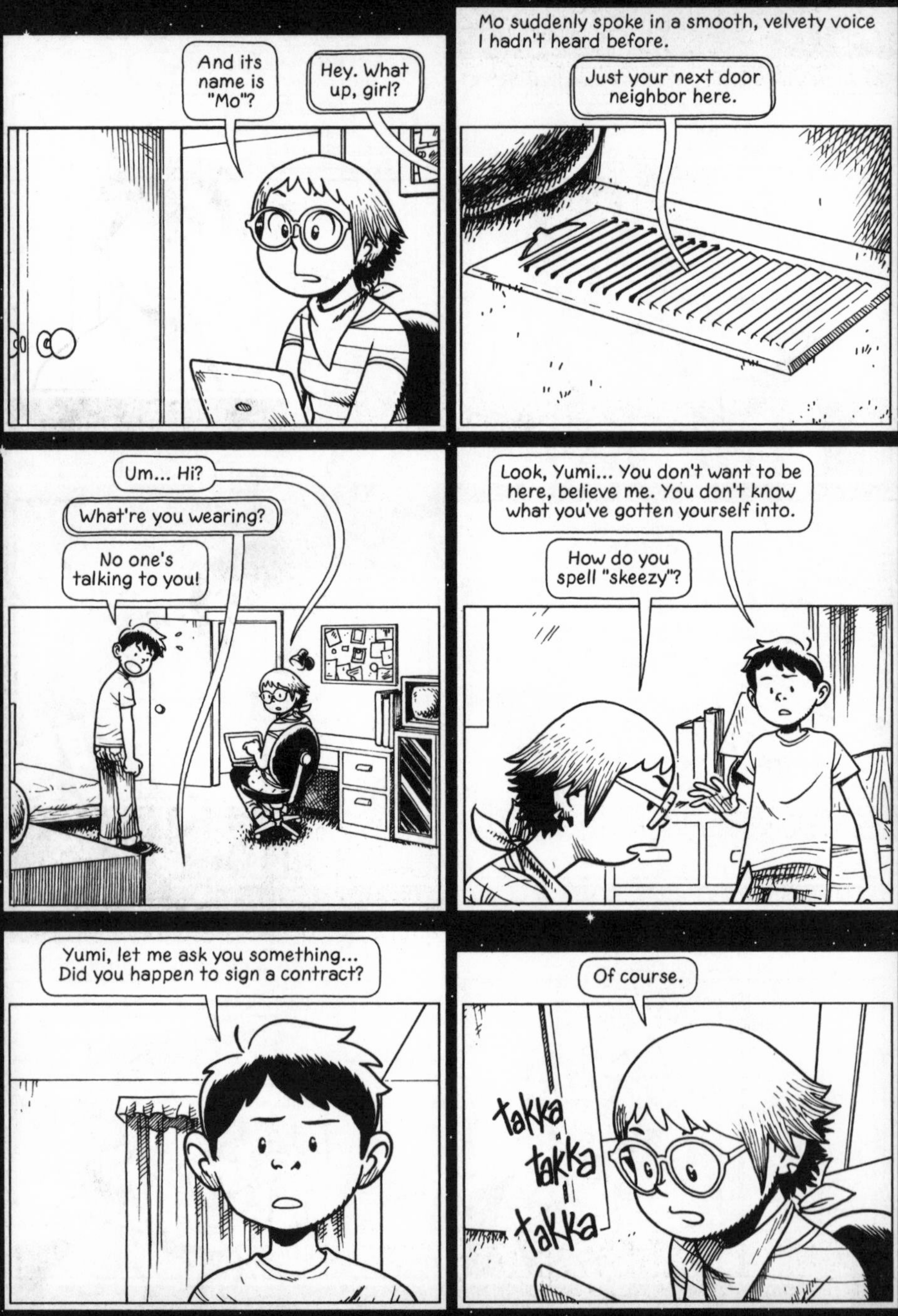
And its name is "Mo"?
Hey. What up, girl?
Mo suddenly spoke in a smooth, velvety voice I hadn't heard before.
Just your next door neighbor here.
Um... Hi?
What're you wearing?
No one's talking to you!
Look, Yumi... You don't want to be here, believe me. You don't know what you've gotten yourself into.
How do you spell "skeezy"?
Yumi, let me ask you something... Did you happen to sign a contract?
Of course.
takka takka takka

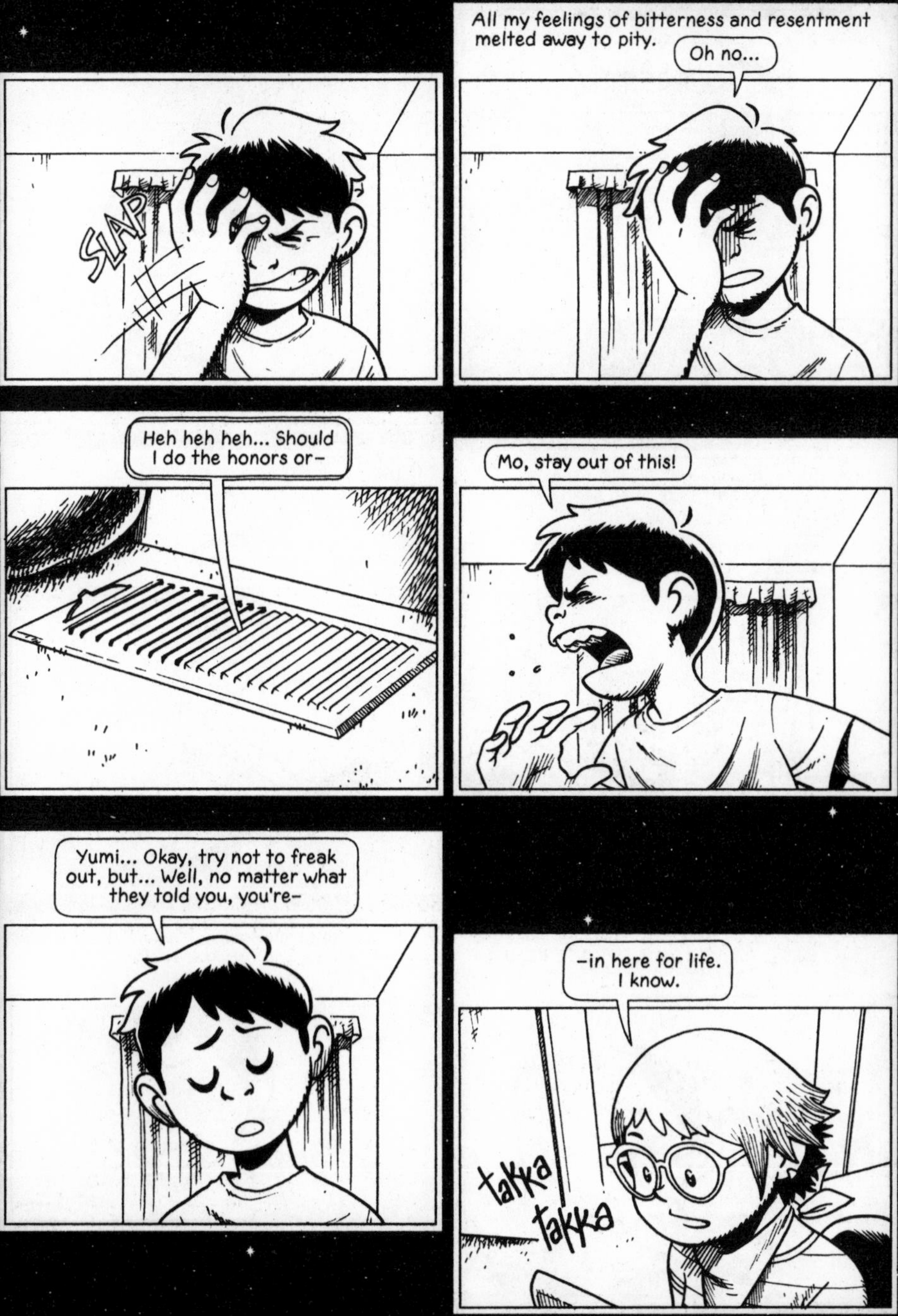
SLAP
All my feelings of bitterness and resentment melted away to pity.
Oh no...
Heh heh heh... Should I do the honors or-
Mo, stay out of this!
Yumi... Okay, try not to freak out, but... Well, no matter what they told you, you're-
-in here for life. I know.
takka takka

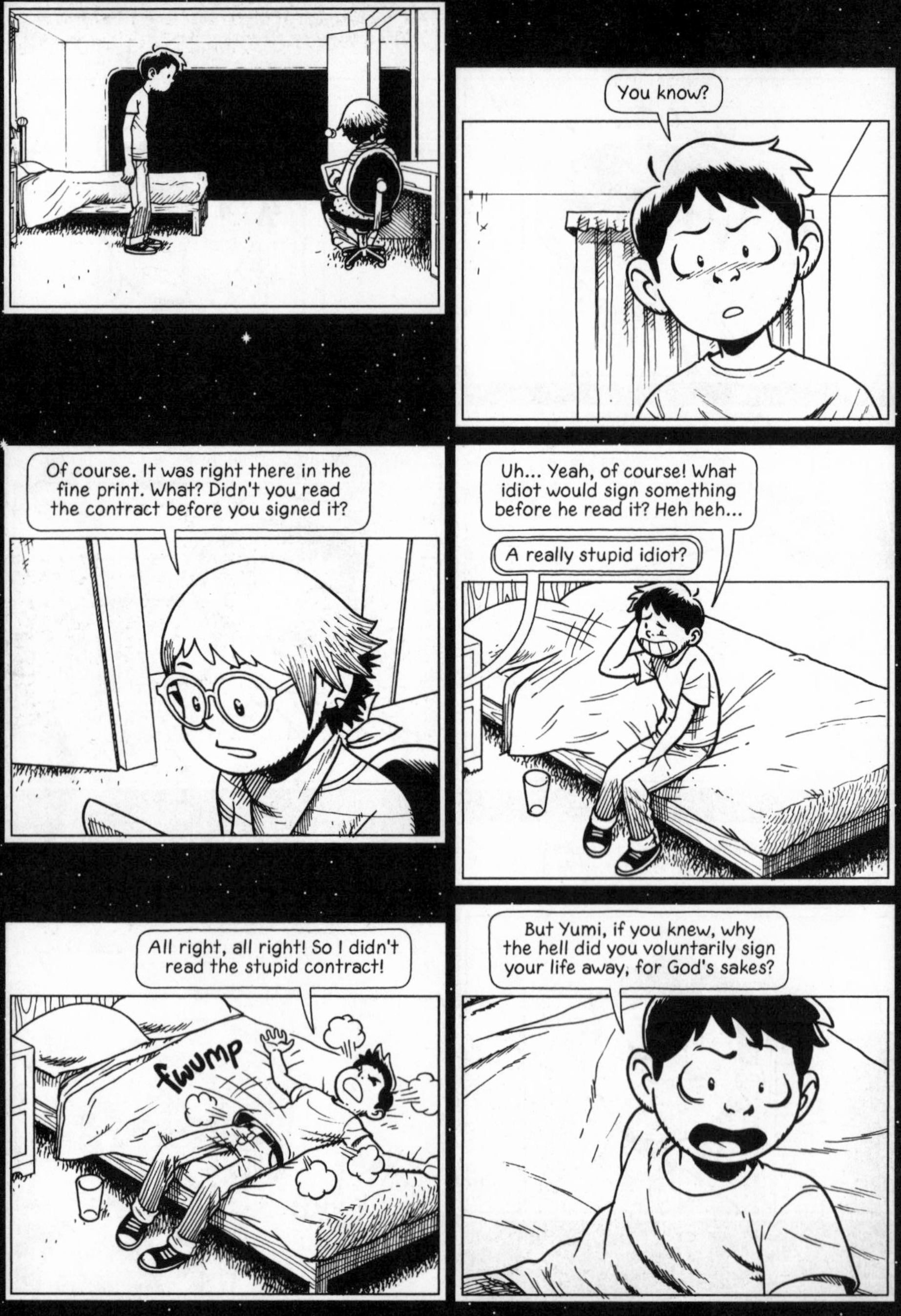
You know?
Of course. It was right there in the fine print. What? Didn't you read the contract before you signed it?
Uh... Yeah, of course! What idiot would sign something before he read it? Heh heh...
A really stupid idiot?
All right, all right! So I didn't read the stupid contract!
fwump
But Yumi, if you knew, why the hell did you voluntarily sign your life away, for God's sakes?

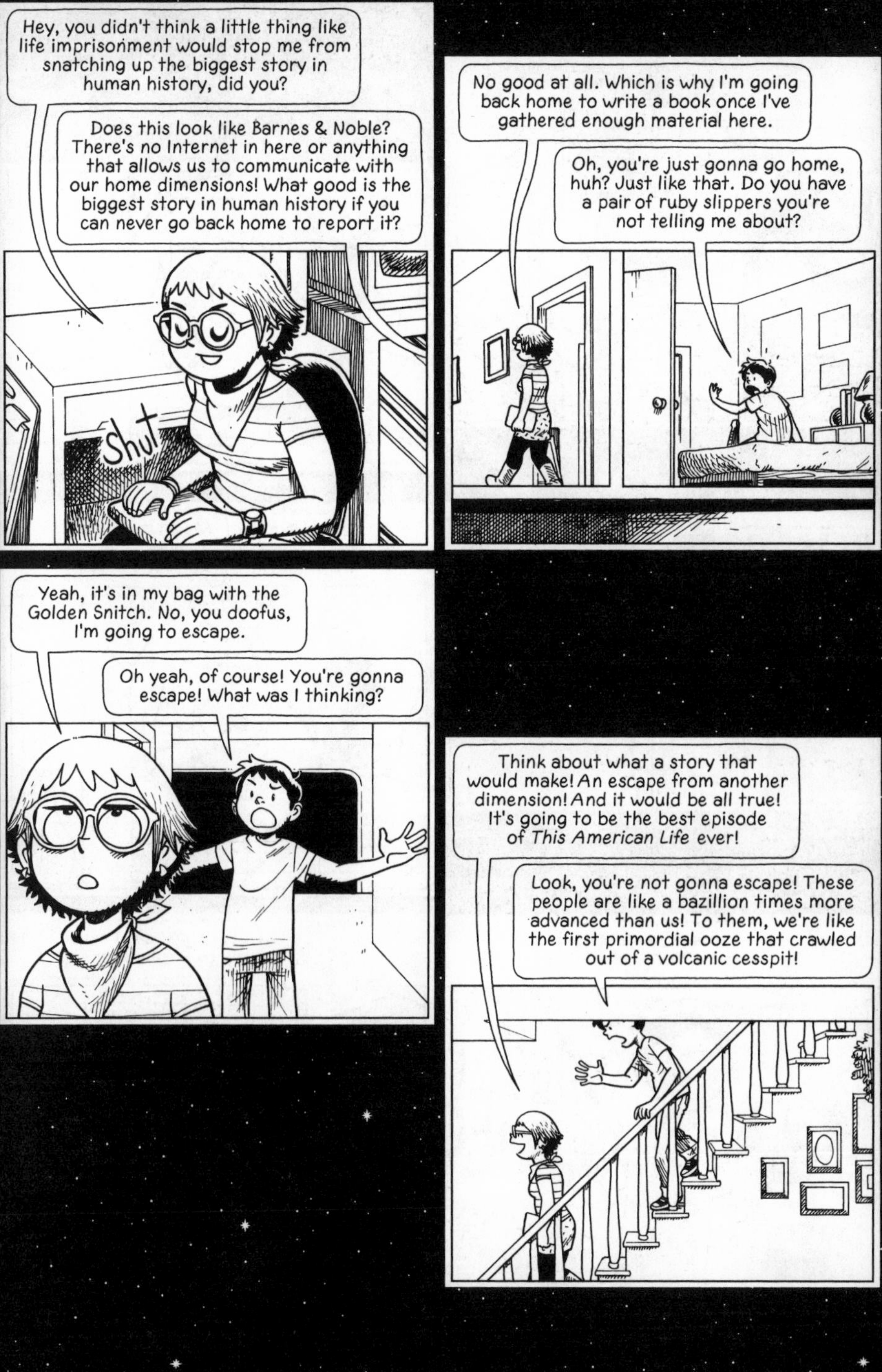

Hey, you didn't think a little thing like life imprisonment would stop me from snatching up the biggest story in human history, did you?
Does this look like Barnes & Noble? There's no Internet in here or anything that allows us to communicate with our home dimensions! What good is the biggest story in human history if you can never go back home to report it?
Shut
No good at all. Which is why I'm going back home to write a book once I've gathered enough material here.
Oh, you're just gonna go home, huh? Just like that. Do you have a pair of ruby slippers you're not telling me about?
Yeah, it's in my bag with the Golden Snitch. No, you doofus, I'm going to escape.
Oh yeah, of course! You're gonna escape! What was I thinking?
Think about what a story that would make! An escape from another dimension! And it would be all true! It's going to be the best episode of *This American Life* ever!
Look, you're not gonna escape! These people are like a bazillion times more advanced than us! To them, we're like the first primordial ooze that crawled out of a volcanic cesspit!

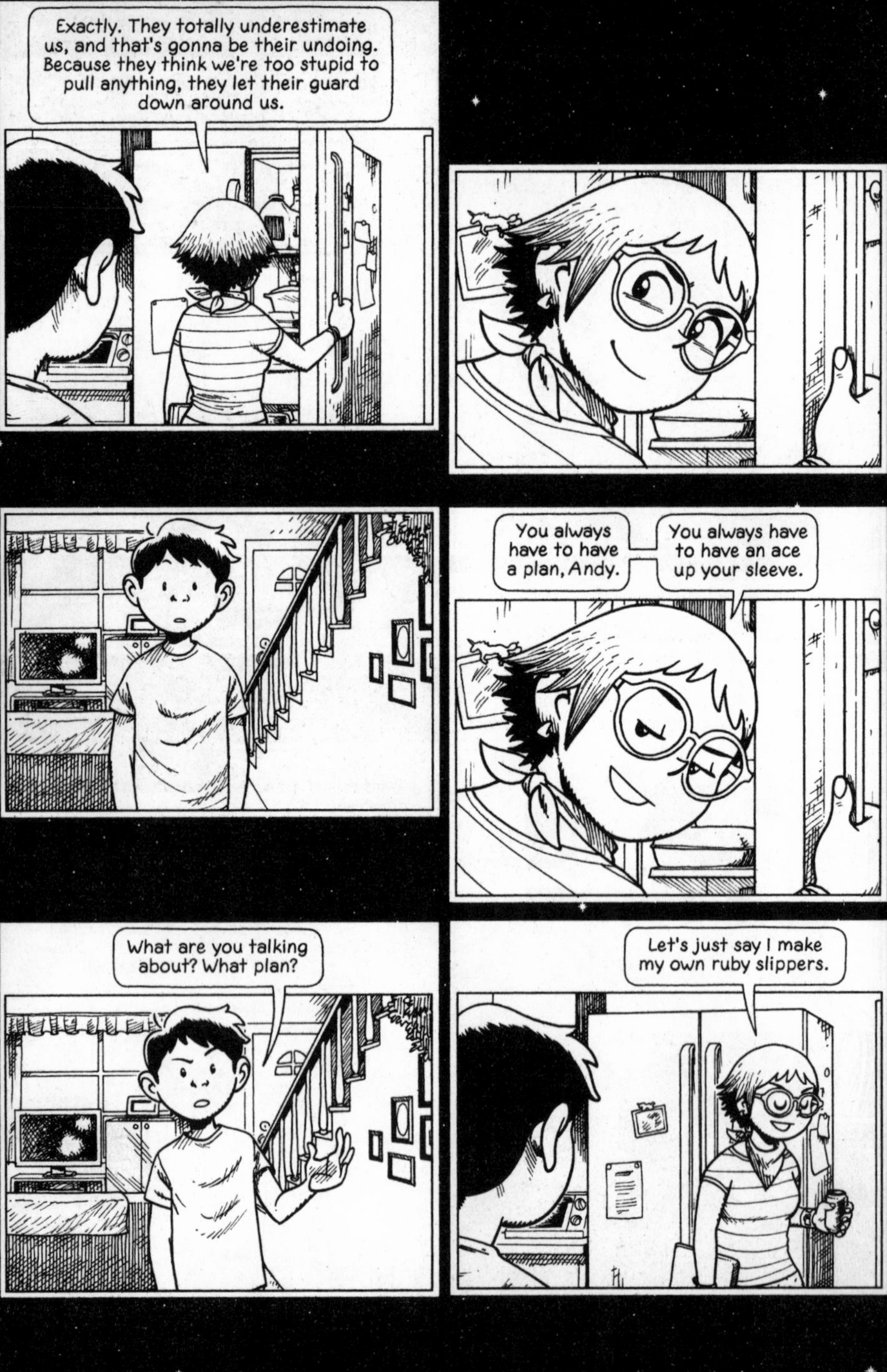
Exactly. They totally underestimate us, and that's gonna be their undoing. Because they think we're too stupid to pull anything, they let their guard down around us.
You always have to have a plan, Andy.
You always have to have an ace up your sleeve.
What are you talking about? What plan?
Let's just say I make my own ruby slippers.

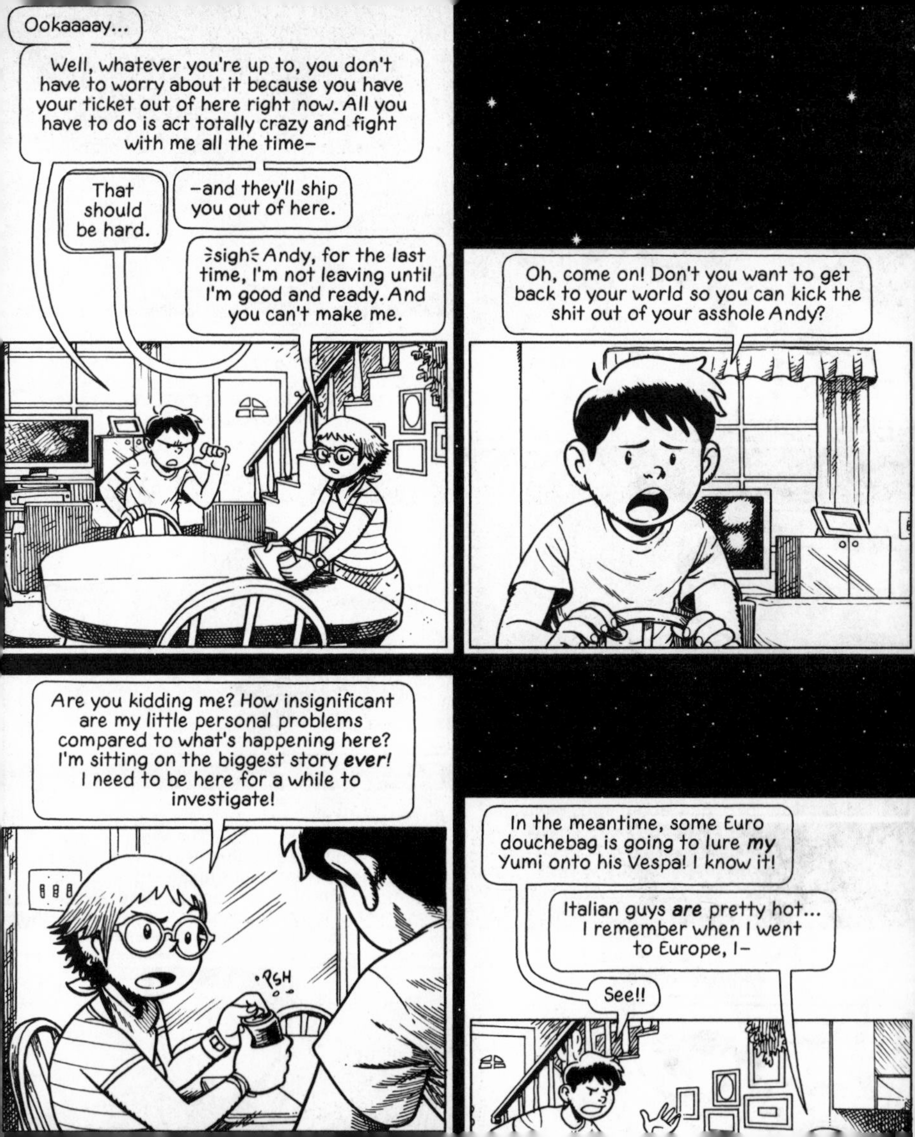
Ookaaaay...
Well, whatever you're up to, you don't have to worry about it because you have your ticket out of here right now. All you have to do is act totally crazy and fight with me all the time–
That should be hard.
–and they'll ship you out of here.
sigh Andy, for the last time, I'm not leaving until I'm good and ready. And you can't make me.
Oh, come on! Don't you want to get back to your world so you can kick the shit out of your asshole Andy?
Are you kidding me? How insignificant are my little personal problems compared to what's happening here? I'm sitting on the biggest story ever! I need to be here for a while to investigate!
PSH
In the meantime, some Euro douchebag is going to lure my Yumi onto his Vespa! I know it!
Italian guys are pretty hot... I remember when I went to Europe, I–
See!!

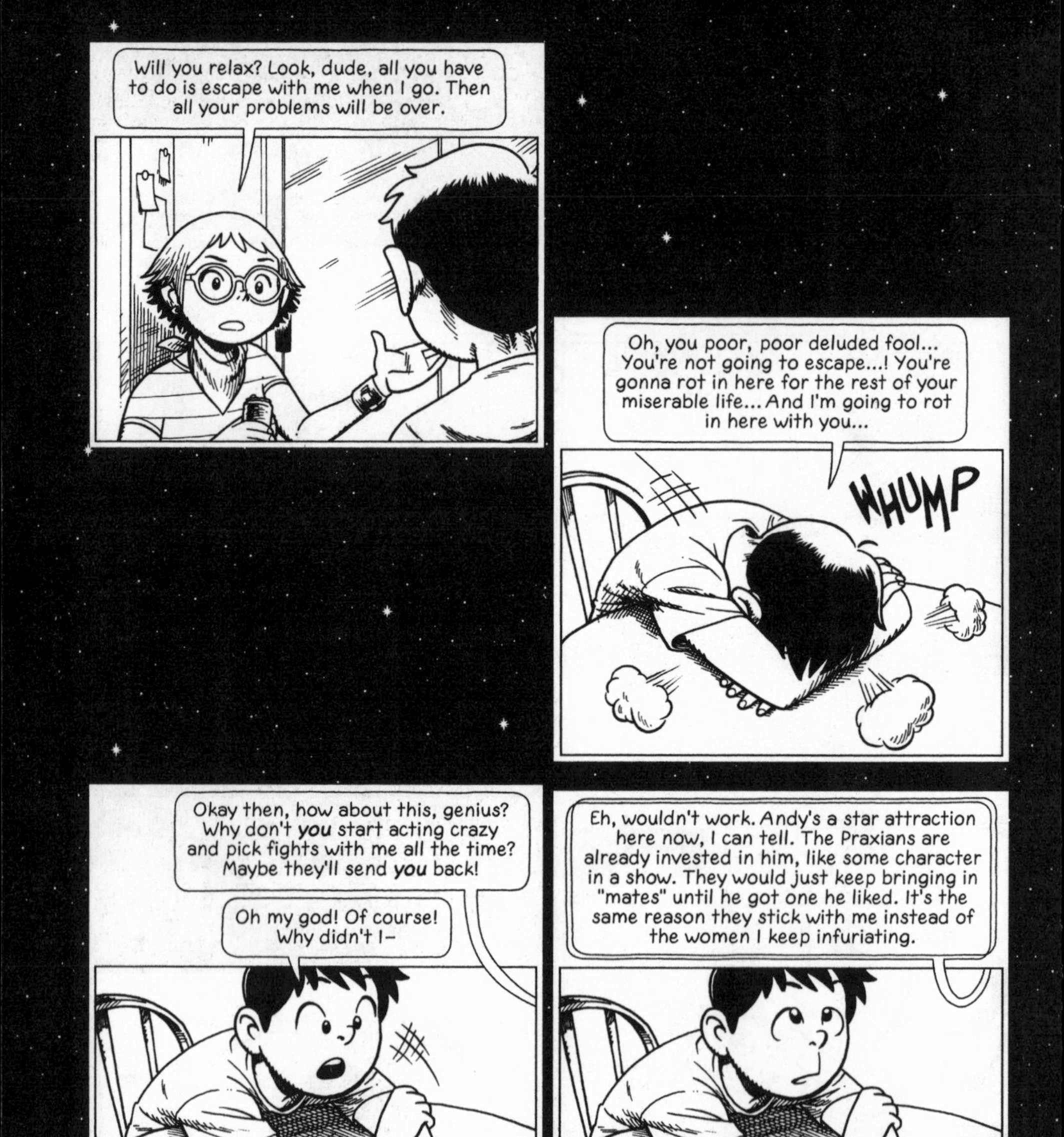
Will you relax? Look, dude, all you have to do is escape with me when I go. Then all your problems will be over.
Oh, you poor, poor deluded fool... You're not going to escape...! You're gonna rot in here for the rest of your miserable life... And I'm going to rot in here with you...
WHUMP
Okay then, how about this, genius? Why don't *you* start acting crazy and pick fights with me all the time? Maybe they'll send *you* back!
Oh my god! Of course! Why didn't I–
Eh, wouldn't work. Andy's a star attraction here now, I can tell. The Praxians are already invested in him, like some character in a show. They would just keep bringing in "mates" until he got one he liked. It's the same reason they stick with me instead of the women I keep infuriating.

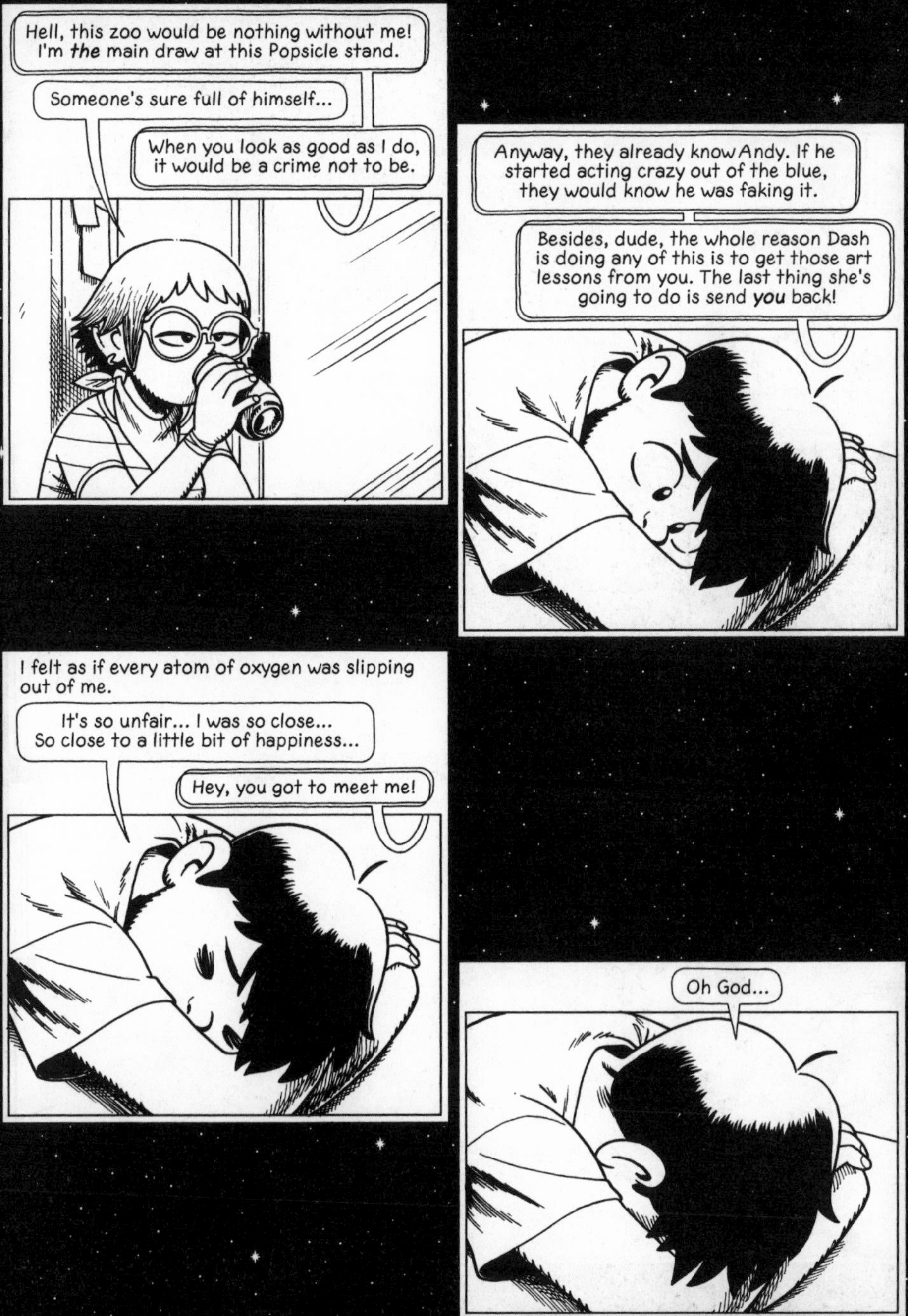
Hell, this zoo would be nothing without me! I'm *the* main draw at this Popsicle stand.
Someone's sure full of himself...
When you look as good as I do, it would be a crime not to be.
Anyway, they already know Andy. If he started acting crazy out of the blue, they would know he was faking it.
Besides, dude, the whole reason Dash is doing any of this is to get those art lessons from you. The last thing she's going to do is send *you* back!
I felt as if every atom of oxygen was slipping out of me.
It's so unfair... I was so close... So close to a little bit of happiness...
Hey, you got to meet me!
Oh God...

CHAPTER 18

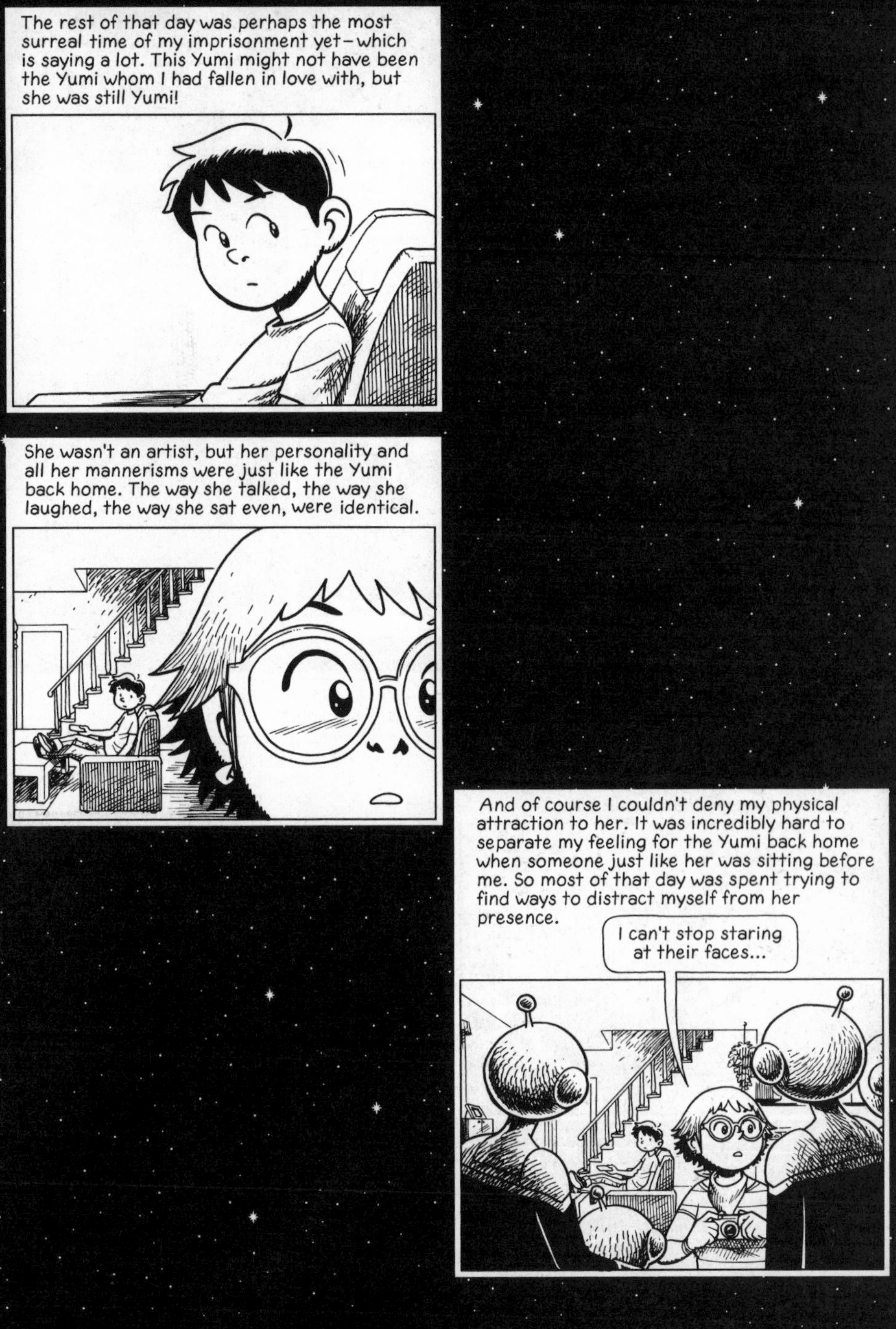
The rest of that day was perhaps the most surreal time of my imprisonment yet–which is saying a lot. This Yumi might not have been the Yumi whom I had fallen in love with, but she was still Yumi!
She wasn't an artist, but her personality and all her mannerisms were just like the Yumi back home. The way she talked, the way she laughed, the way she sat even, were identical.
And of course I couldn't deny my physical attraction to her. It was incredibly hard to separate my feeling for the Yumi back home when someone just like her was sitting before me. So most of that day was spent trying to find ways to distract myself from her presence.
I can't stop staring at their faces...

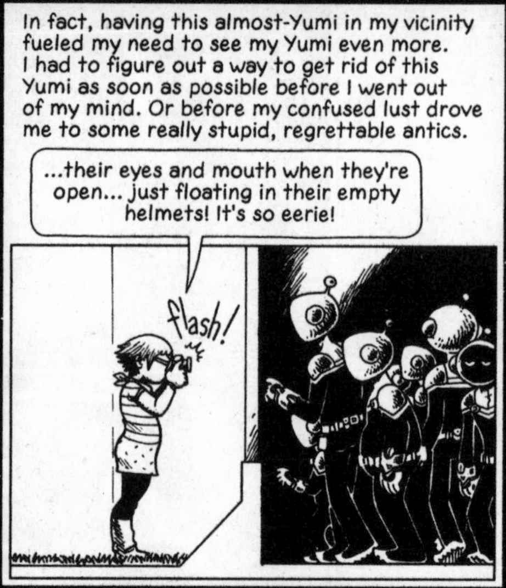
In fact, having this almost-Yumi in my vicinity fueled my need to see my Yumi even more. I had to figure out a way to get rid of this Yumi as soon as possible before I went out of my mind. Or before my confused lust drove me to some really stupid, regrettable antics.
...their eyes and mouth when they're open... just floating in their empty helmets! It's so eerie!
flash!
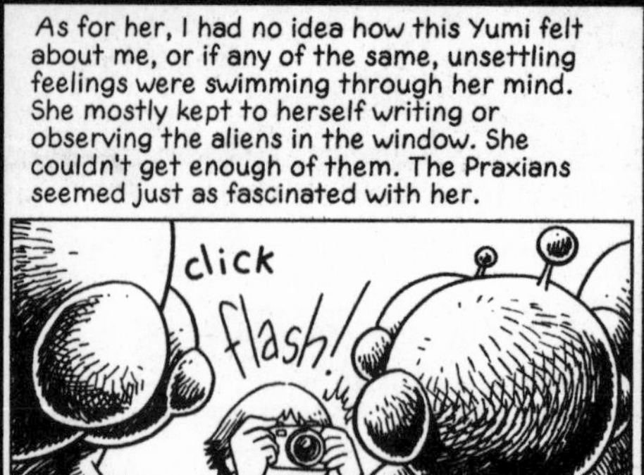
As for her, I had no idea how this Yumi felt about me, or if any of the same, unsettling feelings were swimming through her mind. She mostly kept to herself writing or observing the aliens in the window. She couldn't get enough of them. The Praxians seemed just as fascinated with her.
click
flash!
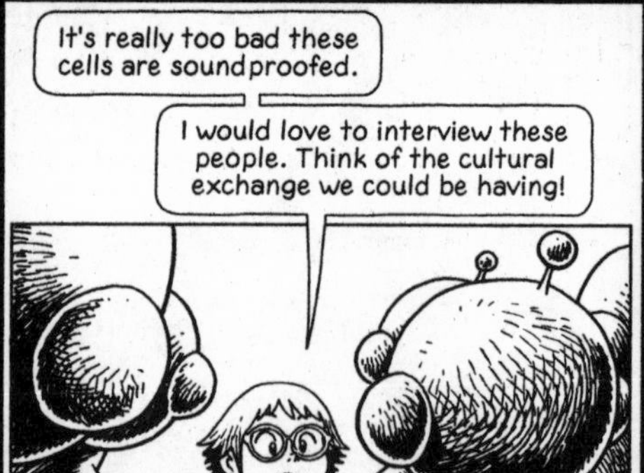
It's really too bad these cells are soundproofed.
I would love to interview these people. Think of the cultural exchange we could be having!

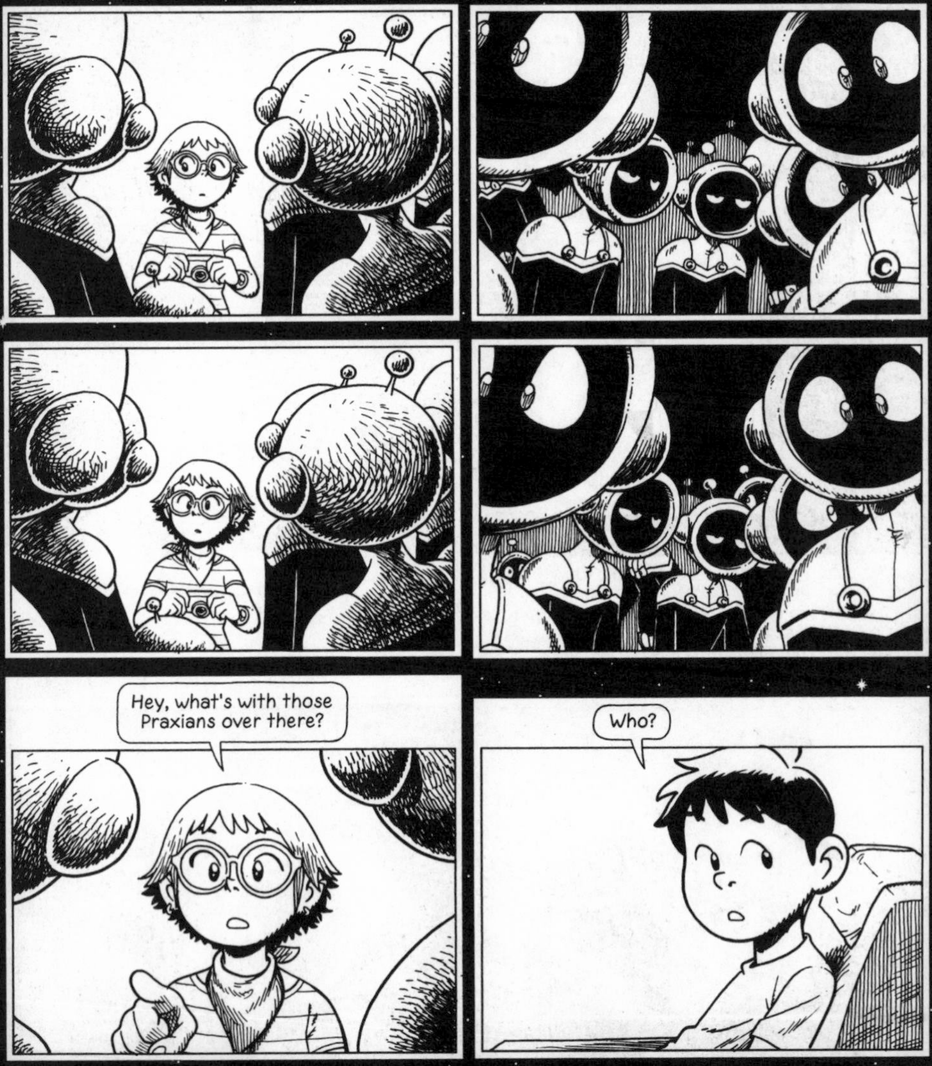

Hey, what's with those Praxians over there?
Who?

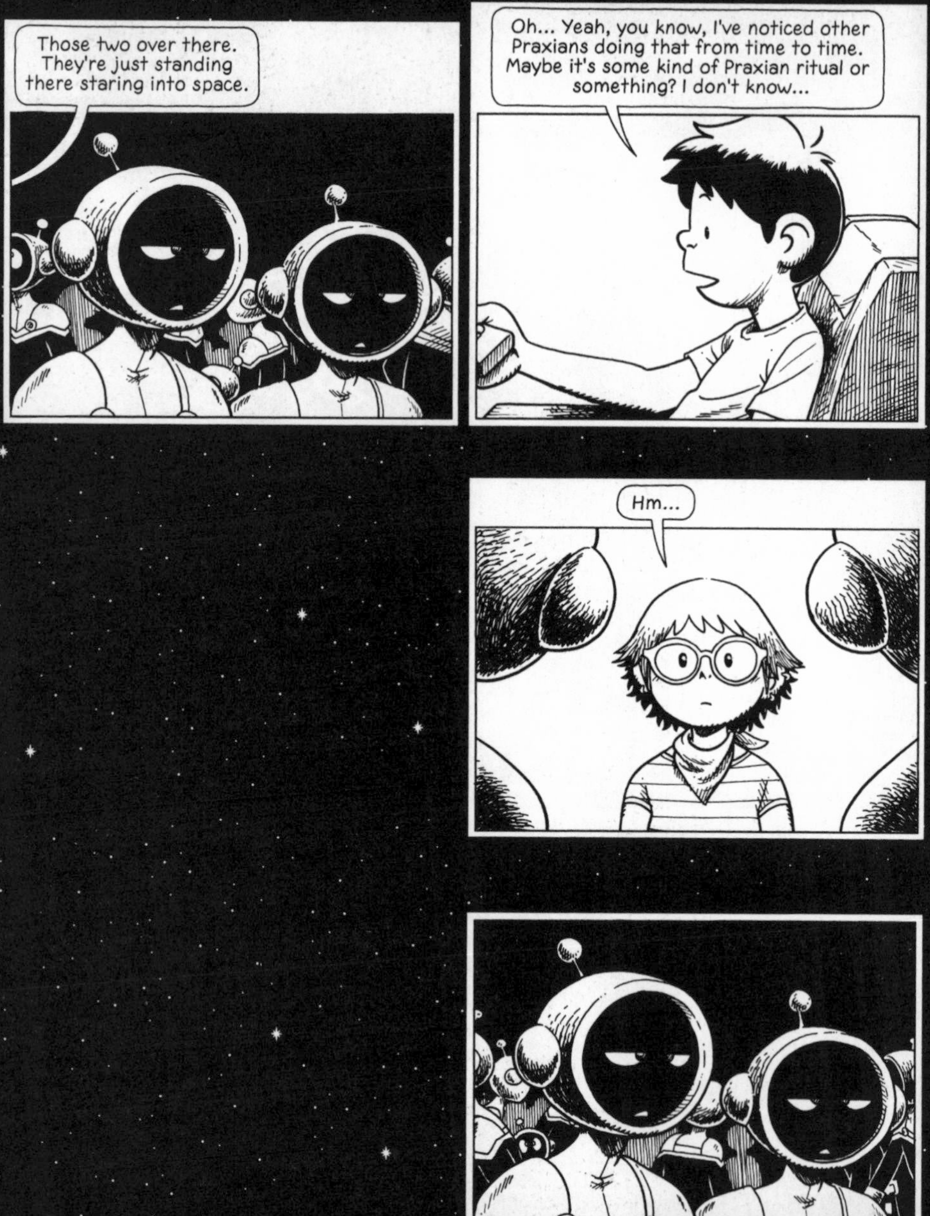
Those two over there. They're just standing there staring into space.
Oh... Yeah, you know, I've noticed other Praxians doing that from time to time. Maybe it's some kind of Praxian ritual or something? I don't know...
Hm...

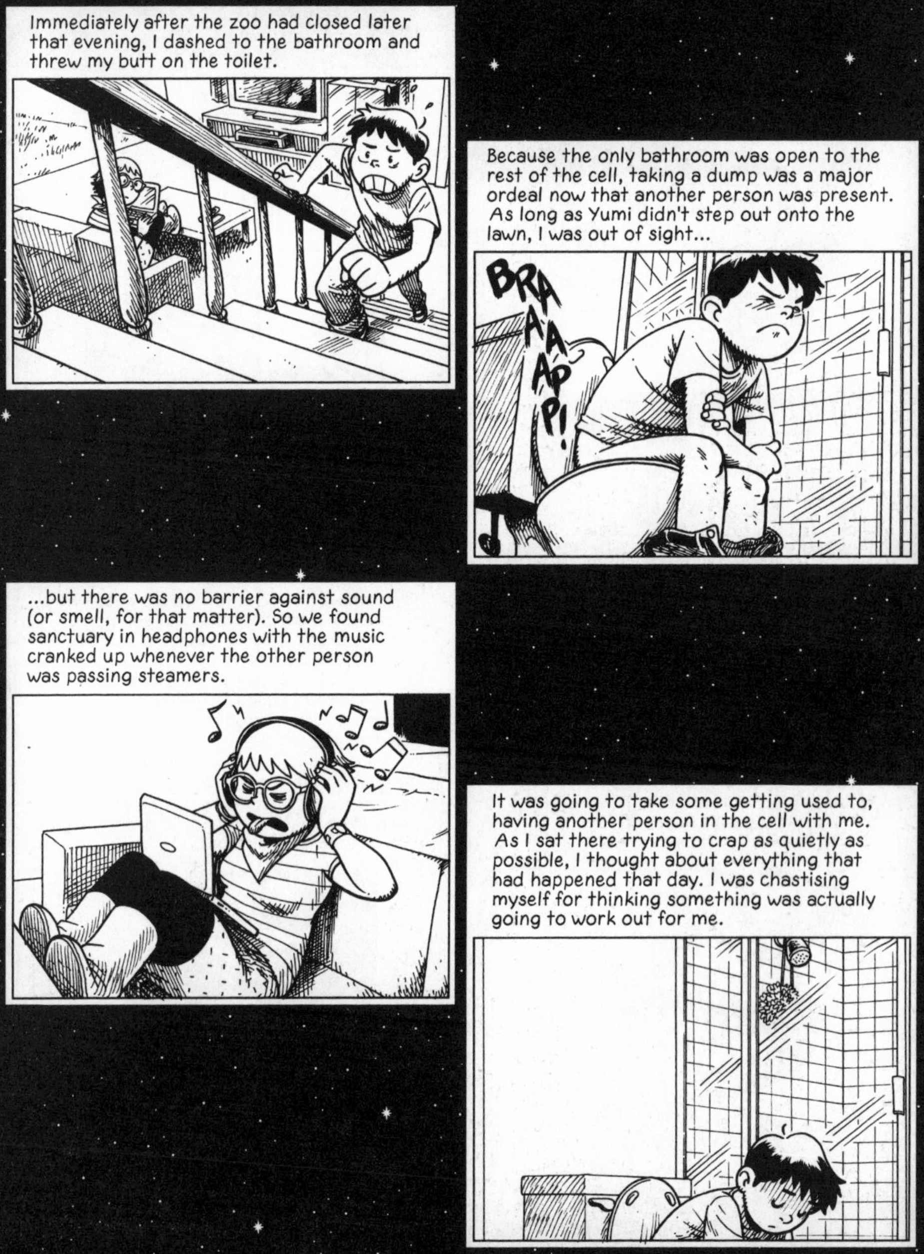
Immediately after the zoo had closed later that evening, I dashed to the bathroom and threw my butt on the toilet.
Because the only bathroom was open to the rest of the cell, taking a dump was a major ordeal now that another person was present. As long as Yumi didn't step out onto the lawn, I was out of sight...
BRAAAAPP!
...but there was no barrier against sound (or smell, for that matter). So we found sanctuary in headphones with the music cranked up whenever the other person was passing steamers.
It was going to take some getting used to, having another person in the cell with me. As I sat there trying to crap as quietly as possible, I thought about everything that had happened that day. I was chastising myself for thinking something was actually going to work out for me.

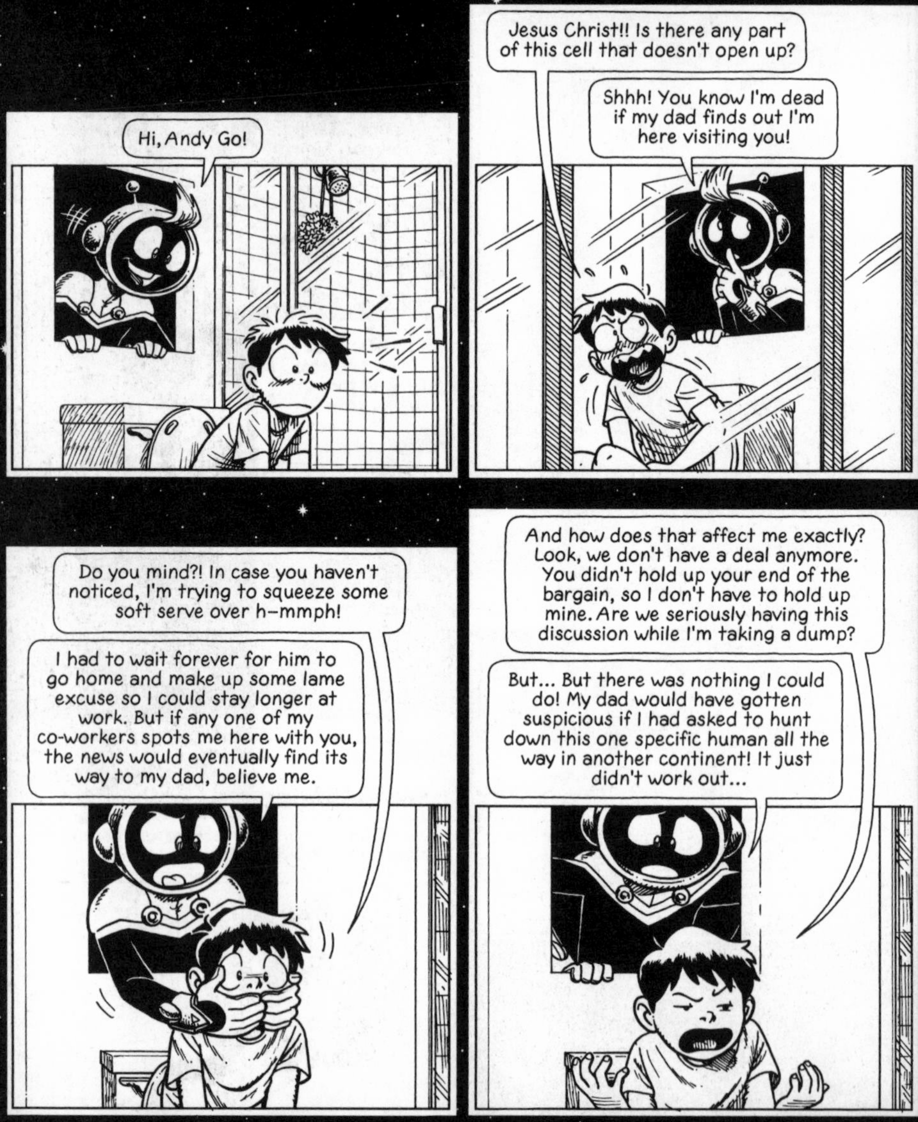
Hi, Andy Go!
Jesus Christ!! Is there any part of this cell that doesn't open up?
Shhh! You know I'm dead if my dad finds out I'm here visiting you!
Do you mind?! In case you haven't noticed, I'm trying to squeeze some soft serve over h—mmph!
I had to wait forever for him to go home and make up some lame excuse so I could stay longer at work. But if any one of my co-workers spots me here with you, the news would eventually find its way to my dad, believe me.
And how does that affect me exactly? Look, we don't have a deal anymore. You didn't hold up your end of the bargain, so I don't have to hold up mine. Are we seriously having this discussion while I'm taking a dump?
But... But there was nothing I could do! My dad would have gotten suspicious if I had asked to hunt down this one specific human all the way in another continent! It just didn't work out...

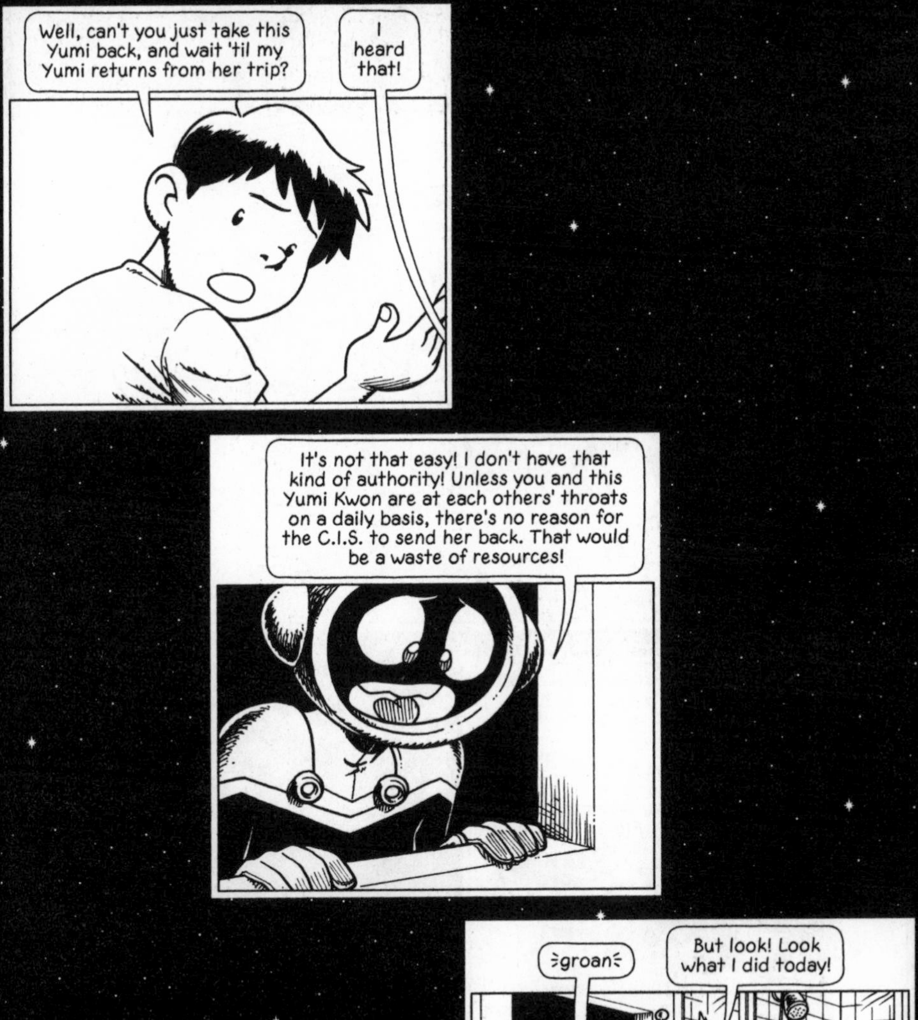
Well, can't you just take this Yumi back, and wait 'til my Yumi returns from her trip?
I heard that!
It's not that easy! I don't have that kind of authority! Unless you and this Yumi Kwon are at each others' throats on a daily basis, there's no reason for the C.I.S. to send her back. That would be a waste of resources!
groan
But look! Look what I did today!

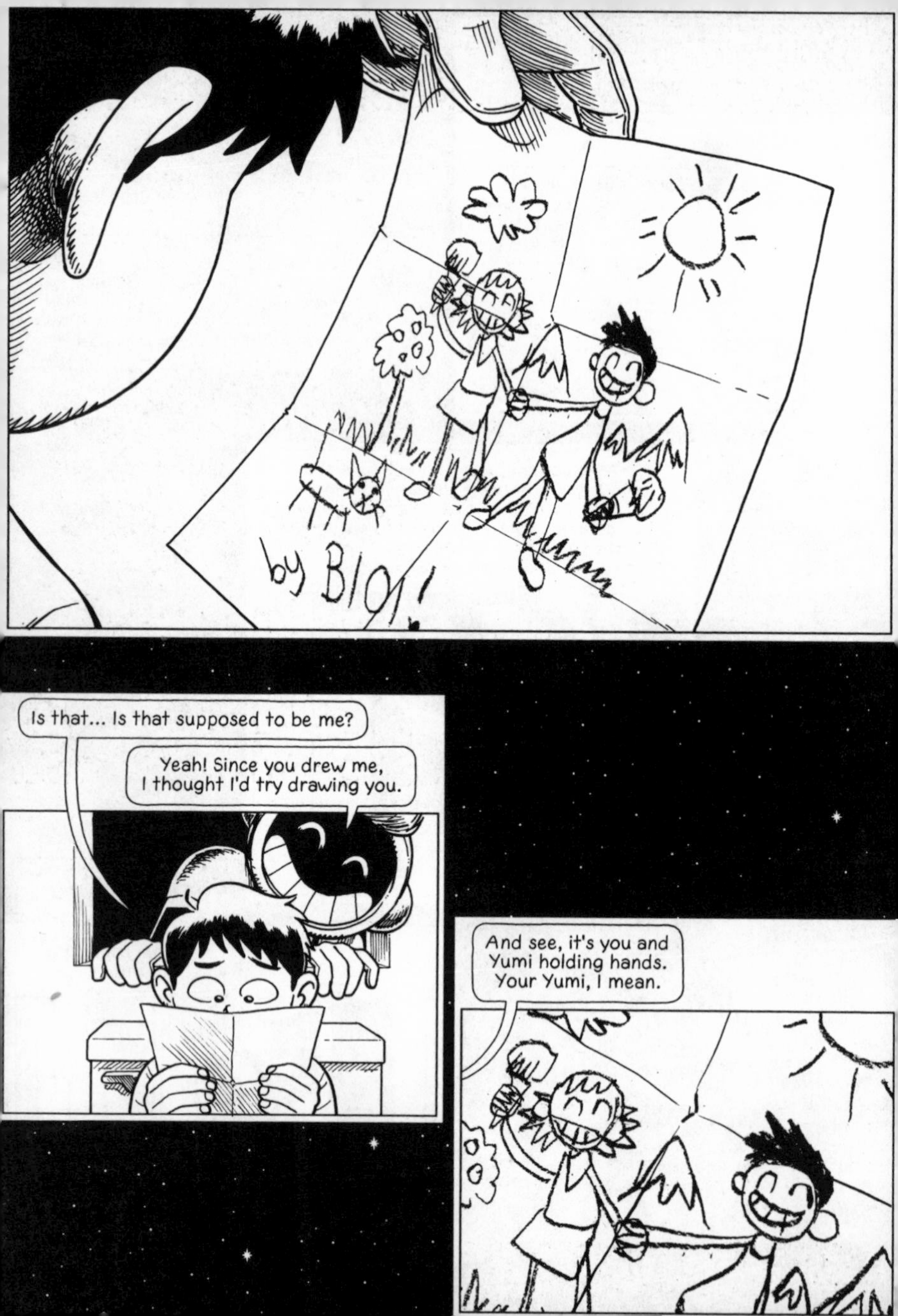
by BIOI!
Is that... Is that supposed to be me?
Yeah! Since you drew me, I thought I'd try drawing you.
And see, it's you and Yumi holding hands. Your Yumi, I mean.

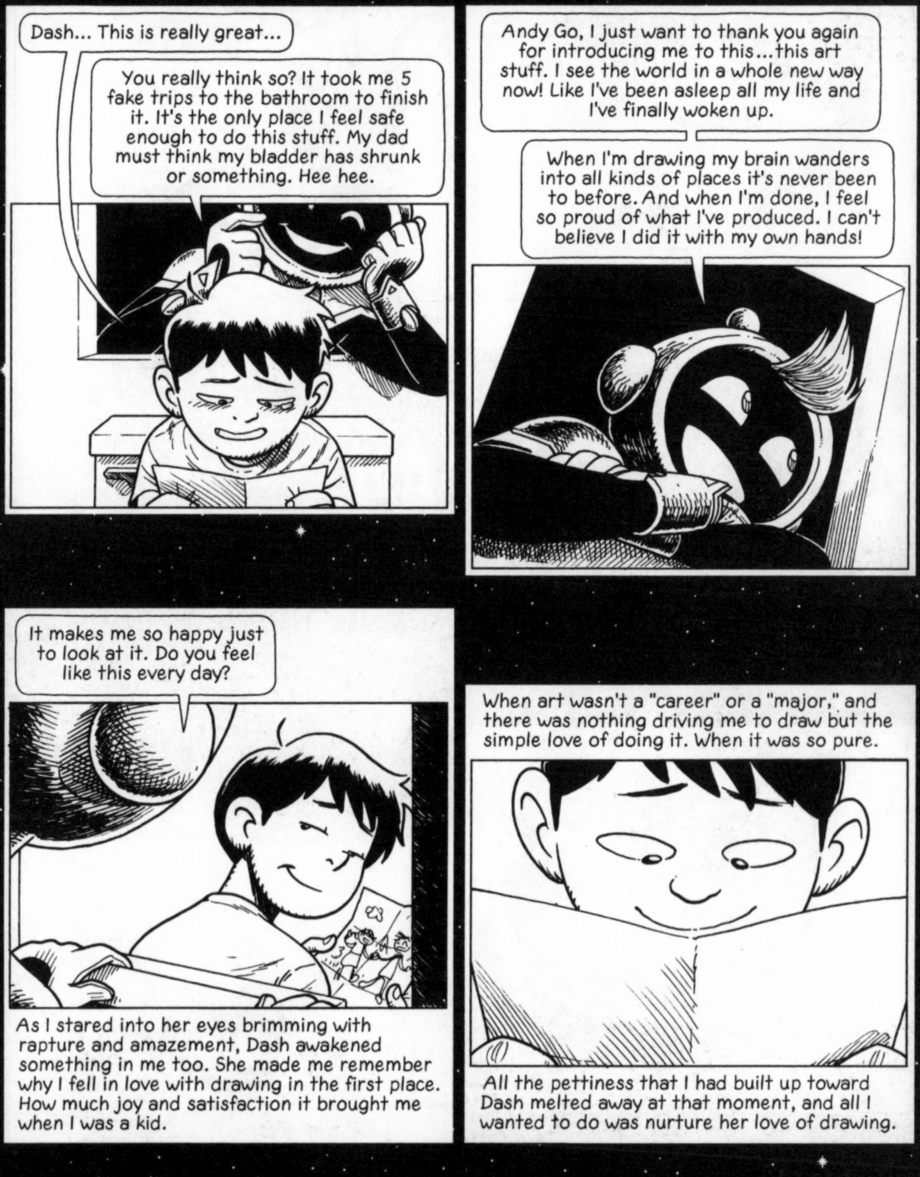
Dash... This is really great...
You really think so? It took me 5 fake trips to the bathroom to finish it. It's the only place I feel safe enough to do this stuff. My dad must think my bladder has shrunk or something. Hee hee.
Andy Go, I just want to thank you again for introducing me to this...this art stuff. I see the world in a whole new way now! Like I've been asleep all my life and I've finally woken up.
When I'm drawing my brain wanders into all kinds of places it's never been to before. And when I'm done, I feel so proud of what I've produced. I can't believe I did it with my own hands!
It makes me so happy just to look at it. Do you feel like this every day?
As I stared into her eyes brimming with rapture and amazement, Dash awakened something in me too. She made me remember why I fell in love with drawing in the first place. How much joy and satisfaction it brought me when I was a kid.
When art wasn't a "career" or a "major," and there was nothing driving me to draw but the simple love of doing it. When it was so pure.
All the pettiness that I had built up toward Dash melted away at that moment, and all I wanted to do was nurture her love of drawing.

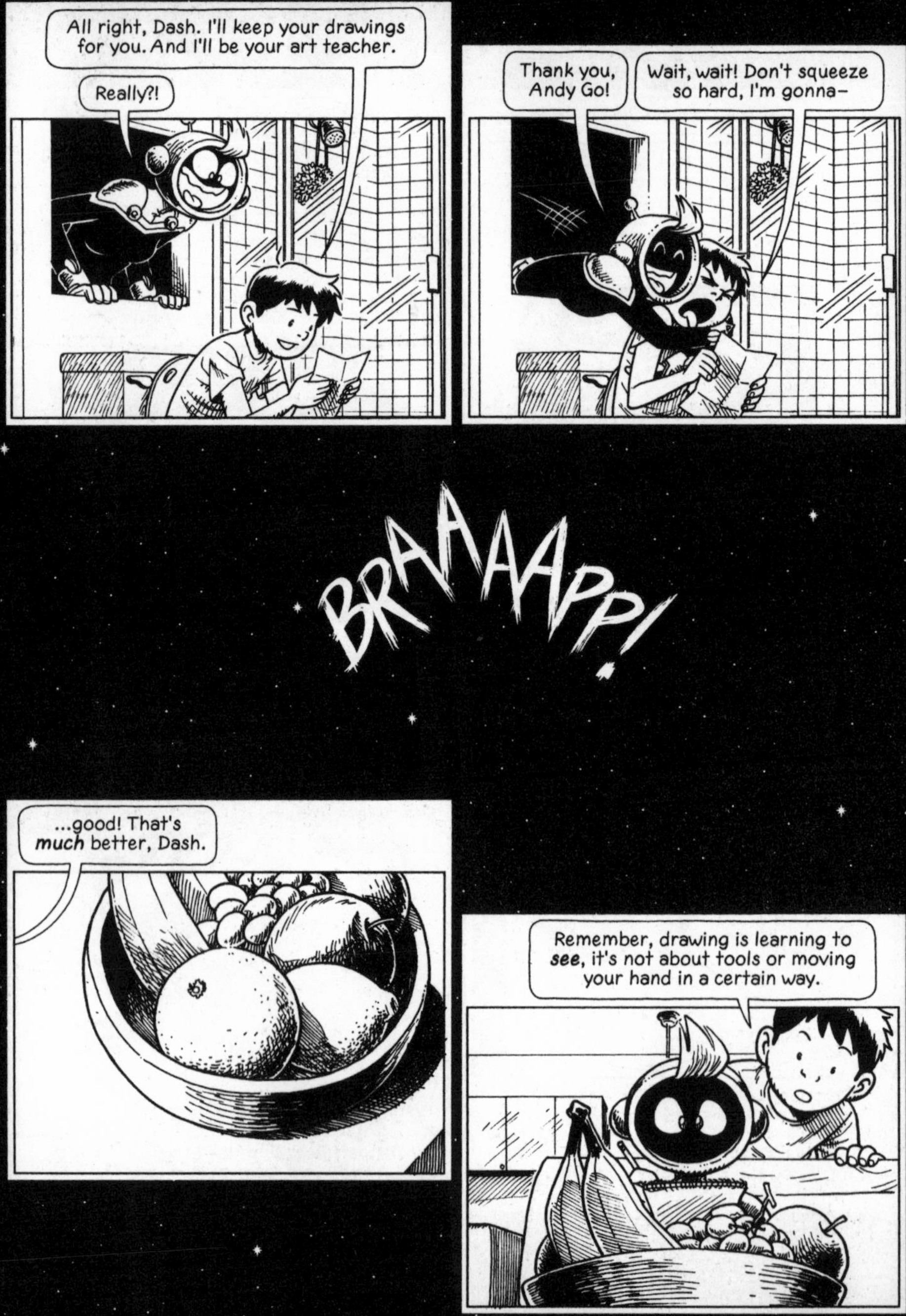
All right, Dash. I'll keep your drawings for you. And I'll be your art teacher.
Really?!
Thank you, Andy Go!
Wait, wait! Don't squeeze so hard, I'm gonna–
BRAAAAPP!
...good! That's *much* better, Dash.
Remember, drawing is learning to *see*, it's not about tools or moving your hand in a certain way.

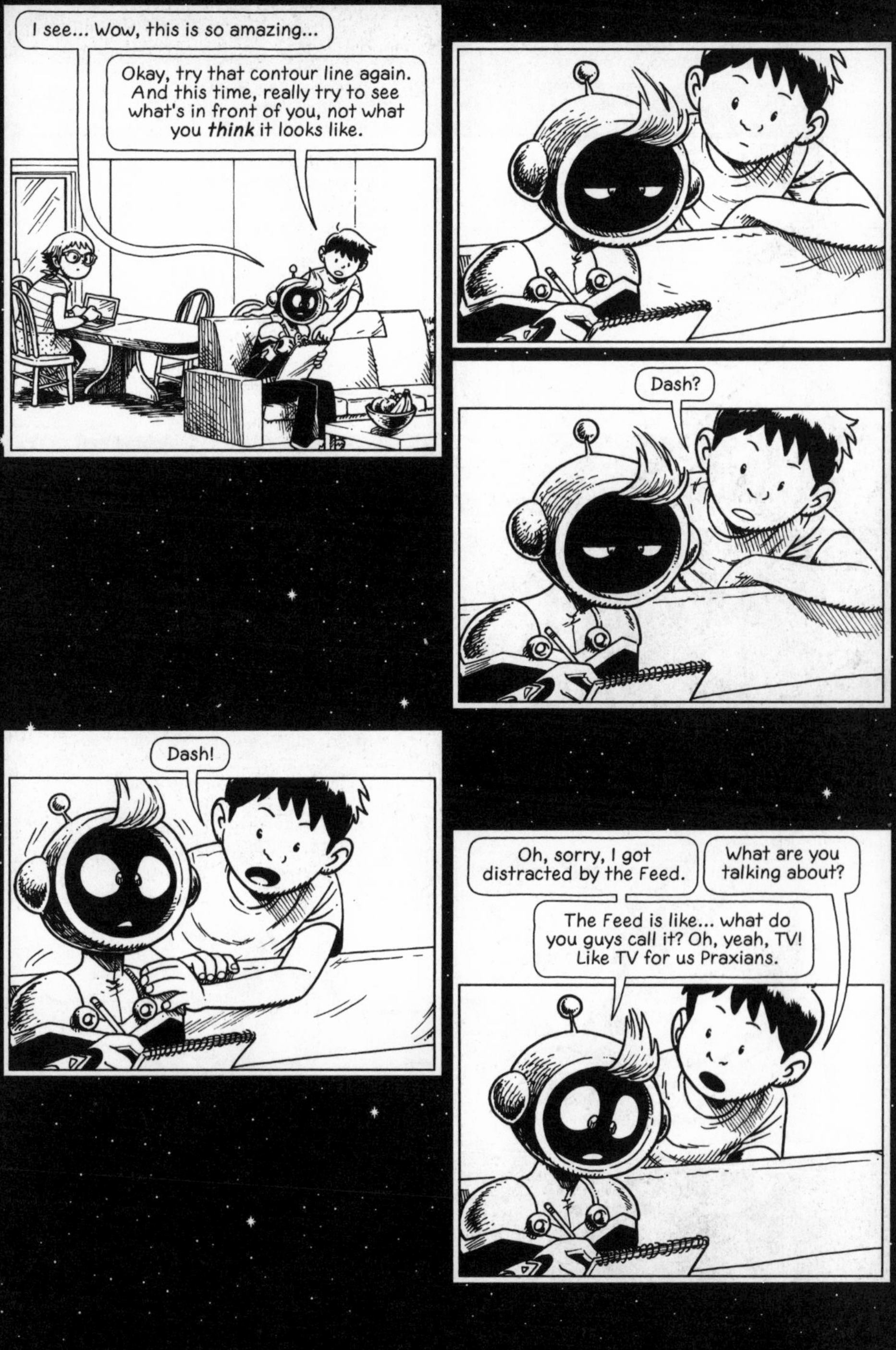
I see... Wow, this is so amazing...
Okay, try that contour line again. And this time, really try to see what's in front of you, not what you *think* it looks like.
Dash?
Dash!
Oh, sorry, I got distracted by the Feed.
What are you talking about?
The Feed is like... what do you guys call it? Oh, yeah, TV! Like TV for us Praxians.

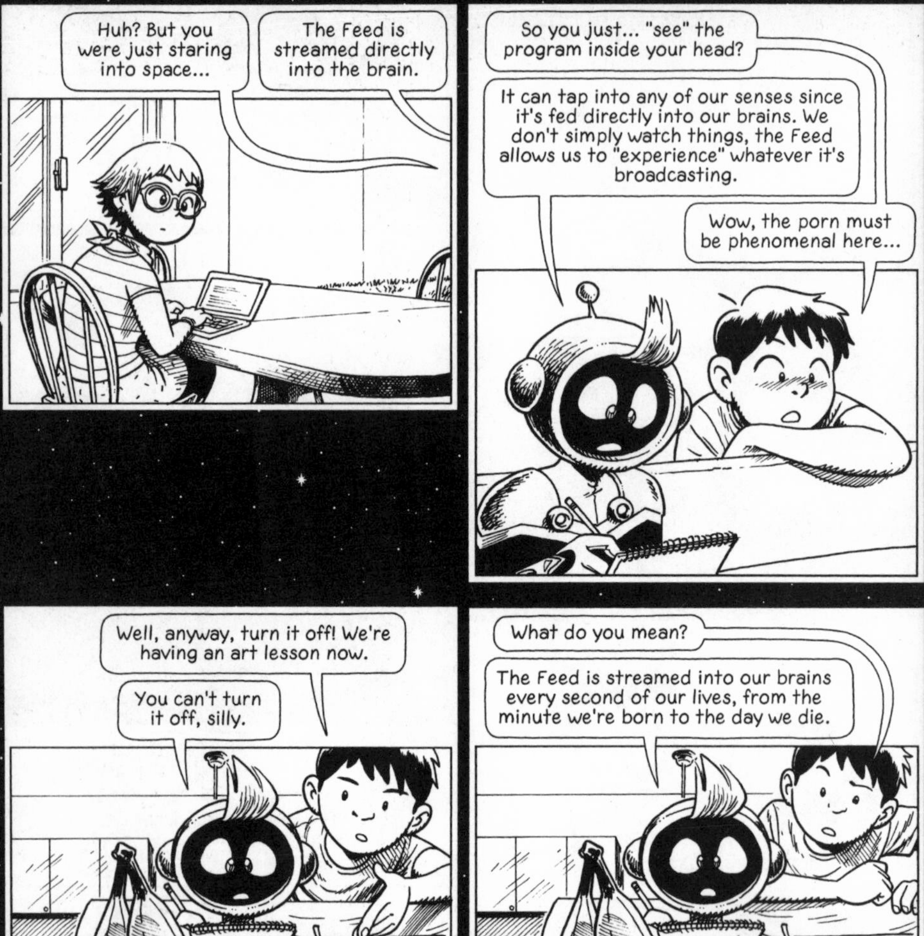

Huh? But you were just staring into space...
The Feed is streamed directly into the brain.
So you just... "see" the program inside your head?
It can tap into any of our senses since it's fed directly into our brains. We don't simply watch things, the Feed allows us to "experience" whatever it's broadcasting.
Wow, the porn must be phenomenal here...
Well, anyway, turn it off! We're having an art lesson now.
You can't turn it off, silly.
What do you mean?
The Feed is streamed into our brains every second of our lives, from the minute we're born to the day we die.

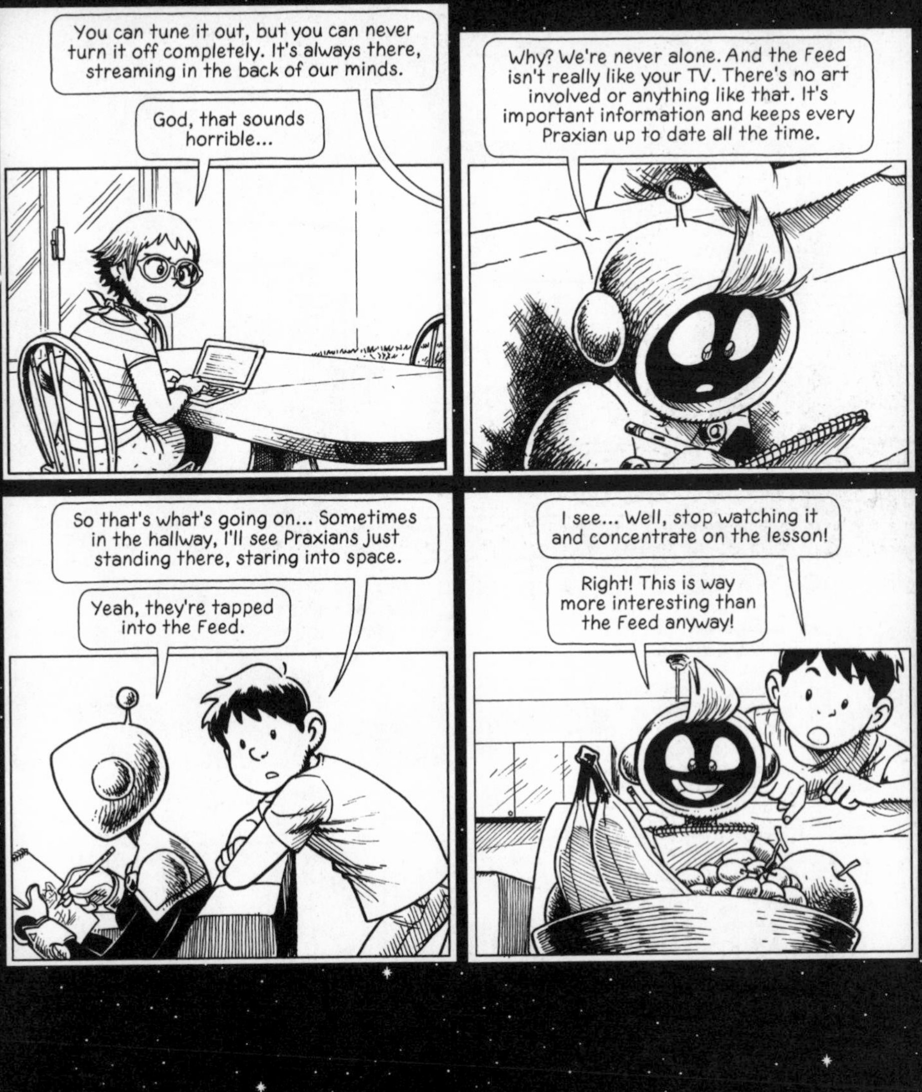
You can tune it out, but you can never turn it off completely. It's always there, streaming in the back of our minds.
God, that sounds horrible...
Why? We're never alone. And the Feed isn't really like your TV. There's no art involved or anything like that. It's important information and keeps every Praxian up to date all the time.
So that's what's going on... Sometimes in the hallway, I'll see Praxians just standing there, staring into space.
Yeah, they're tapped into the Feed.
I see... Well, stop watching it and concentrate on the lesson!
Right! This is way more interesting than the Feed anyway!

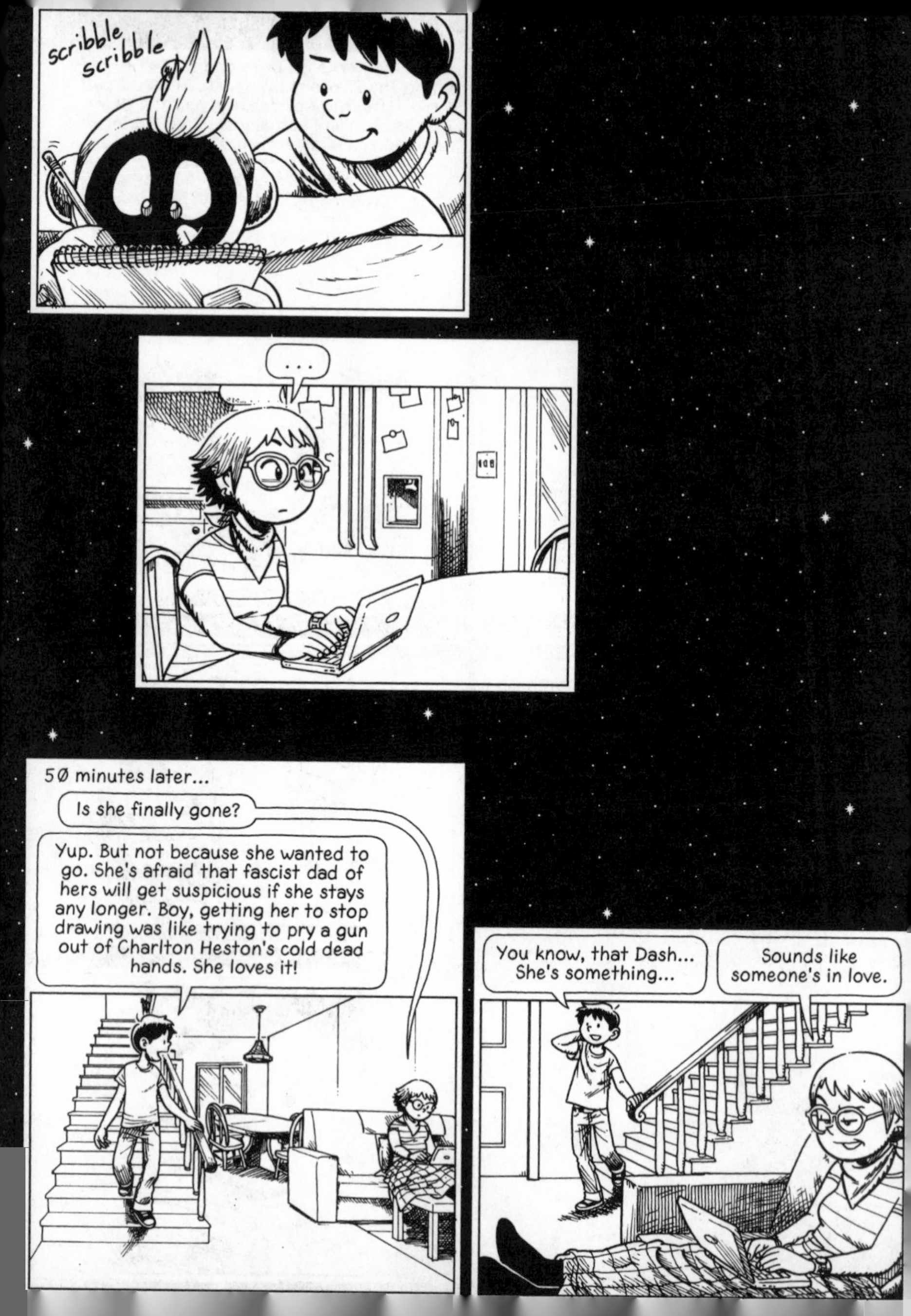
scribble scribble
. . .
50 minutes later...
Is she finally gone?
Yup. But not because she wanted to go. She's afraid that fascist dad of hers will get suspicious if she stays any longer. Boy, getting her to stop drawing was like trying to pry a gun out of Charlton Heston's cold dead hands. She loves it!
You know, that Dash... She's something...
Sounds like someone's in love.

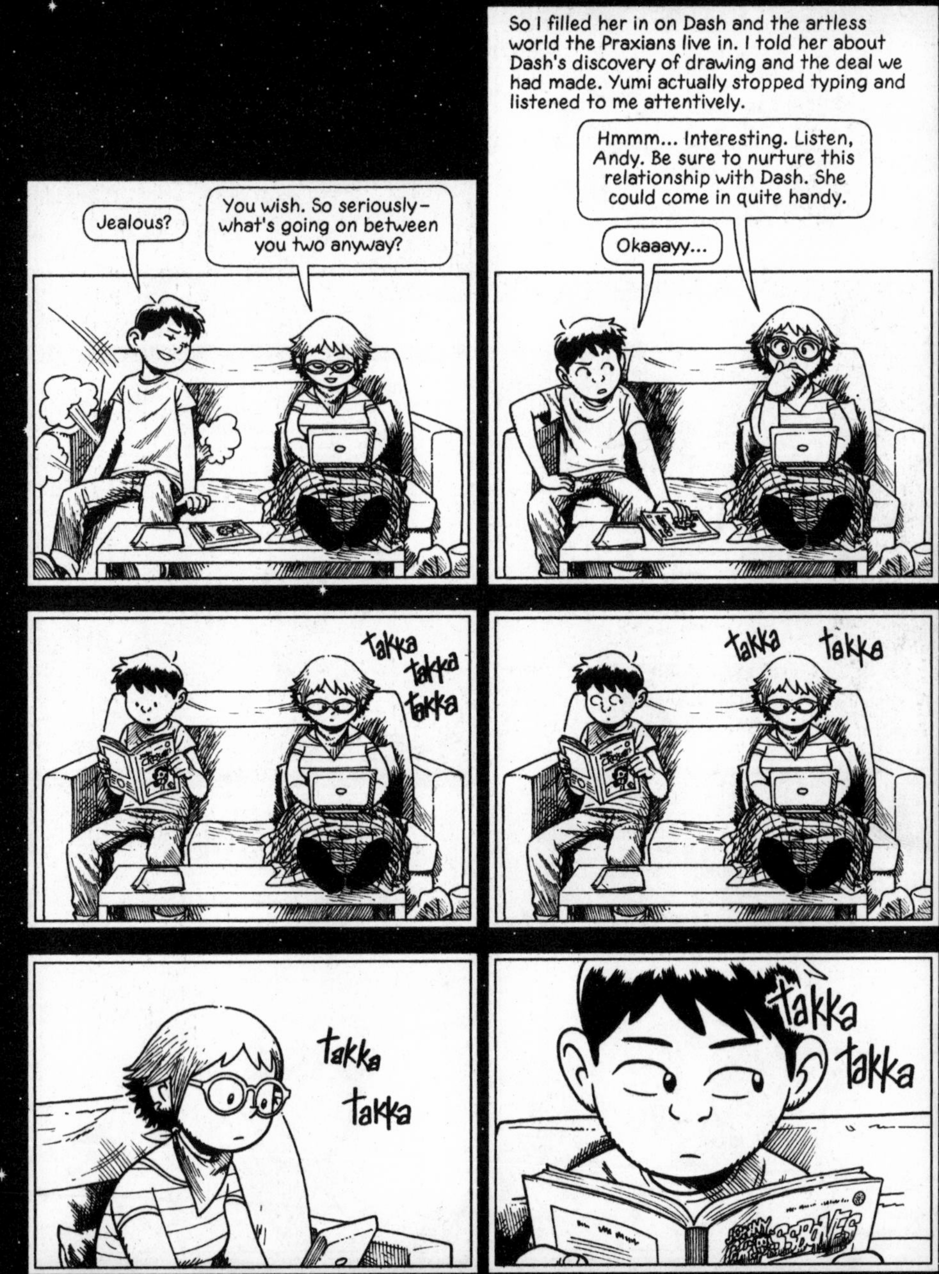
Jealous?
You wish. So seriously–what's going on between you two anyway?
So I filled her in on Dash and the artless world the Praxians live in. I told her about Dash's discovery of drawing and the deal we had made. Yumi actually stopped typing and listened to me attentively.
Hmmm... Interesting. Listen, Andy. Be sure to nurture this relationship with Dash. She could come in quite handy.
Okaaayy...
takka takka takka
takka takka
takka takka
takka takka

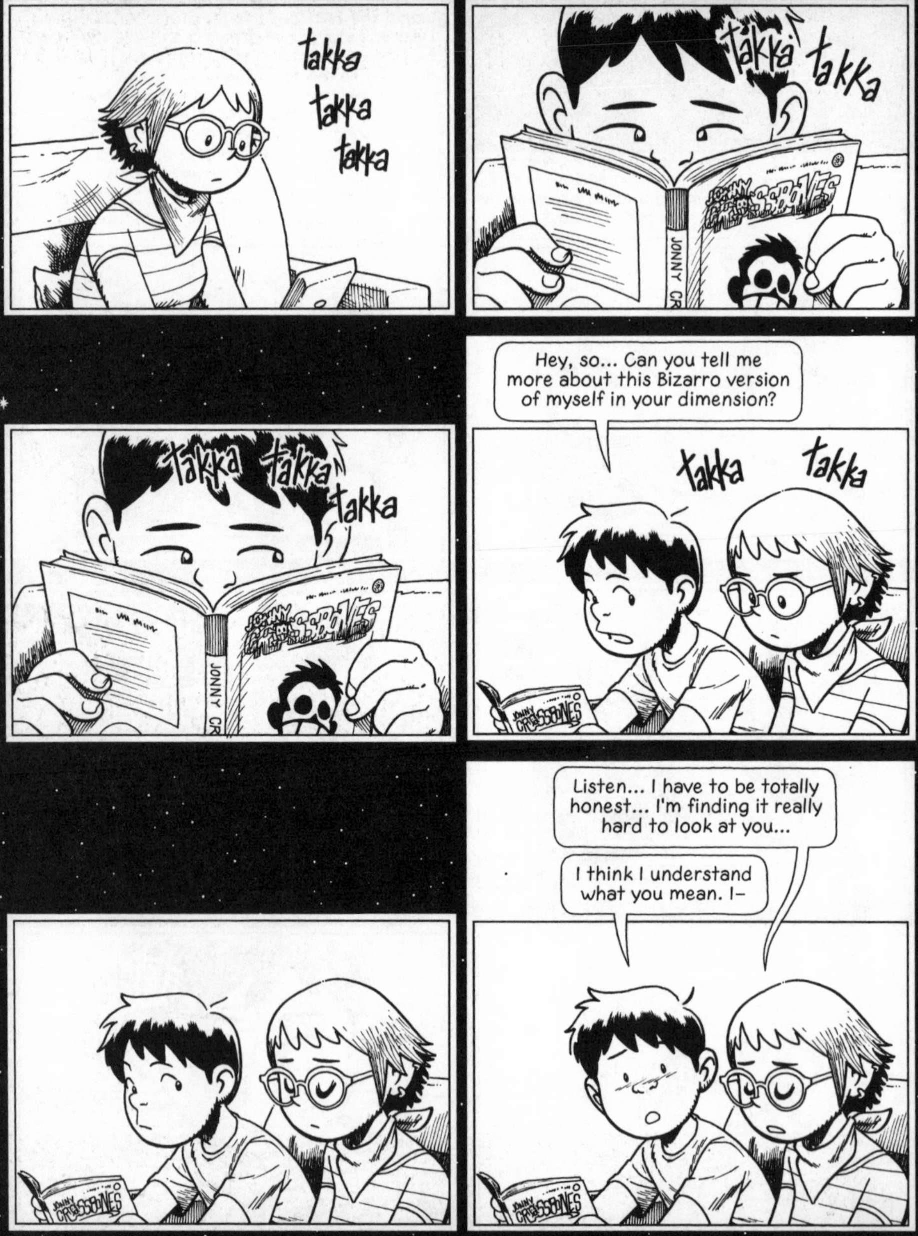
takka
takka
takka
takka
takka
takka
takka
takka
Hey, so... Can you tell me more about this Bizarro version of myself in your dimension?
takka
takka
Listen... I have to be totally honest... I'm finding it really hard to look at you...
I think I understand what you mean. I–

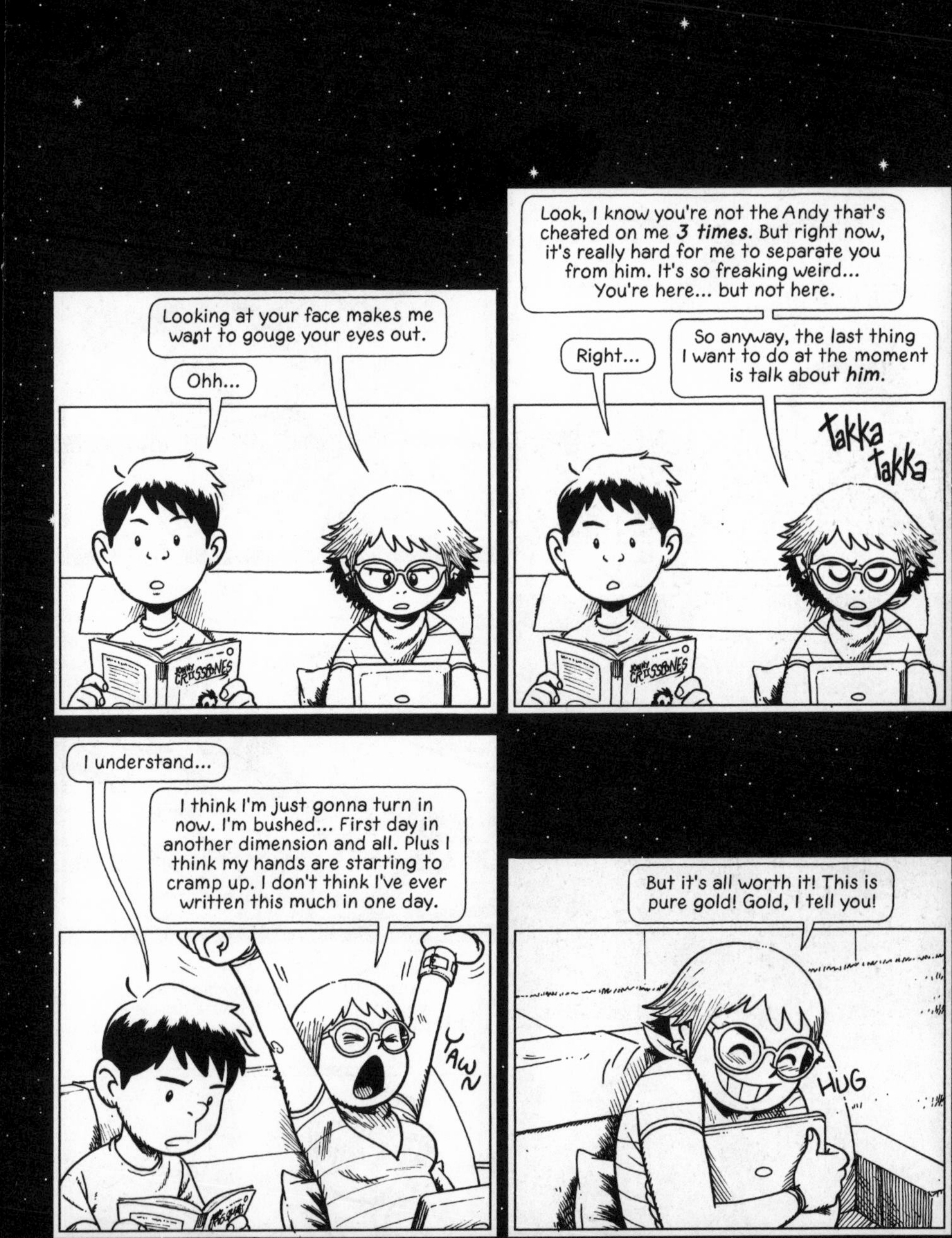
Looking at your face makes me want to gouge your eyes out.
Ohh...
Look, I know you're not the Andy that's cheated on me *3 times*. But right now, it's really hard for me to separate you from him. It's so freaking weird... You're here... but not here.
Right...
So anyway, the last thing I want to do at the moment is talk about *him*.
TAKKA TAKKA
I understand...
I think I'm just gonna turn in now. I'm bushed... First day in another dimension and all. Plus I think my hands are starting to cramp up. I don't think I've ever written this much in one day.
YAWN
But it's all worth it! This is pure gold! Gold, I tell you!
HUG

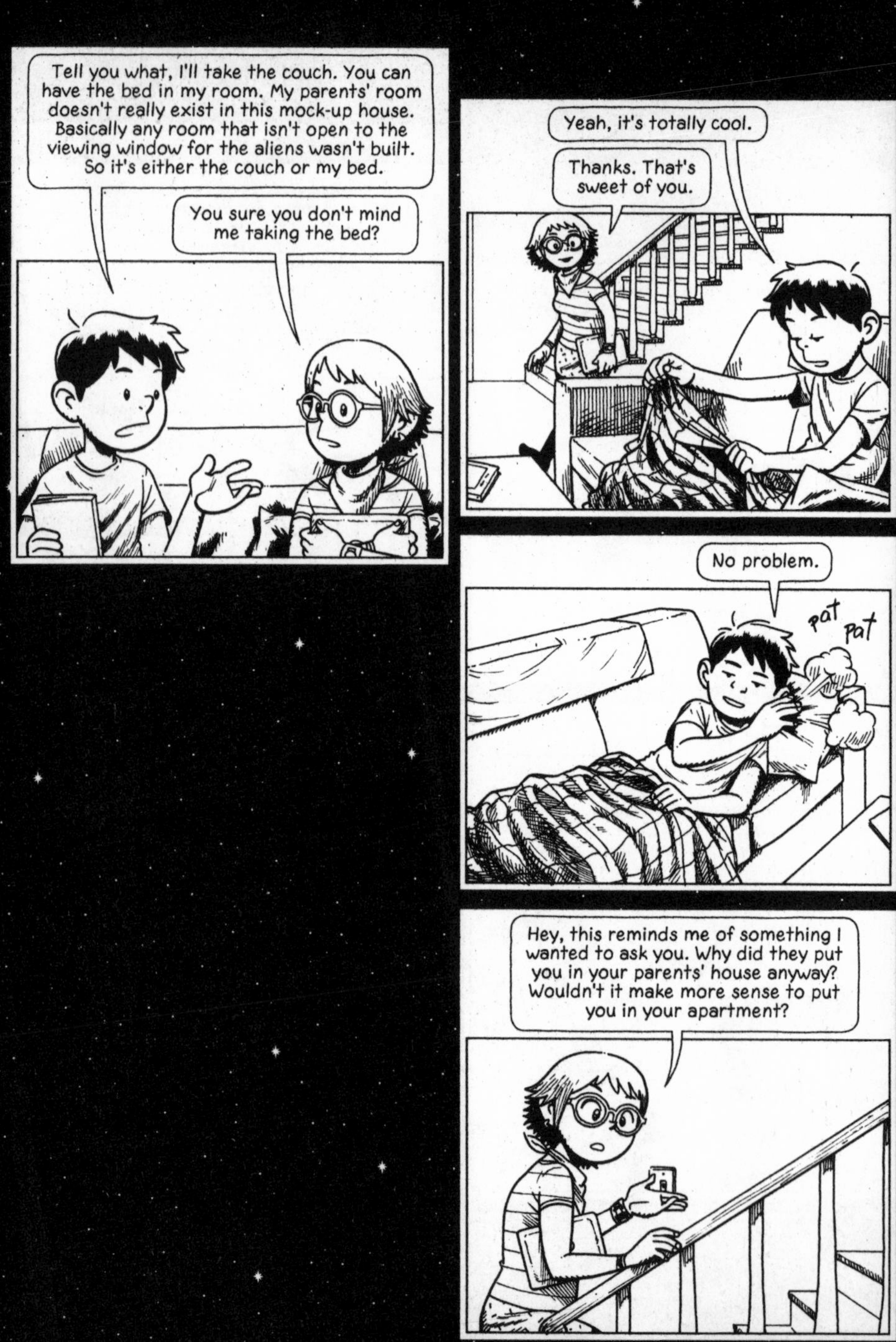

Tell you what, I'll take the couch. You can have the bed in my room. My parents' room doesn't really exist in this mock-up house. Basically any room that isn't open to the viewing window for the aliens wasn't built. So it's either the couch or my bed.
You sure you don't mind me taking the bed?
Yeah, it's totally cool.
Thanks. That's sweet of you.
No problem.
pat pat
Hey, this reminds me of something I wanted to ask you. Why did they put you in your parents' house anyway? Wouldn't it make more sense to put you in your apartment?

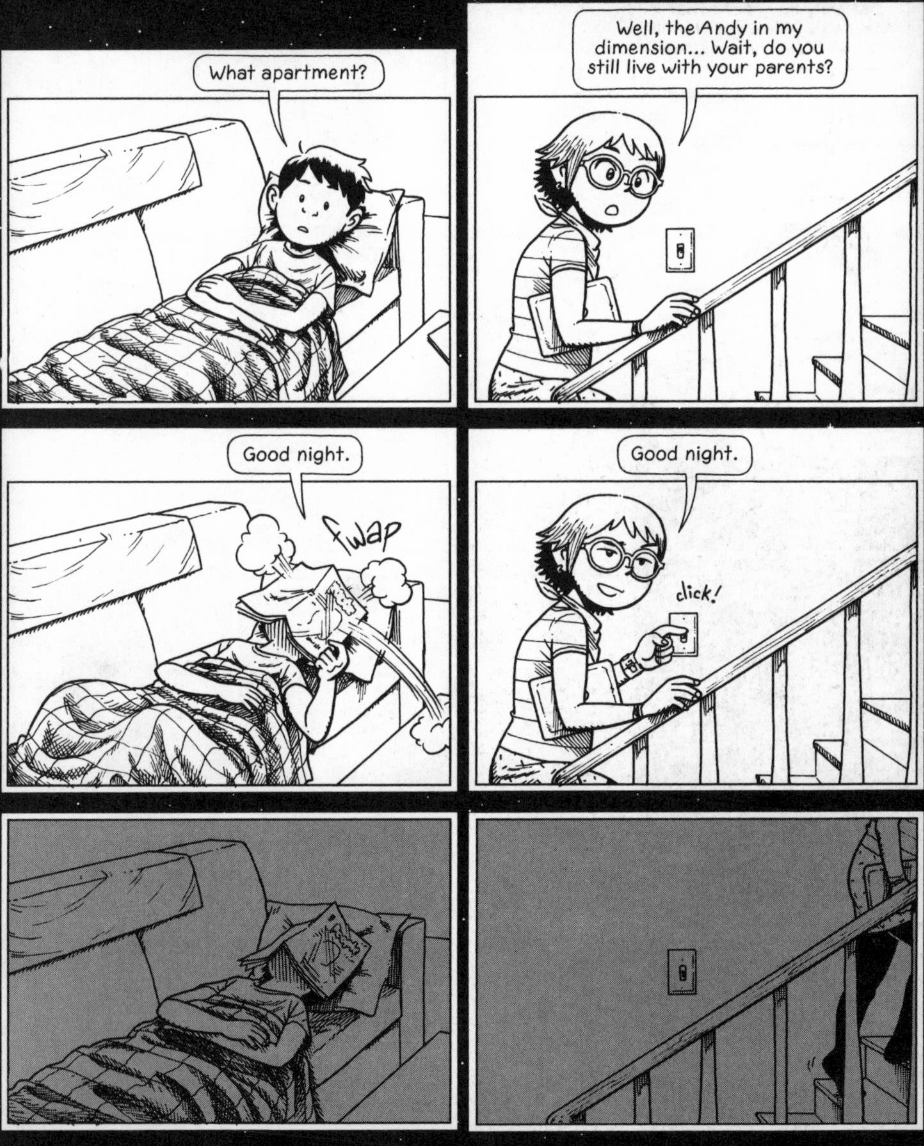
What apartment?
Well, the Andy in my dimension... Wait, do you still live with your parents?
Good night.
fwap
Good night.
click!

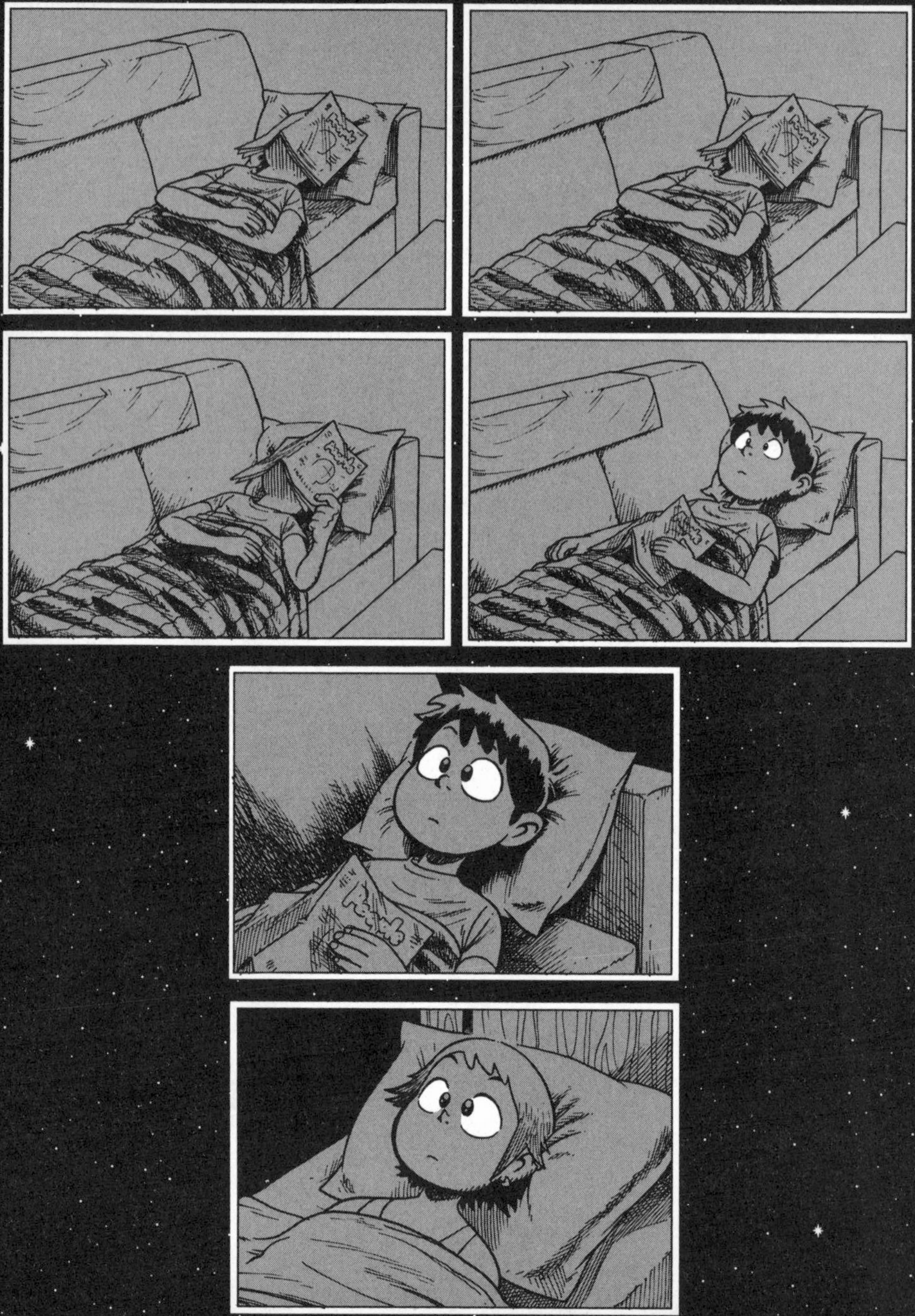

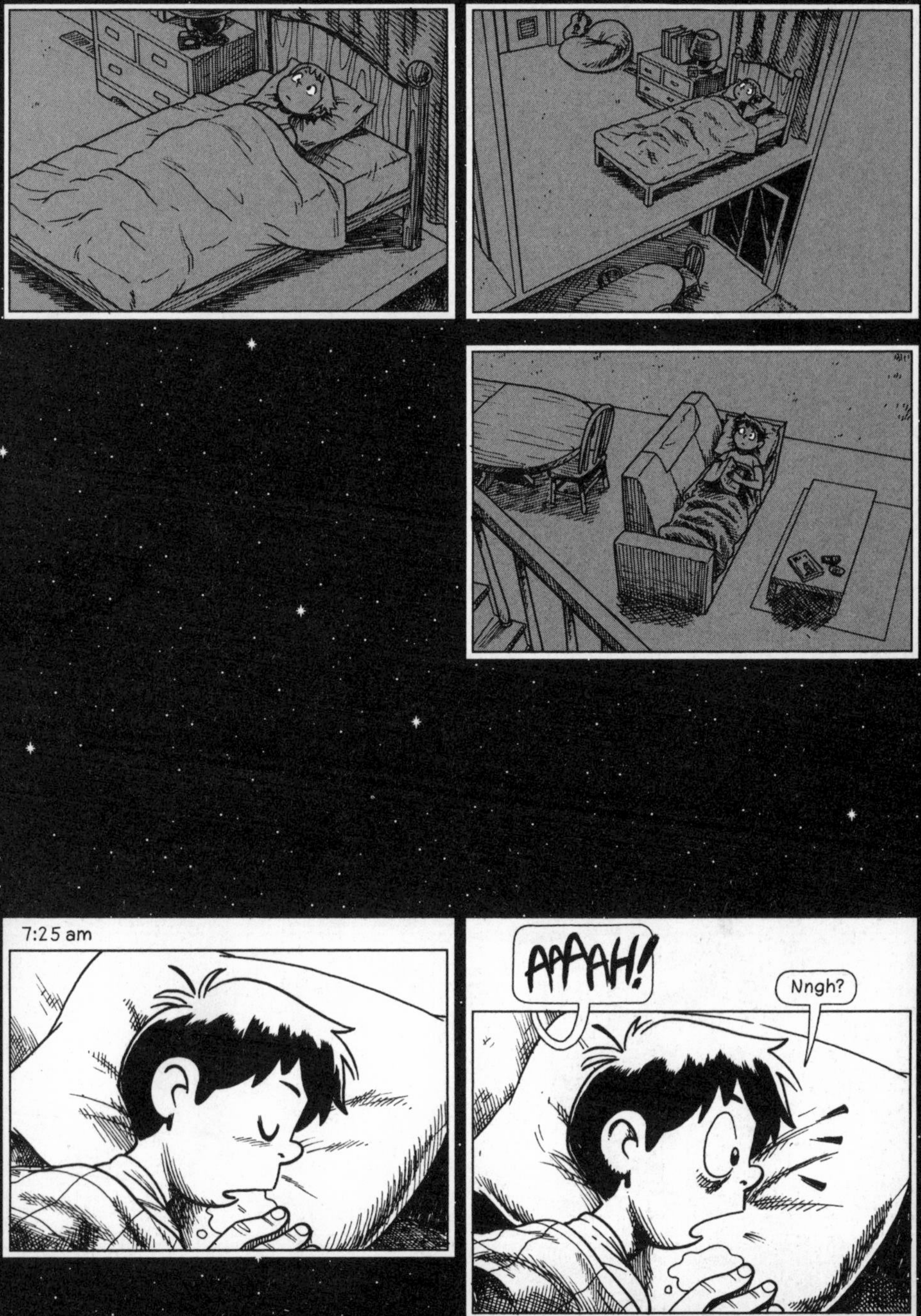
7:25 am
AAAAH!
Nngh?

Yumi?!
DASH!
Yumi! Are you okay? What's wrong?
Gyaah!
BAM!
What?! What is it?
S-s-spider!!!
??
ZIP!

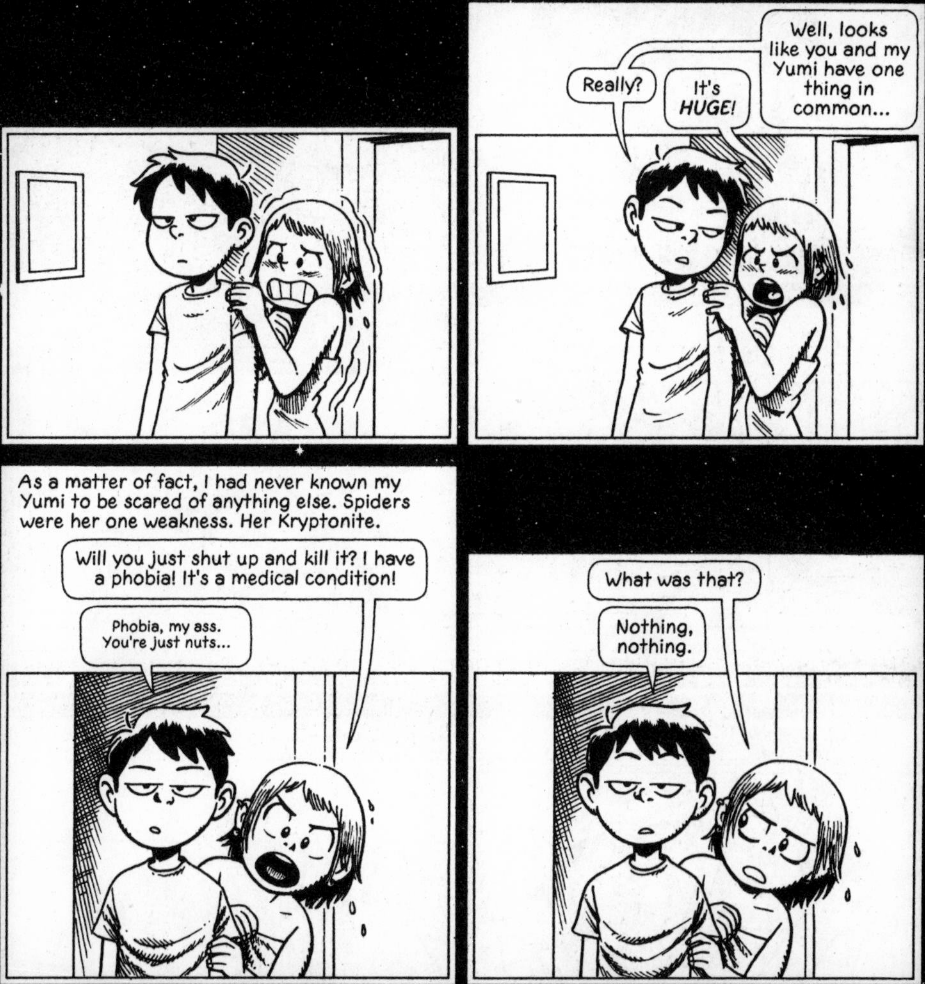
Well, looks like you and my Yumi have one thing in common...
It's *HUGE!*
Really?
As a matter of fact, I had never known my Yumi to be scared of anything else. Spiders were her one weakness. Her Kryptonite.
Will you just shut up and kill it? I have a phobia! It's a medical condition!
Phobia, my ass. You're just nuts...
What was that?
Nothing, nothing.

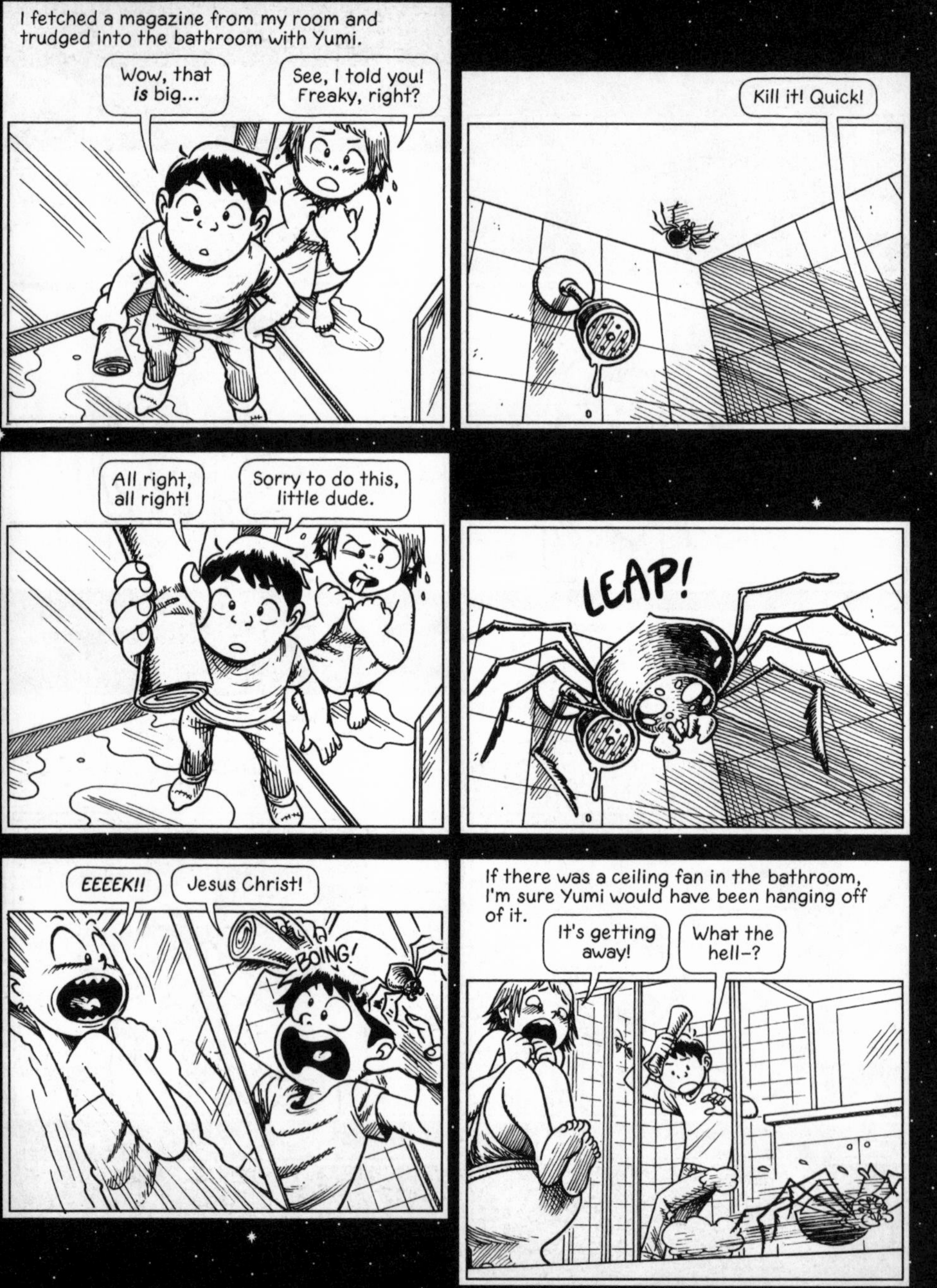

I fetched a magazine from my room and trudged into the bathroom with Yumi.
Wow, that *is* big...
See, I told you! Freaky, right?
Kill it! Quick!
All right, all right!
Sorry to do this, little dude.
LEAP!
EEEEK!!
Jesus Christ!
BOING!
If there was a ceiling fan in the bathroom, I'm sure Yumi would have been hanging off of it.
It's getting away!
What the hell–?

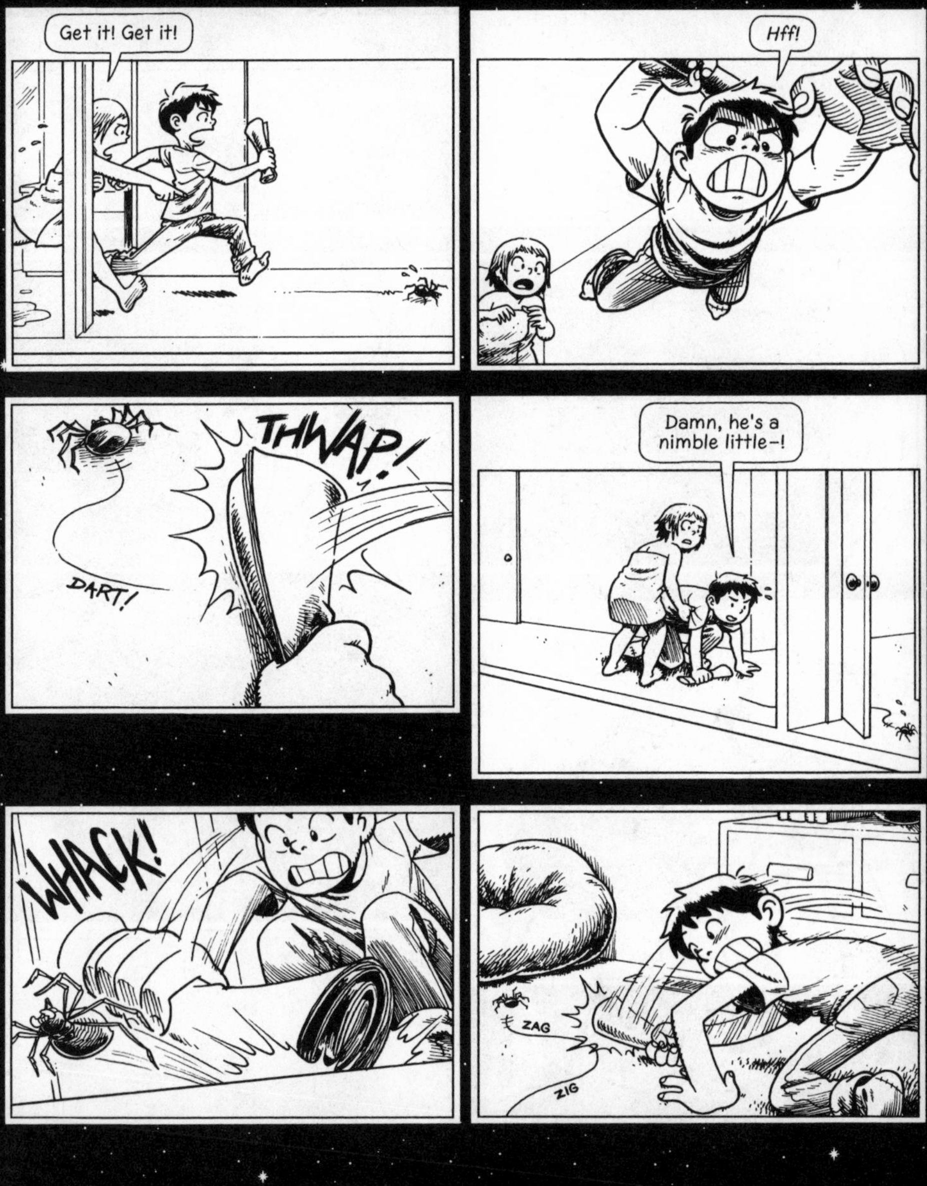
Get it! Get it!
Hff!
THWAP!
DART!
Damn, he's a nimble little-!
WHACK!
ZAG
ZIG

ZIP!

There he is! Quick! Come on, Andy!

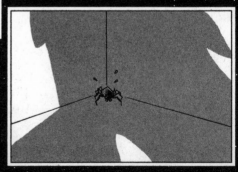

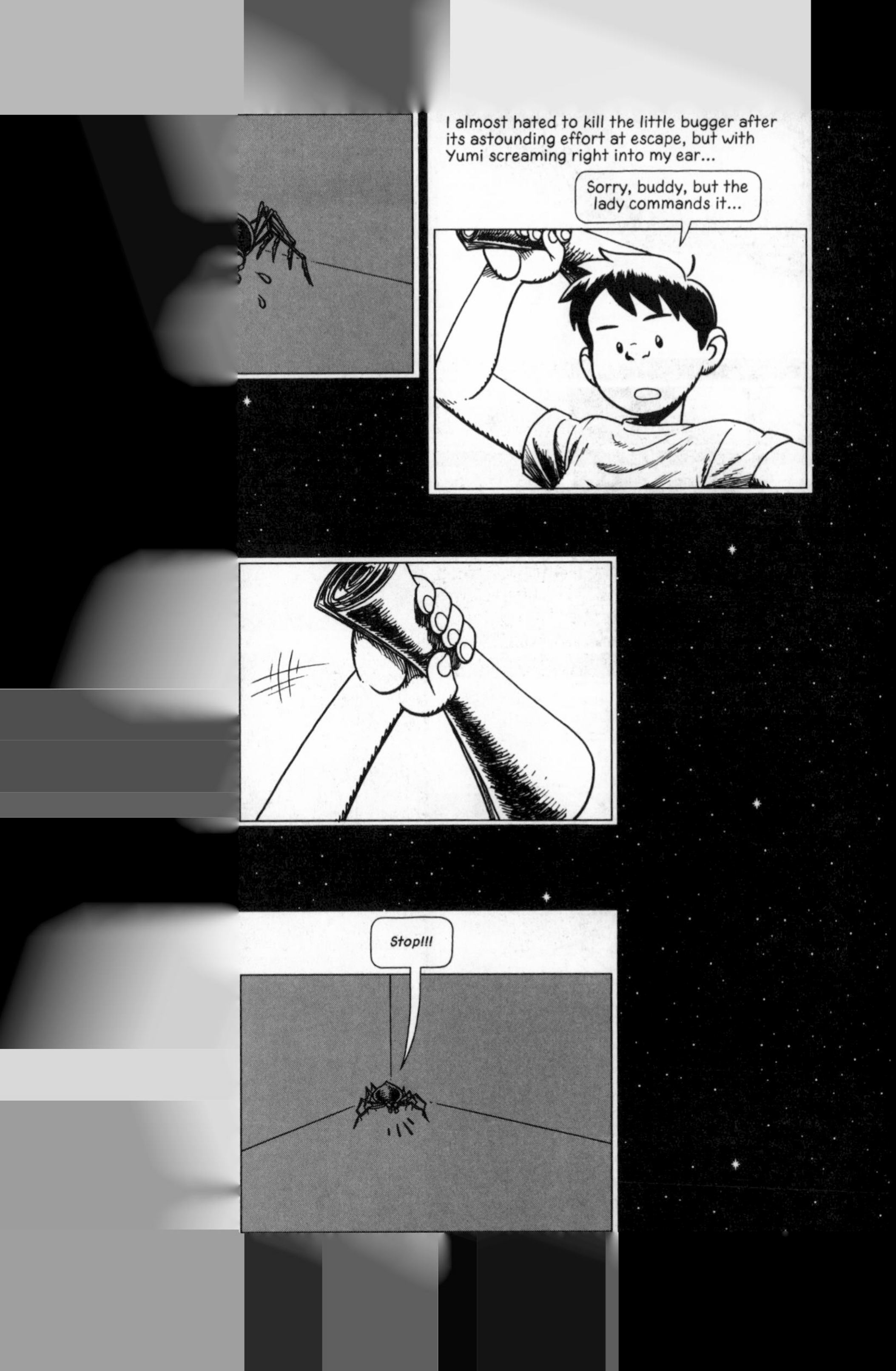
I almost hated to kill the little bugger after its astounding effort at escape, but with Yumi screaming right into my ear...
Sorry, buddy, but the lady commands it...
Stop!!!

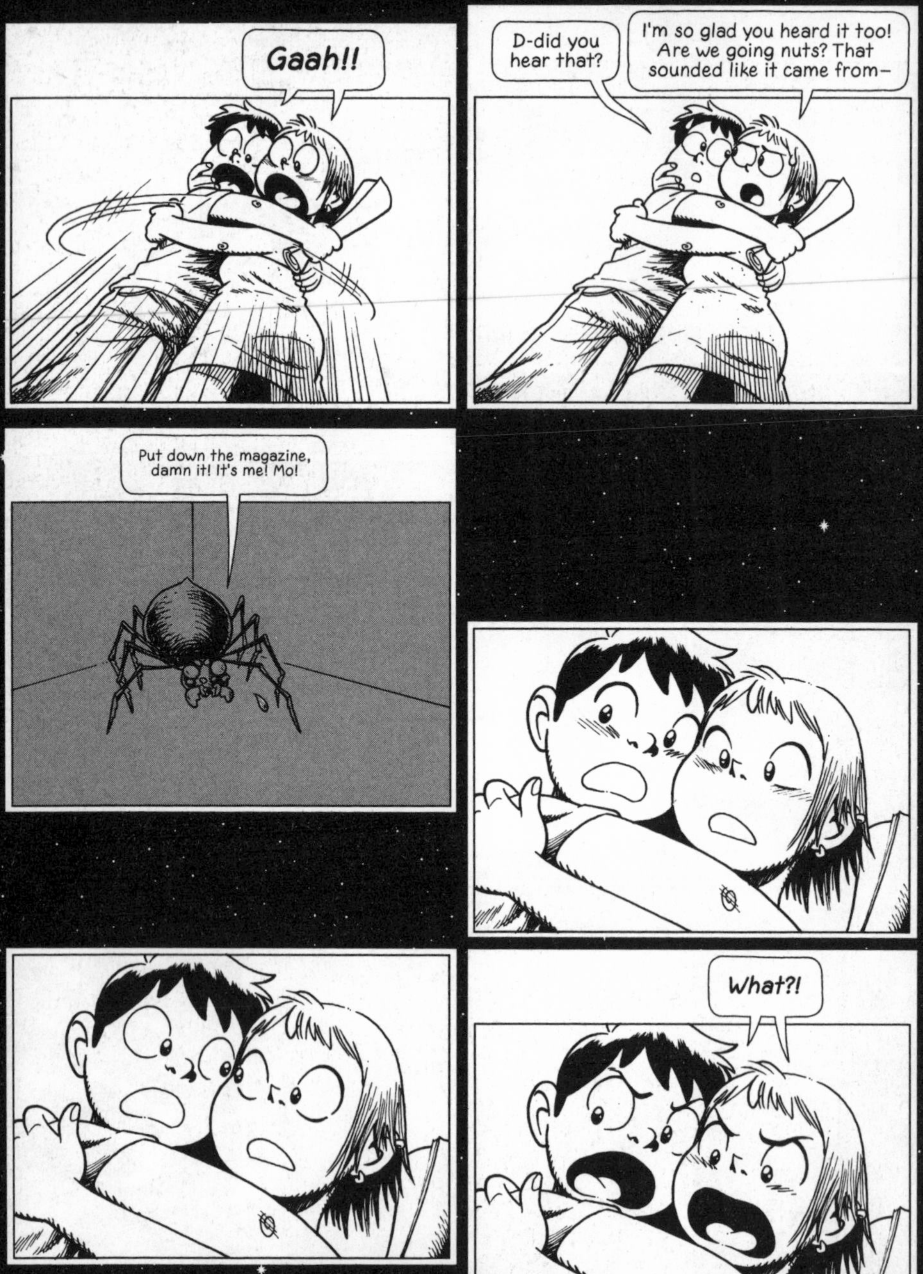
Gaah!!
D-did you hear that?
I'm so glad you heard it too! Are we going nuts? That sounded like it came from–
Put down the magazine, damn it! It's me! Mo!
What?!

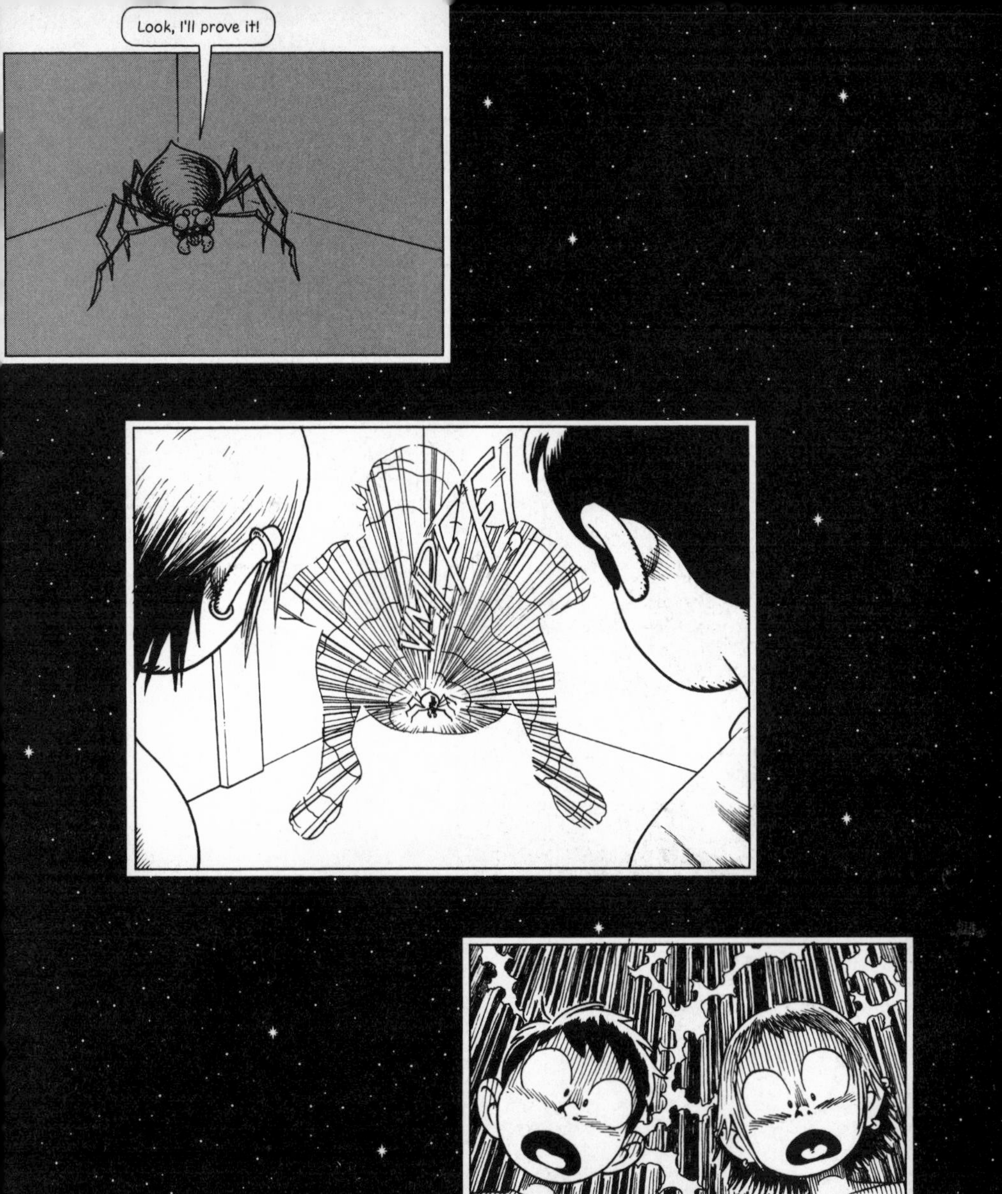

Look, I'll prove it!
WMPFF!

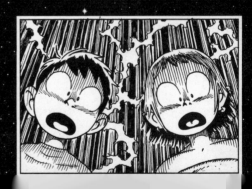

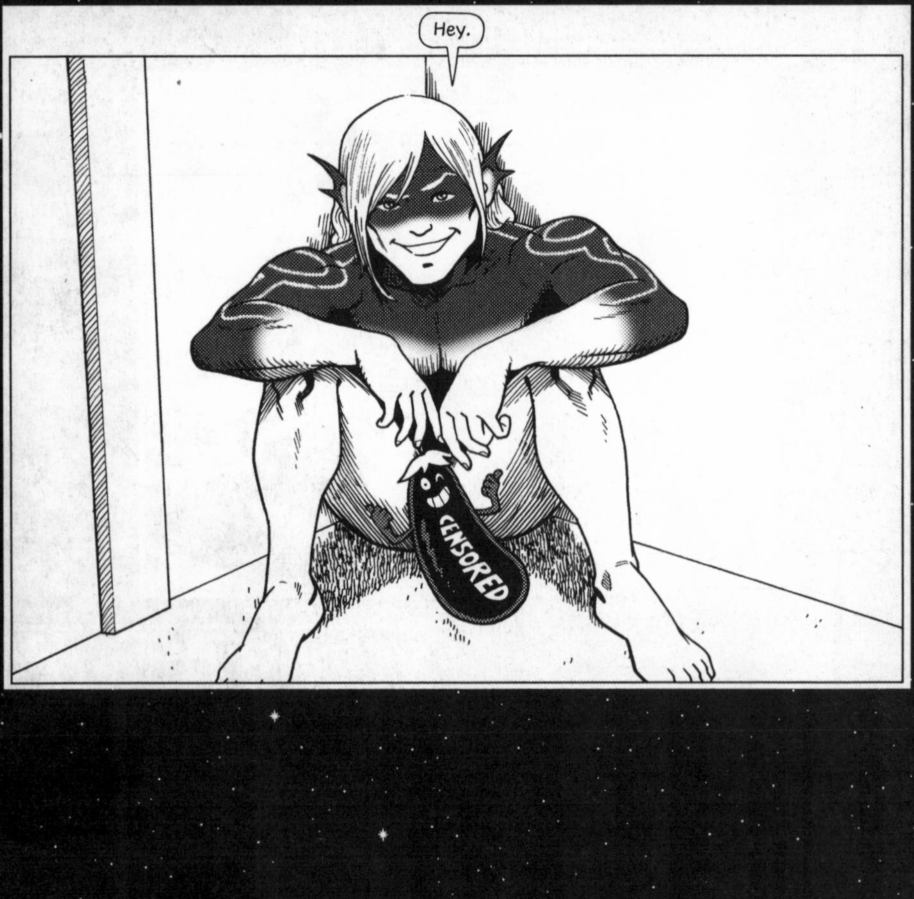
Hey.
CENSORED

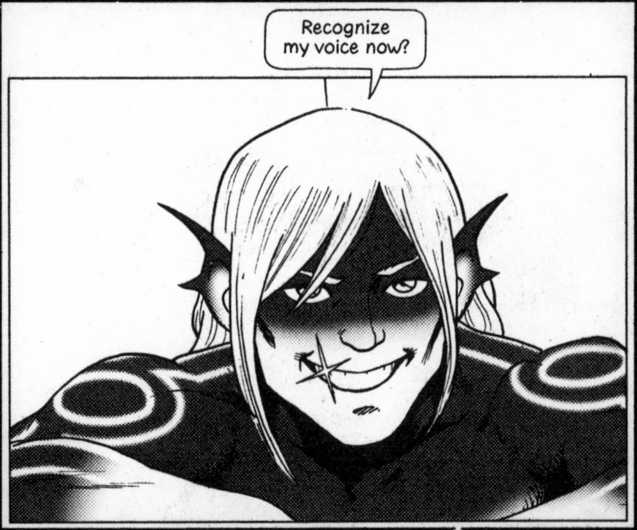
Recognize
my voice now?

TO BE CONTINUED...

WWW.TUNECOMIC.COM

First Second

Text copyright © 2013 by Derek Kirk Kim
Art copyright © 2013 by Les McClaine

Special thanks to Michel Stupin

Published by First Second
First Second is an imprint of Roaring Brook Press, a division of Holtzbrinck Publishing Holdings Limited Partnership
175 Fifth Avenue, New York, New York 10010
All rights reserved

Cataloging-in-Publication Data is on file at the Library of Congress.

ISBN 978-1-59643-760-9

First Second books may be purchased for business or promotional use. For information on bulk purchases, please contact Macmillan Corporate and Premium Sales Department at (800) 221-7945 ext. 5442 or by e-mail at specialmarkets@macmillan.com.

First edition 2013
Book design by Ananth Panagariya
Printed in the United States of America

10 9 8 7 6 5 4 3 2 1